WE THE PEOPLES

HE
PEOPLES

A UN FOR THE
21ST CENTURY

BY

KOFI ANNAN

EDITED BY

EDWARD MORTIMER

PARADIGM PUBLISHERS
Boulder & London

"A Girl Born Today in Afghanistan" appearing in Chapter 1: Copyright © The Nobel Foundation (2001). Source: Nobelprize.org. Reprinted with permission.

Published in the United States by Paradigm Publishers, 5589 Arapahoe Avenue, Boulder, CO 80303 USA.

Paradigm Publishers is the trade name of Birkenkamp & Company, LLC, Dean Birkenkamp, President and Publisher.

Library of Congress Cataloging-in-Publication Data

Annan, Kofi A. (Kofi Atta)
 We the peoples : a UN for the 21st century / Kofi Annan ; edited by Edward Mortimer.
   pages cm
 Includes index.
 ISBN 978-1-61205-558-9 (hardcover : alk. paper)—
 ISBN 978-1-61205-652-4 (library ebook)
 ISBN 978-1-61205-653-1 (consumer ebook)
  1. Globalization. 2. United Nations. 3. Security, International. 4. Sustainable development. I. Title.
 JZ1318.A6652 2014
 341.23—dc23

                                                         2013043211

Designed and typeset by Straight Creek Bookmakers

Printed and bound in the United States of America on acid-free paper that meets the standards of the American National Standard for Permanence of Paper for Printed Library Materials.

18 17 16 15 14 1 2 3 4 5

❊

CONTENTS

Introduction

The Secretary-General of the United Nations is expected to play several different roles. The Charter defines him as "the chief administrative officer of the Organization" (Article 97) and requires him to make an annual report to the General Assembly (Article 98). But it also allows him to "bring to the attention of the Security Council any matter which in his opinion may threaten the maintenance of international peace and security" (Article 99)—a clearly political responsibility. In practice, he is frequently called on to use his "good offices" to resolve or manage disputes through quiet diplomacy. Besides, the Member States often look to him for guidance on procedural matters, and sometimes for a lead on substantive ones, to help them find a common position.

But the Secretary-General is also a public figure who is expected to represent the UN, and its principles and ideals, to the world at large. This was anticipated by the Preparatory Commission of the United Nations in its report of 23 December 1945, just a few weeks before the first Secretary-General was appointed. "The United Nations," said the Commission, "cannot prosper, nor can its aims be realized, without the active and steadfast support of the peoples of the world…. The Secretary-General, more than anyone else, will stand for the United Nations as a whole. In the eyes of the world, no less than in the eyes of his own staff, he must embody the principles and ideals of the Charter to which the Organization seeks to give effect."

In the early years of the Organization, this was a fairly small part of his job. Trygve Lie, the first Secretary-General, is remembered for having settled the United Nations in New York—he persuaded John D. Rockefeller to donate the site on the East River and he assembled the outstanding team of architects who designed the building—but he is not recalled for any of his public statements. It was Dag Hammarskjöld who first discovered that he could use his office as Theodore Roosevelt had used the US presidency, as a "bully pulpit," from which to influence public opinion and thereby give himself some room to resist the pressure of powerful Member States. Hammarskjöld made some very fine speeches, particularly the Oxford lecture on "The International Civil Servant in Law and in Fact," to which I referred in my own Dag Hammarskjöld lecture, the first item in this volume. But he had to choose his words and his themes with great care, navigating skillfully in the small space that the cold war allowed him. And after his death the three Secretaries-General who held office in the remaining decades of the cold war were similarly constrained.

By the time that I was appointed, at the end of 1996, the world had changed almost beyond recognition. The cold war had ended, with the result that the Security Council was no longer in a state of structural and permanent deadlock. Of course that did not mean that its members were able or willing to agree on an effective course of action in every case, as we quickly and painfully discovered in Somalia, in Rwanda, and in the former Yugoslavia. But it did mean that UN officials could speak up for some of the principles set out in the Charter and the Universal Declaration of Human Rights and sound as if they meant it, without automatically bringing down the wrath of one of the permanent members of the Council on their heads or causing a crisis that would paralyze the whole system.

And the world had changed in another respect, too—perhaps an even more important one. We had embarked on the communications revolution, which gave a whole new meaning to the phrase "public figure." Any event, and any remark, could be instantly beamed around the world, and the person who in the eyes of the world stood for the United Nations was expected to react instantly. To say nothing was in itself considered a reaction and often was simply not an option. I found myself continuously in the media spotlight, whether I liked it or not.

This was a burden, but I soon realized that it was also an opportunity. I was well aware that I had no "hard power": no armored divisions or bombers or battleships at my beck and call that I could deploy quickly in times of crisis. But I did have some "soft power," in the phrase coined by Joseph Nye. The idea that there could be such a thing as world public opinion was no longer completely fanciful. People in different parts of the world were following the same events on their radios and TV sets, and increasingly on their cell phones or computer screens, in "real time." They were becoming aware that certain issues—such as endemic poverty, infectious disease, climate change, population growth, drugs, organized crime, migration, energy, and food supplies—were not confined within national borders and could not be dealt with by any one nation-state working alone. They saw the need for international cooperation, and they looked to the UN—often with very little knowledge or understanding of its history or its methods—as the body that should get nations working together for global solutions to global problems.

In other words, there was a global agenda and a global public. But someone needed to articulate that agenda and speak to that public. And it could not be just anyone. It had to be someone with a status that governments would recognize, someone with the authority to speak for humanity as a whole. Who could that be, if not the Secretary-General of the United Nations?

That may sound an absurdly ambitious thought, but I felt that I had little to lose by being ambitious. The times required it. And the time was propitious in another respect, too, which may seem trivial but which I believe was psychologically very important. I was appointed in 1996 for a five-year term, which therefore spanned the year 2000. On my watch, something was about to happen that everyone in the world would notice and that would not happen again for another thousand years: one millennium would end and a new one would begin. If ever there were a moment for the nations of the world to take stock of their situation collectively, to measure what they had achieved and to set themselves goals for the future, this was surely it. And it was only through the United Nations that such a collective stocktaking and goal-setting exercise could conceivably happen. Someone had to take the lead, and who else if not the Secretary-General?

So I suggested that the opening of the 55th session of the General Assembly, in September 2000, should be the occasion for a "Millennium Summit," attended by as many as possible of the national leaders of the UN's Member States. The Assembly agreed and asked me to propose "a number of forward-looking and widely relevant topics that could help to focus the Millennium Summit within the context of an overall theme."

This was the origin of my Millennium Report, which included at the end a draft statement "for consideration by the Summit." This in turn formed the basis for the Millennium Declaration adopted by the Summit, which included what were to become the Millennium Development Goals: a set of simple, quantified targets for the world to achieve by 2015, including halving extreme poverty, establishing universal primary education, and halting the spread of HIV/AIDS.

Taken together, these factors convinced me that public activity, and public words, would be an important part of my work—perhaps a bigger part than for any of my predecessors. I needed to propose and advocate some compelling ideas and to do so in clear language that would be noticed and understood by a public well beyond the captive audience of UN "insiders." I therefore paid a great deal of attention to my speeches and other public statements. I was helped greatly in this by my strategic advisor for the first four years, John Ruggie, and by a team of speechwriters, to whom my most important guidance was, "I don't want to address the world in UN-speak!"

Of course, all these statements were made for specific times and places, and all of them are available to diligent researchers who know where and how to look for them. In this book I have assembled a small selection of those I think may deserve a wider readership, even a decade or more after they were delivered.

This book is intended to complement and amplify the narrative of my time in office, which I published in 2012,[1] by giving examples of what I was actually saying at the time, to different audiences and on different themes. It is arranged in nine thematic chapters, with chronologically ordered statements within each chapter.

The first chapter deals with the UN itself, that precious but imperfect instrument for handling global problems, which we inherit from an earlier generation, which we have to make the most of, and which it fell to me to try to steer through ten years of dramatic change, stress, and opportunity. It includes the Nobel Lecture that I gave in Oslo in 2001 when accepting the Nobel Peace Prize awarded jointly to myself

---

1. Kofi Annan with Nader Mousavizadeh, *Interventions: A Life in War and Peace* (New York: Penguin Press, 2012).

and to the United Nations "for their work for a better organized and more peaceful world."

Chapter 2 follows next, on development, economics, and civil society—themes that I saw as central to my mandate. Development may seem an abstract concept to people living in rich countries, but to the vast majority of men and women it is *the* global issue: the one in which success or failure will determine whether they and their children have a real prospect of living a decent life. Naturally they judge the UN by the contribution it makes, or does not make, to the success of development worldwide. Yet one of the messages I had to get across was that development depends on economic factors and policies over which the UN has little influence, let alone control. Of course I was an advocate—how could I not be?—for more generous development assistance from rich countries to poor, as well as fairer rules in trade, finance, and investment and better representation for developing countries in global financial institutions. But I had to stress repeatedly that development can only happen *in* developing countries and therefore depends crucially on conditions in those countries and the policies that *their* governments adopt; that it cannot happen unless women and girls (who make up half the human race and at least half of its potential) are enabled to play their full part in all societies, including in their leadership; and that development will be of no use to our children and grandchildren if it so damages our planet and its ecosystems that it cannot be sustained.

I also had to appeal to partners beyond the world of governments where the UN, as an association of sovereign states, habitually operates. One of these partners was the business community, to which I proposed the Global Compact in 1999. But no less important was civil society, in all its myriad forms: the people who voluntarily come together in many different kinds of groups—locally, nationally, and internationally—to push forward one or another aspect of human progress. I was convinced that the UN would achieve little in the twenty-first century unless it reached out to such people and convinced them that it was a useful ally, able and willing to work with them to achieve common objectives. That is why I kept reminding the world that the Charter was issued in the name not of "we the states" but of "we the peoples," choosing those words as the title of my Millennium Report, and of this book.

Chapter 3 deals with peace and security, the very first task that the world's peoples assigned to the UN: "to save succeeding generations from the scourge of war." Success here is vital in itself, for the preservation of human life and also for the cause of development, because conflict is in many places the biggest obstacle that prevents development and social progress. I saw the prevention of conflict as equal in importance with development and inseparably connected. It was therefore immensely useful to me that, soon after I became Secretary-General, the Carnegie Commission on Preventing Deadly Conflict, chaired by David Hamburg and Cyrus Vance, produced its groundbreaking final report on that subject.

I welcomed the report and tried to apply many of its ideas in the practical work of the UN. But I also had, of course, to deal with the major crises of war and peace that arose during my time in office: the Kosovo war in 1999, the terrorist attacks on New York and Washington in 2001, and the Iraq war in 2003. And these led me to wrestle with some of the most fundamental issues for our international order in the new century: how to make decisions collectively rather than unilaterally, particularly on the use of force; how to confront international terrorism; and how to deal with nuclear weapons, not only to prevent them from spreading further but also to move towards disarmament.

Alongside these two themes—development, and peace and security—there was a third, which the Charter actually puts second after preventing war: fundamental human rights, the subject of Chapter 4. This is a particularly difficult issue for the UN: as an association of sovereign states, it has to persuade its members to uphold human rights, even though the membership includes the main violators of human rights. But I was, and remain, firmly convinced that this is not an issue the UN can afford to duck.

Peace and development are not just about facts and figures; they are about the fate of individual human beings. So we cannot achieve peace or development in any meaningful sense unless individuals and their rights are protected by the rule of law, instead of being at the mercy of arbitrary power. Indeed, numerous studies have shown that human rights violations on a large scale are one of the most reliable predictors of conflict in a country. This means that, unless people are able to organize themselves and claim their rights by peaceful agitation or protest, neither peace nor development can be considered secure. So in 2005, in my report *In Larger Freedom*,[2] I proclaimed human rights the "third pillar" of the United Nations, which needed its own Council, alongside the Security Council and the Economic and Social Council. It is a theme whose relevance and importance continues in my current work, which is why I have included here a speech that I made after leaving office, on the bicentenary of what may well be considered the first great victory of the human rights movement: the abolition of the slave trade by the British parliament in 1807.

The most original contribution the UN has made to conflict prevention is the invention of peacekeeping—the idea that neutral, lightly armed forces can help preserve a truce by interposing themselves between opposing parties and building confidence on each side that the other will not be able to launch a surprise attack. Over the decades this role has expanded and peacekeepers have become peace-builders: outsiders sent by the international community to help a society recover from conflict and make the transition to lasting peace. Before I became Secretary-General, I was privileged to serve as the first head of the UN's Department of Peacekeeping Operations. So it is natural that I wanted to include in this book, as Chapter 5, two speeches devoted to that aspect of the UN's work and what we have learnt from it.

After that come two chapters on specific regions of the world that, between them, have the misfortune to provide a very large share of the UN's security agenda and therefore take up a lot of every Secretary-General's time. The first of these regions is my own continent, Africa, considered in Chapter 6. Africa has too often presented itself to the world as a helpless and needy victim, riven with conflict and in desperate need of assistance. I am glad to see that this is now changing, and we read much more about Africa as a continent of opportunity and rapid growth. That does not mean that all the problems have miraculously disappeared, but it does reflect the fact that, over the past twenty years or so, Africans have been facing up to them and have been willing to make some difficult choices.

---

2. UN General Assembly, *In Larger Freedom: Towards Development, Security and Human Rights for All*, Report of the Secretary-General, 21 March 2005, A/59/2005. http://www.un.org/en/ga/search/view_doc.asp?symbol=A/59/2005.

I am glad to remember that, as the UN's second African Secretary-General (and the first from sub-Saharan Africa), I always felt it was my responsibility to speak candidly to African leaders and to voice the concerns of ordinary African people, especially on the scourge of HIV/AIDS, which is probably the single biggest tragedy the continent has had to cope with in my lifetime. Here, too, I have included a speech made shortly after I left office, on the occasion of my home country's golden jubilee as an independent state, since this gave me the chance to sum up some of the changes that had been happening in Africa and the reasons to feel hopeful about its future.

The other region that takes up so much of the UN's time and energy is, of course, the Middle East, the subject of Chapter 7. Here I refer mainly to the Arab-Israeli conflict rather than Iraq and the wider Middle East, although one point I had to make repeatedly was that this is a conflict that, perhaps more than any other, has the capacity to draw in people beyond its immediate theater, indeed virtually throughout the world.

The "question of Palestine" is one that has preoccupied the UN from its very beginnings. Israel derives its international legitimacy from a General Assembly resolution, passed in 1947, that authorized the partition of the then British-mandate territory of Palestine into a Jewish and an Arab state. The first UN peacekeeping force was deployed on the Israeli-Egyptian border in 1956, and the UN still has forces on Israel's borders with Lebanon and Syria, as well as maintains the Truce Supervision Organization (UNTSO), based in Jerusalem, which dates back to 1948, and a major humanitarian operation, the Relief and Works Agency for Palestine Refugees (UNRWA). Yet, when I became Secretary-General, the UN had been virtually excluded from political efforts to resolve the conflict for a quarter of a century, because Israel perceived it as hostile. That seemed to me wrong, and I did what I could to change it. We did play a vital role in certifying Israel's withdrawal from Lebanon in 2000, and from 2002 onwards we were involved in all the peace efforts through the Quartet.[3] I only wish those efforts had had more success.

---

3. During this period the United Nations, United States, European Union, and Russian Federation met regularly as "the Quartet" in an attempt to encourage and guide the Israeli-Palestinian peace process.

Chapter 8 is about a particular issue—the prevention of genocide—in which I felt deeply and personally involved, partly because my wife, Nane, is the niece of Raoul Wallenberg, the heroic Swedish diplomat who saved tens of thousands of Jews from the Nazi death camps, but mainly because, during my time as head of UN peacekeeping, I had to take responsibility for the UN's failure to prevent genocide in Rwanda in 1994 and at Srebrenica in Bosnia in 1995.

I was determined to prevent such failures from being repeated, if I possibly could. As Secretary-General I gave strong support to the creation of the International Criminal Court, to ensure that in future such crimes could not be committed with impunity. I published a hard-hitting report[4] that found that "through error, misjudgment and an inability to recognize the scope of the evil confronting us, we failed to do our part to help save the people of Srebrenica from the Serb campaign of mass murder"; and I commissioned an independent report[5] that found that "the overriding failure of the United Nations before and during the genocide in Rwanda can be summarized as a lack of resources and a lack of will to take on the commitment which would have been necessary to prevent or to stop the genocide." In response to this I produced a UN action plan for the prevention of future genocides, which I announced in the Commission on Human Rights in 2004, on the tenth anniversary of the Rwanda genocide in 2004. In 1999 I persuaded President B. J. Habibie of Indonesia to prevent further bloodshed in East Timor by withdrawing his army and allowing an international force to come in; and later I pleaded with Member States to take a stronger line in dealing with atrocities in Darfur and elsewhere. I also persuaded the General Assembly, in 2005, to commemorate those who had perished sixty years earlier in the worst of all genocides, the Nazi Holocaust.

Most of all, I wrestled with the issue of humanitarian intervention: the need, in extreme cases, for whomever is able to intervene and put a stop to genocide or mass atrocities to go ahead and do so. This is an especially difficult issue for the United Nations because it may involve intervening "in matters which are essentially within the domestic jurisdiction" of a

4. Report of the Secretary-General Pursuant to General Assembly Resolution 53/55, Entitled "The Fall of Srebrenica," A/54/549, 15 November 1999.
5. Report of the Independent Inquiry into the Actions of the United Nations during the 1994 Genocide in Rwanda, UN document S/1999/1257, 16 December 1999.

Member State—something that the Charter expressly forbids (Article 2.7). But the same article says that this "shall not prejudice the application of enforcement measures under Chapter VII," meaning measures taken by the Security Council when there is a threat to international peace and security. I argued that sovereignty entails the responsibility of a state to protect its citizens against extreme violations and that when a state fails flagrantly to do this, the Security Council may need to intervene.

That is what became known as the doctrine of "responsibility to protect," and it is perhaps the issue with which I am most closely associated in public memory. This may have given some people the impression that I am someone who likes military intervention and is always prepared to speak up for it. It is even possible that the title of my memoir, *Interventions*, has strengthened that impression. But anyone who actually reads that book will quickly find that nothing could be further from the truth. As explained in the speech "On Intervention" in *this* book, I believe that intervention can take many forms, that the vast majority of interventions are entirely peaceful, and that whenever there is a choice, non-violent means are to be preferred to violent ones.

In the rare cases where there is no longer a choice and using force becomes the lesser evil, it always means that earlier and better chances to avoid bloodshed have been missed. Prevention is better than cure. And before embarking on such a drastic "cure" as military intervention, one must be very sure that it is not going to make the situation even worse. It is for that reason that, in the last two years, I have not felt able to encourage military intervention in Syria, despite the many atrocities to which its people have been subjected.

Genocide involves an attempt by one group of human beings to exterminate another, almost always because they have convinced themselves that this other group poses a threat to their own existence. You kill in order not to be killed. I believe that this perception of difference as a threat lies at the root of much of the evil in human affairs. If the United Nations is about anything, I believe it must be about the *celebration* of difference, about convincing people that diversity is something to be welcomed as a source of wealth and pleasure and knowledge, not shunned as a source of fear and danger. In the last chapter of this book, therefore, I have gathered a few statements devoted to that idea.

Overall, I remain convinced that the United Nations belongs not only to the governments of its Member States but above all to their peoples, in whose name it was founded. That means that it must become more democratic by ensuring that *all* the world's peoples, and not only the richest and most powerful, have a voice and also that those who make the decisions genuinely represent their peoples and are accountable to them. The peoples must insist that this precious instrument is truly in their hands, so that together they can face the challenges and exploit the opportunities of the twenty-first century.

I hope that some of the ideas set out in this book will help them do so.

Kofi Annan
Geneva, 2013

❊ CHAPTER ONE ❊

THE UNITED NATIONS

❄

The Legacy of Dag Hammarskjöld

Fourth Dag Hammarskjöld Lecture
Uppsala, Sweden
6 September 2001

Annan delivered this lecture on "Dag Hammarskjöld and the 21st Century" in Sweden just twelve days before the fortieth anniversary of Hammarskjöld's death. Annan had just completed an extensive tour of southern and central Africa, which included a visit to the Democratic Republic of Congo. The speech was an opportunity for him to reflect on the changing role of the United Nations and particularly on his own office as Secretary-General. From Sweden he returned to New York where, only five days later, the international scene was to be transformed by the 9/11 attacks.

A s Secretary-General of the United Nations, I have given many speeches, and even quite a few lectures. But I can think of no invitation to speak that is a greater honor, or a greater challenge, than this one.

It will not surprise you to hear that Dag Hammarskjöld is a figure of great importance to me—as he must be for any Secretary-General. His life and his death, his words and his actions, have done more to shape public expectations of the office, and indeed of the Organization, than those of any other man or woman in its history.

His wisdom and his modesty, his unimpeachable integrity and his single-minded devotion to duty, have set a standard for all servants of the international community—and especially, of course, for his successors—which is simply impossible to live up to. There can be no better rule of thumb for a Secretary-General, as he approaches each new challenge or crisis, than to ask himself, "How would Hammarskjöld have handled this?"

If that is true for any Secretary-General, how much more so for one of my generation, who came of age during the years when Dag Hammarskjöld personified the United Nations, and began my own career in the UN system within a year of his death....

So you see, it is quite a solemn thing for me to give this lecture, especially so close to the fortieth anniversary of Hammarskjöld's death. And I feel all the more solemn about it coming here, as I do, directly from the part of Africa where he met that death—and where, 40 years later, the United Nations is again struggling to restore unity and peace to the Democratic Republic of Congo.

I can tell you that the Congolese have never forgotten Dag Hammarskjöld.

Four days ago, during my visit to the Congo, I met with a group of representatives of parties involved in the Inter-Congolese Dialogue as part of the peace process.

Their spokesman began the meeting by telling me how much they appreciated the late Secretary-General's dedication, and the fact that he gave his life for peace in their country. And he asked us to pay tribute to Hammarskjöld's memory by observing a minute of silence. Everyone got up. I found it very moving that people could feel like that about him after 40 years....

If Dag were to walk through that door just now, and ask me what are the main problems the United Nations is dealing with today, I could easily answer in a way that would make him think nothing much had changed.

I could talk to him not only about the Congo, but about the Middle East, or Cyprus, or the relations between India and Pakistan, and it would all seem very familiar.

But I could also tell him things that he would find very *un*familiar—though some would surprise him less than others, and some would gratify him more than others.

He would probably be relieved, but not surprised, to hear that China is now represented at the United Nations by the government that actually governs the vast majority of Chinese people.

It would surprise him much more to learn that the Soviet Union no longer exists. But he could only be pleased to find that there is no longer an unbridgeable ideological difference between the permanent Members of the Security Council.

He might be struck by the number of conflicts that the United Nations is dealing with today that are within, rather than between, States—though the experience of the Congo would have prepared him for this—and also by the number of regional organizations that have developed as partners for the United Nations in different parts of the world.

I feel sure, in any case, that he would be pleased to see the way United Nations peacekeeping has developed, from the model that he and Lester Pearson so brilliantly improvised in 1956 to something much more diverse and complex, which is often more accurately described as peace-building.

And I imagine he would be equally impressed by the wide range of issues that the United Nations is now called upon to face outside the traditional security arena—from climate change to HIV/AIDS.

He would be gratified, and perhaps not all that surprised, to hear that human rights and democracy are now generally accepted as world norms—though he might well be distressed to see how far, in many countries, the practice still falls short of the rhetoric.

He would definitely be distressed to learn that, within the last decade, genocide had again disfigured the face of humanity—and that well over a billion people today are living in extreme poverty. I think he would see preventing the recurrence of the former, and putting an end to the latter, as the most urgent tasks confronting us in this new century.

He would no doubt be impressed by the speed and intensity of modern communications, and momentarily confused by talk of faxes and satellite phones—let alone e-mails and the Internet. But I'm sure he would be quick to grasp the advantages and disadvantages of all these innovations, both for civilization as a whole and for the conduct of diplomacy in particular.

What is clear is that his core ideas remain highly relevant in this new international context. The challenge for us is to see how they can be adapted to take account of it in this new environment.

One idea which inspired all his words and actions as Secretary-General was his belief that the United Nations had to be a dynamic instrument, through which its Members would collectively develop forms of executive action.

During his time in office he became increasingly sensitive to the fact that some Member States did not share this vision, but regarded the United Nations as only a static conference machinery for resolving conflicts of interests and ideologies with a view to peaceful coexistence.

In the Introduction to his last Annual Report—a magisterial work, which reads almost as if he was consciously writing his political testament—Hammarskjöld argued that those who regarded the Organization in this way were not paying adequate attention to certain essential principles of the Charter.

He showed that the Charter clearly implies the existence of "an international community, for which the Organization is an instrument and an expression." The overriding purpose of this community was to save succeeding generations from the scourge of war, and to do this it had to follow certain key principles.

These were

* First, "*equal political rights*"—which encompassed both the "sovereign equality" of all Member States, in Article 2 of the Charter, and "respect for human rights and fundamental freedoms," in Article 1.
* Second, "*equal economic opportunities*"—spelt out in Article 55 as the promotion of "higher standards of living, full employment, and conditions of economic and social progress and development," as well as "solutions of international economic, social, health, and related problems."
* Third, "*justice*"—by which he meant that the international community must be "based on law ... with a judicial procedure through which law and justice could be made to apply."
* And, finally, the "*prohibition of the use of armed force*," "save in the common interest."

These principles, Hammarskjöld argued, are incompatible with the idea of the United Nations as merely a conference or debating chamber—as indeed is the authority the Charter gives to its principal organs, and particularly to the Security Council, which clearly has both legislative and executive powers.

The context in which he put forward these arguments was, of course, the cold war, and particularly the Soviet campaign against him during the Congo crisis of 1960–61.

That campaign is happily long past. But we still face, from time to time, attempts by Member States to reduce the United Nations to a conference mechanism.

Those attempts no longer come systematically from one particular ideological camp. Instead, they tend to vary according to the subject under discussion.

Broadly speaking, industrialized countries remain reluctant to see the United Nations act on Hammarskjöld's second principle—the promotion of "equal economic opportunities." And the governments of some other countries are equally loath to see it actively promote "respect for, and observance of, human rights and fundamental freedoms for all."

In both cases, I believe the Secretary-General has no choice. He has to follow in the footsteps of Hammarskjöld, upholding the right and duty of the United Nations to pursue the aims laid down for it by the Charter.

Of course there is always a need for negotiation and discussion on the appropriate forms of action. But the United Nations will fail in its duty to the world's peoples, who are the ultimate source of its authority, if it allows itself to be reduced to a mere static conference, whether on economic and social rights or on civil and political ones.

The same applies to Hammarskjöld's exalted view of the international civil servant, which he also pursued in that last annual report, and in a lecture given that same summer at Oxford University.

His argument here was that the people charged with carrying out the executive functions of the United Nations could not be neutral in relation to the principles of the Charter. Nor could they be regarded, or allowed to regard themselves, as nominees or representatives of their own nations. They had to represent the international community as a whole.

Here, too, Hammarskjöld based his argument on a very careful reading of the Charter itself—in this case Articles 100 and 101.

Article 100 forbids the Secretary-General or any of his staff either to seek or to receive instructions from States. And Article 101 prescribes "the highest standards of efficiency, competence, and integrity" as "the paramount consideration in the employment of the staff."

Once again, Hammarskjöld was arguing in the context of the cold war, in which first one side and then the other had tried to insist on the right to be represented, within the Secretariat, by people who were loyal to its political or ideological point of view.

Again, the context has changed, and I am glad to say that States today, while extremely keen to see their nationals appointed to senior positions, no longer seek—or, at least, not in the same way—to exercise political control over them, once appointed.

But the principle of an independent international civil service, to which Dag Hammarskjöld was so attached, remains as important as ever. Each successive Secretary-General must be vigilant in defending it, even if, on occasion, changing times require us to depart from the letter of his views, in order to preserve the spirit.

To give just one example: Hammarskjöld insisted that the bulk of United Nations staff should have permanent appointments and expect to spend their whole career with the Organization.

That may have been appropriate in his time. It is less so now that the role of the United Nations has expanded, and more than half of our employees are serving in missions in the field. This is a development which Hammarskjöld would surely have welcomed, since it reflects a transition from the static conference model to the dynamic instrument model which he so strongly believed in.

But what is clear is that his ideal of the United Nations as an expression of the international community, whose staff carry out decisions taken by States collectively rather than bending to the will of any one of them, is just as relevant in our times as in his.

And that, of course, has very important implications for the role of the Secretary-General himself.

Hammarskjöld pointed out that Article 99 of the Charter—which allows the Secretary-General, on his own initiative, to bring matters to the Security Council's attention when in his view they may threaten the maintenance of international peace and security—makes him clearly a political rather than a purely administrative official.

In practice, successive Secretaries-General, including Hammarskjöld, have invoked this article very sparingly. I myself have never yet found it necessary to do so. But the fact that the Secretary-General has this power crucially affects the way he is treated by the Security Council, and by the General Assembly.

Few people now question the responsibility of the Secretary-General to act politically, or to make public pronouncements on political issues.

In fact, the boot today is if anything on the other foot: I find myself called on to make official statements on almost everything that happens in the world today, from royal marriages to the possibility of human cloning!

I do my best to satisfy this demand with due respect for the decisions of the Security Council and General Assembly. But those bodies would find it very strange if on each occasion I sought their approval before opening my mouth!

Their members can, and do, take exception to some of my statements—and thank goodness they do. There must be freedom of speech for governments, as well as for international officials! But they do not question my right to make such statements, according to my own understanding of the purposes and principles of the United Nations as set out in the Charter.

No doubt Hammarskjöld would also disagree with some of the specific positions I have taken. But I suspect he would envy me the discretion I enjoy in deciding what to say, and what topics to comment on. And I have no doubt he would strongly endorse the principle that the Secretary-General must strive to make himself an authentic and independent voice of the international community.

What he might not have foreseen is the way our concept of that community has developed in recent years. In his time it was essentially a community of separate nations or peoples, who for all practical purposes were represented by States.

So if we go back to the things about today's world that we would have to explain to him, if he were to unexpectedly join us now, probably the most difficult for him to adjust to would be the sheer complexity of a world in which individuals and groups of all kinds are constantly interacting—across frontiers and across oceans, economically, socially, culturally, politically—without expecting or receiving any permission, let alone assistance, from their national governments.

He might well find it difficult to identify the precise role, in such a world, for a body like the United Nations, whose Charter presupposes the division of the world into sovereign and equal States, and in which the peoples of the world are represented essentially by their governments.

He might find that difficult—and if so, he would not be alone! But I am convinced he would relish the challenge. And I am sure he would not stray from his fundamental conviction that the essential task of the United Nations is to protect the weak against the strong.

In the long term, the vitality and viability of the Organization depend on its ability to perform that task, by adapting itself to changing realities. That, I believe, is the biggest test it faces in the new century.

How would Hammarskjöld approach that task?

First of all he would insist, quite correctly, that States are still the main holders of political authority in the world, and are likely to remain so. Indeed, the more democratic they become—the more genuinely representative of, and accountable to, their peoples—the greater also will be their political legitimacy. And therefore it is entirely proper, as well as inevitable, that they will remain the political masters of the United Nations.

He would also insist, I am sure, on the continuing responsibility of States to maintain international order—and, indeed, on their collective responsibility, which their leaders solemnly recognized in last year's Millennium Declaration, "to uphold the principles of human dignity, equality and equity at the global level."

And he might well say that, with a few honorable exceptions, the more fortunate countries in this world are not living up to that responsibility, so long as they do not fulfill their long-standing commitments to much higher levels of development assistance, to much more generous debt relief, and to duty- and quota-free access for exports from the least developed countries.

But then he would also see that his own lifetime coincided, in most countries, with the high watermark of State control over the lives of citizens. And he would see that States today generally tax and spend a smaller proportion of their citizens' wealth than they did 40 years ago.

From this he might well conclude that we should not rely exclusively on State action to achieve our objectives on the international level either.

A great deal, he would think, is likely to depend on non-State actors in the system—private companies, voluntary agencies or pressure groups, philanthropic foundations, universities and think tanks, and, of course, creative individuals.

And that thought would surely feed into his reflection on the role of the United Nations.

Can it confine itself, in the twenty-first century, to the role of coordinating action by States? Or should it reach out further?

Is it not obliged, in order to fulfill the purposes of the Charter, to form partnerships with all these different actors? To listen to them, to guide them, and to urge them on?

Above all, to provide a framework of shared values and understanding, within which their free and voluntary efforts can interact, and reinforce each other, instead of getting in each other's way?

Perhaps it is presumptuous of me to suggest that this would be part of Hammarskjöld's vision of the role of the United Nations in the twenty-first century—because it is, of course, my own vision.

No doubt if he were alive today he would offer us something nobler and more profound.

But I like to think that what I have just described would find some place in that vision.

※

A Girl Born Today in Afghanistan

Nobel Lecture
Oslo, Norway
10 December 2001

One month after the 9/11 attacks, the Norwegian Nobel Committee awarded the centennial Nobel Peace Prize jointly to Kofi Annan and the United Nations "for their work for a better organized and more peaceful world." This speech is the Nobel Lecture that Annan delivered on receiving the Prize in Oslo City Hall.

Today, in Afghanistan, a girl will be born. Her mother will hold her and feed her, comfort her and care for her just as any mother would anywhere in the world. In these most basic acts of human nature, humanity knows no divisions. But to be born a girl in today's Afghanistan is to begin life centuries away from the prosperity that one small part of humanity has achieved. It is to live under conditions that many of us in this hall would consider inhuman. Truly, it is as if it were a tale of two planets.

I speak of a girl in Afghanistan, but I might equally well have mentioned a baby boy or girl in Sierra Leone. No one today is unaware of this divide between the world's rich and poor. No one today can claim ignorance of the cost that this divide imposes on the poor and dispossessed who are no less deserving of human dignity, fundamental freedoms, security, food and education than any of us. The cost, however, is not borne by them alone. Ultimately, it is borne by all of us—North and South, rich and poor, men and women of all races and religions.

Today's real borders are not between nations, but between powerful and powerless, free and fettered, privileged and humiliated. Today, no walls can separate humanitarian or human rights crises in one part of the world from national security crises in another.

Scientists tell us that the world of nature is so small and interdependent that a butterfly flapping its wings in the Amazon rainforest can generate a violent storm on the other side of the earth. This principle is known as the "Butterfly Effect." Today, we realize, perhaps more than ever, that the world of human activity also has its own "Butterfly Effect"—for better or for worse.

We have entered the third millennium through a gate of fire. If today, after the horror of 11 September, we see better, and we see further—we will realize that humanity is indivisible. New threats make no distinction between races, nations or regions. A new insecurity has entered every mind, regardless of wealth or status. A deeper awareness of the bonds that bind us all—in pain as in prosperity—has gripped young and old.

In the early beginnings of the twenty-first century—a century already violently disabused of any hopes that progress towards global peace and prosperity is inevitable—this new reality can no longer be ignored. It must be confronted.

The twentieth century was perhaps the deadliest in human history, devastated by innumerable conflicts, untold suffering, and unimaginable crimes. Time after time, a group or a nation inflicted extreme violence on another, often driven by irrational hatred and suspicion, or unbounded arrogance and thirst for power and resources. In response to these cataclysms, the leaders of the world came together at mid-century to unite the nations as never before.

A forum was created—the United Nations—where all nations could join forces to affirm the dignity and worth of every person, and to secure peace and development for all peoples. Here States could unite to strengthen the rule of law, recognize and address the needs of the poor, restrain man's brutality and greed, conserve the resources and beauty of nature, sustain the equal rights of men and women, and provide for the safety of future generations.

We thus inherit from the twentieth century the political, as well as the scientific and technological, power which—if only we have the will to use them—give us the chance to vanquish poverty, ignorance and disease.

In the twenty-first century I believe the mission of the United Nations will be defined by a new, more profound, awareness of the sanctity and dignity of every human life, regardless of race or religion. This will require us to look beyond the framework of States, and beneath the surface of nations or communities. We must focus, as never before, on improving the conditions of the individual men and women who give the State or nation its richness and character. We must begin with the young Afghan girl, recognizing that saving that one life is to save humanity itself.

Over the past five years, I have often recalled that the United Nations' Charter begins with the words "we the peoples." What is not always recognized is that "we the peoples" are made up of individuals whose claims to the most fundamental rights have too often been sacrificed in the supposed interests of the State or the nation.

A genocide begins with the killing of one man—not for what he has done, but because of who he is. A campaign of "ethnic cleansing" begins with one neighbor turning on another. Poverty begins when even one child is denied his or her fundamental right to education. What begins with the failure to uphold the dignity of one life, all too often ends with a calamity for entire nations.

In this new century, we must start from the understanding that peace belongs not only to States or peoples, but to each and every member of those communities. The sovereignty of States must no longer be used as a shield for gross violations of human rights. Peace must be made real and tangible in the daily existence of every individual in need. Peace must be sought, above all, because it is the condition for every member of the human family to live a life of dignity and security.

The rights of the individual are of no less importance to immigrants and minorities in Europe and the Americas than to women in Afghanistan or children in Africa. They are as fundamental to the poor as to the rich; they are as necessary to the security of the developed world as to that of the developing world.

From this vision of the role of the United Nations in the next century flow three key priorities for the future: eradicating poverty, preventing conflict, and promoting democracy. Only in a world that is rid of poverty can all men and women make the most of their abilities. Only where individual rights are respected can differences be channelled politically and resolved peacefully. Only in a democratic environment, based on respect for diversity and dialogue, can individual self-expression and self-government be secured, and freedom of association be upheld.

Throughout my term as Secretary-General, I have sought to place human beings at the center of everything we do—from conflict prevention to development to human rights. Securing real and lasting improvement in the lives of individual men and women is the measure of all we do at the United Nations.

It is in this spirit that I humbly accept the Centennial Nobel Peace Prize. Forty years ago today, the Prize for 1961 was awarded for the first time to a Secretary-General of the United Nations—posthumously, because Dag Hammarskjöld had already given his life for peace in Central Africa. And on the same day, the Prize for 1960 was awarded for the first time to an African—Albert Luthuli, one of the earliest leaders of the struggle against apartheid in South Africa. For me, as a young African beginning his career in the United Nations a few months later, those two men set a standard that I have sought to follow throughout my working life.

This award belongs not just to me. I do not stand here alone. On behalf of all my colleagues in every part of the United Nations, in every corner of the globe, who have devoted their lives—and in many instances risked or given their lives in the cause of peace—I thank the Members of the Nobel Committee for this high honor....

Most nations have monuments or memorials to war, bronze salutations to heroic battles, archways of triumph. But peace has no parade, no pantheon of victory.

What it does have is the Nobel Prize—a statement of hope and courage with unique resonance and authority. Only by understanding and addressing the needs of individuals for peace, for dignity, and for security can we at the United Nations hope to live up to the honor conferred today, and fulfil the vision of our founders. This is the broad mission of peace that United Nations staff members carry out every day in every part of the world.

A few of them, women and men, are with us in this hall today. Among them, for instance, are a Military Observer from Senegal who is helping to provide basic security in the Democratic Republic of the Congo; a Civilian Police Adviser from the United States who is helping to improve the rule of law in Kosovo; a UNICEF Child Protection Officer from Ecuador who is helping to secure the rights of Colombia's most vulnerable citizens; and a World Food Programme Officer from China who is helping to feed the people of North Korea.

The idea that there is one people in possession of the truth, one answer to the world's ills, or one solution to humanity's needs, has done untold harm throughout history—especially in the last century. Today, however, even amidst continuing ethnic conflict around the world, there is a growing understanding that human diversity is both the reality that makes dialogue necessary, and the very basis for that dialogue.

We understand, as never before, that each of us is fully worthy of the respect and dignity essential to our common humanity. We recognize that we are the products of many cultures, traditions and memories;

that mutual respect allows us to study and learn from other cultures; and that we gain strength by combining the foreign with the familiar.

In every great faith and tradition one can find the values of tolerance and mutual understanding. The Qur'an, for example, tells us that "We created you from a single pair of male and female and made you into nations and tribes, that you may know each other." Confucius urged his followers, "When the good way prevails in the State, speak boldly and act boldly. When the State has lost the way, act boldly and speak softly." In the Jewish tradition, the injunction to "love thy neighbor as thyself" is considered to be the very essence of the Torah.

This thought is reflected in the Christian Gospel, which also teaches us to love our enemies and pray for those who wish to persecute us. Hindus are taught that "truth is one, the sages give it various names." And in the Buddhist tradition, individuals are urged to act with compassion in every facet of life.

Each of us has the right to take pride in our particular faith or heritage. But the notion that what is ours is necessarily in conflict with what is theirs is both false and dangerous. It has resulted in endless enmity and conflict, leading men to commit the greatest of crimes in the name of a higher power.

It need not be so. People of different religions and cultures live side by side in almost every part of the world, and most of us have overlapping identities which unite us with very different groups. We can love what we are, without hating what—and who—we are not. We can thrive in our own tradition, even as we learn from others, and come to respect their teachings.

This will not be possible, however, without freedom of religion, of expression, of assembly, and basic equality under the law. Indeed, the lesson of the past century has been that where the dignity of the individual has been trampled or threatened—where citizens have not enjoyed the basic right to choose their government, or the right to change it regularly—conflict has too often followed, with innocent civilians paying the price, in lives cut short and communities destroyed.

The obstacles to democracy have little to do with culture or religion, and much more to do with the desire of those in power to maintain their position at any cost. This is neither a new phenomenon nor one confined to any particular part of the world. People of all cultures value their freedom of choice, and feel the need to have a say in decisions affecting their lives.

The United Nations, whose membership comprises almost all the States in the world, is founded on the principle of the equal worth of every human being. It is the nearest thing we have to a representative institution that can address the interests of all States, and all peoples. Through this universal, indispensable instrument of human progress, States can serve the interests of their citizens by recognizing common interests and pursuing them in unity. No doubt, that is why the Nobel Committee says that it "wishes, in its centenary year, to proclaim that the only negotiable route to global peace and cooperation goes by way of the United Nations."

I believe the Committee also recognizes that this era of global challenges leaves no choice but cooperation at the global level. When States undermine the rule of law and violate the rights of their individual citizens, they become a menace not only to their own people, but also to their neighbors, and indeed the world. What we need today is better governance—legitimate, democratic governance that allows each individual to flourish, and each State to thrive.

You will recall that I began my address with a reference to the girl born in Afghanistan today. Even though her mother will do all in her power to protect and sustain her, there is a one-in-four risk that she will not live to see her fifth birthday. Whether she does is just one test of our common humanity—of our belief in our individual responsibility for our fellow men and women. But it is the only test that matters.

Remember this girl and then our larger aims—to fight poverty, prevent conflict, or cure disease—will not seem distant, or impossible. Indeed, those aims will seem very near, and very achievable—as they should. Because beneath the surface of States and nations, ideas and language, lies the fate of individual human beings in need. Answering their needs will be the mission of the United Nations in the century to come.

※

Unhealable Wounds: The Colleagues We Lost in Iraq

Address to UN Staff
New York, New York
19 September 2003

On August 19, 2003, the Canal Hotel in Baghdad, which was the UN headquarters in Iraq, was destroyed by a truck bomb. Twenty-three people were killed, including Sergio Vieira de Mello, the UN High Commissioner for Human Rights, whom Annan had persuaded to go to Iraq for four months to head the UN mission set up after the Anglo-American invasion. (The mission, unlike the invasion, had been authorized by the Security Council.) The event was described by some as "the UN's own 9/11"—a bitter blow to the Organization and to Annan personally. Exactly a month later he made this speech to the staff.

Dear friends, ...
I probably speak for most of us in saying that the past month has been among the longest and blackest in our lifetimes.

Today, we share our shock and sorrow at the loss of people we loved. We meet to bring their families together with our United Nations family. We pray for those who were wounded in this tragedy, for their strength and their recovery. We pray for those who survived, but who have to endure a trauma the rest of us cannot imagine.

We meet to express together what cannot be endured alone.

Even for those of us who have experience in dealing with human loss and suffering on a large scale, this tragedy is different, because it is our own.

When we learned the names of those we had lost on 19 August 2003, the very nature of loss became suddenly and acutely personal.

So many of us knew closely one or more of those who died. Even if we ourselves did not, we knew someone else who did. We felt as if we knew them all.

That is why, a month on, we feel that a deeper meaning has been given to the expression "United Nations family."

And if people need an example of our United Nations family at its best and its brightest, at its most committed and most courageous, they have only to look at the men and women who perished in the Canal Hotel.

Many of them were at the height of their careers. Others were just beginning, and had yet to make their full mark when they volunteered for their assignment in Iraq. All of them were in the prime of life. All of them leave a huge void.

They form a roll call of heroes that would be the envy of any nation.

By no measure of the human imagination can I speak for those who shared their lives. That unwritten history can be informed only by the love of family, friends and close comrades. It forms the most eloquent history of all.

I can speak simply as one who shares in the groundswell of grief, affection and respect that follows their passing. In that spirit, let me try to speak to every one of them today.

First, to our national staff[1]—Raid,[2] Leen,[3] Ihssan,[4] Emaad[5] and Basim[6]—I say: you were not only invaluable to our work in Iraq, and dear members of our UN team there. You formed a precious human bridge between us and the Iraqi people. Many of you had worked for the UN for many years, under difficult circumstances, including at times when we were unable to keep an international presence in Iraq. We can never repay you for your courage.

To our international colleagues, I will speak one by one:

Reham,[7] you were so young, yet had already achieved so much. There would have been no limits to what you could have done with your life.

---

1. Iraqis hired locally to work for the United Nations.
2. Raid Shaker Mustafa al-Mahdawi, electrician with the United Nations Monitoring, Verification and Inspection Commission (UNMOVIC).
3. Leen Assad al-Qadi, Office of the Humanitarian Coordinator for Iraq (UNOHCI).
4. Ihssan Taha Husain, driver with the UN Office for Project Services/Office for the Coordination of Humanitarian Affairs.
5. Emaad Ahmed Salman al-Jobory, electrician with UNMOVIC.
6. Basim Mahmood Utaiwi, security guard, UNOHCI.
7. Reham al-Farra (Jordan), Office of the Spokesman for the Special Representative.

You chose to work for the United Nations because you wanted to do something for others. You went to Iraq to make a contribution to the lives of your Arab brothers and sisters. It is their loss as much as ours that you were denied the chance to do that.

Ranillo,[8] you were quiet, diligent, considerate, and ready to work all the hours God gave you. You showed generosity to everyone around you. And you were such a devoted son and sibling to your family back home. You never let the distance to your homeland, or the years spent away, stand between you and your loved ones.

Rick,[9] as a passionate Arabist, you were driven by an equally passionate commitment to peace, justice and human rights. You dazzled people with your brilliance and scholarship, but you also made friends for life through kindness and wisdom beyond your years. You devoted most of your career—and most of the waking hours in many of your days—to searching for ways to help people in the Middle East and the Arab world. And now you have lost your life while on a mission to the region you loved so dearly. Its people have lost a singularly gifted champion; we have lost a deeply beloved friend.

Reza,[10] in your dedicated work to ease the plight of refugees, you never shied away from challenges or difficult assignments. Nor did you ever fail to win people's affection through your warmth, your good humor and your gift for cooking good food. Your heart was as big as your smile—and that was bigger than most.

Jean-Sélim,[11] wherever you went, you waged your war against indifference with a powerful weapon: a determination to translate your ideas into action, to seek practical ways to help others. A true citizen of the world, you were living proof of what it means to come from a UN family. We grieve with your wife, Laura, who is also our colleague. We send our prayers to your baby son, Mattia-Selim.

Christopher,[12] you energized our work for children wherever you went, from Ethiopia to Kosovo to Iraq. Still young yourself, you were

---

8. Ranillo Buenaventura (Philippines), UNOHCI.
9. Rick Hooper (USA), Senior Adviser in the Office of the Under-Secretary-General for the Department of Political Affairs, on a short-term special assignment to the Office of the Special Representative.
10. Reza Hosseini (Iran), UNOHCI.
11. Jean-Sélim Kanaan (Egypt/France), project officer in the Office of the Special Representative.
12. Christopher Klein-Beekman (Canada), Programme Coordinator for Iraq, UNICEF (UN Children's Fund).

such a gifted advocate of young people's right to health, education and a better future. You were a steadfast source of strength and support for your staff. You leave the finest legacy possible—a legacy of hope in the hearts of children you served.

Martha,[13] you combined deeply held humanitarian ideals with healthy realism. Professional, never pretentious, humorous and hardworking, you were the best kind of colleague anyone could wish for, in any UN mission to fight hunger and hardship. Your leadership qualities helped build team unity in the hardest of circumstances. You were good at what you did because you believed in it so fervently.

Fiona,[14] your talent took you from your native Scotland to the Balkans, from New York to Baghdad. Throughout that journey, you were guided by your exceptionally clear head, steadfast principles, and infallible instinct for the right way forward. Your no-nonsense approach was matched by an equal measure of warmth and compassion. When you were taken from us, your young shoulders had already borne a great deal of responsibility. Invariably, they did so with strength, balance and poise.

Nadia,[15] your wit, irreverence and laughter kept our spirits high. There was never anything affected about you; honesty was your defining characteristic. You set the standard in rising above the fray through confidence and humor. In more than 30 years with the UN, you inspired several generations of young women—and men—by showing that there are no limits to what a person with talent and courage could achieve. And you inspired all of us, regardless of age, by showing us that one can be principled without being pompous. Nadia, whenever we get needlessly overwrought, we will remember your voice telling us to "get a grip," and whenever we are tempted to take ourselves too seriously, we will remember the sound of your laughter.

Finally, Sergio,[16] my dear friend, since you were taken from us, there has been an outpouring of tributes to your achievements, accomplishments and talents. But lest we forget, you were a human being first and foremost. A human being who was exceptionally caring; with an

---

13. Martha Teas (USA), Manager of the Humanitarian Information Centre.
14. Fiona Watson (UK), political affairs officer.
15. Nadia Younes (Egypt), Chief of Staff for the Special Representative.
16. Sergio Vieira de Mello (Brazil), Special Representative of the Secretary-General.

exceptionally strong sense of right and wrong; driven by an exceptional need to go out and right the wrongs of this world.

Sergio, if you showed great confidence at all times, it was because you had so much to be confident about. Why did you never seem tired, even while working 18-hour days? Why did you never look crumpled, even after an 18-hour flight? Why were you never sick? Why were you never grumpy? And you were the only top official in the UN system known to everyone by their first name. Even to those who didn't know you personally, you were always just "Sergio."

Now that you are no longer with us, my dear friend, we must make do with your memory and your legacy. They shine bright, and they always will. Like you, they will never grow tired, or crumpled, or weary. Thank you, Sergio, for illuminating our lives.

Friends,

Today, we also pay tribute to non-UN members of our dedicated and extended family—Saad,[17] Omar[18] and Khidir,[19] all Iraqi nationals; Manuel,[20] who sought to coordinate the work of the Coalition Provisional Authority with that of UN agencies; Gillian,[21] who worked tirelessly for the protection of children in crisis; Arthur,[22] who devoted his life to championing the rights of the forcibly displaced; and Alya,[23] who used to serve as one of our most dedicated and experienced translators in Baghdad.

Dear friends,

The work of our United Nations colleagues in Iraq was driven solely by a desire to help the Iraqi people build a better future.

When we lost them, our Organization also suffered another loss, of a different kind: a loss of innocence for the United Nations.

We, who had assumed that our mission to help others served as its own and ultimate form of protection, now find ourselves threatened and exposed.

---

17. Saad Hermiz Abona, worker at the cafeteria of the Canal Hotel.
18. Omar Kahtan Mohamed al-Orfali, driver/interpreter, Christian Children's Fund.
19. Khidir Saleem Sahir, driver who was outside the Canal Hotel at the time of the blast.
20. Manuel Martín-Oar Fernández-Heredia (Spain), Assistant to the Coalition Provisional Authority, Coordinator with UN Specialized Agencies.
21. Gillian Clark (Canada), Christian Children's Fund.
22. Arthur Helton (USA), Director of Peace and Conflict Studies, Council on Foreign Relations.
23. Alya Ahmad Sousa (Iraq), World Bank; former translator, United Nations Iraq-Kuwait Observation Mission.

We, who have tried from the beginning to serve those targeted by violence and destruction, have become a target ourselves.

That means we will need to adapt the way we work to our new environment. We will have to learn to balance our mission on behalf of other people with the need to protect our own.

But our commitment—our pledge in the name of "we the peoples"—must never change. Today, let us renew that commitment in the name of our irreplaceable, inimitable, unforgettable friends. Let us work to heal these unhealable wounds, by working every day to live up to the standard they set us.

❉

Pushing Rocks to the Top of the Mountain

Address to the General Assembly
New York, New York
16 September 2006

In September each year, high-level representatives of all the United Nations' Member States—usually including many heads of state or government, as well as foreign ministers—gather in New York for the "General Debate" at the beginning of the General Assembly session. Before the debate opens, it is customary for the Secretary-General to address them, formally to present his annual report on the work of the Organization but in practice to say whatever he thinks it is most important for them to hear. In September 2006 Annan gave the following as his tenth and last opening address.

When I first spoke to you from this podium, in 1997, it seemed to me that humanity faced three great challenges. One was to ensure that globalization would benefit the human race as a whole, not only its more fortunate members.

Another was to heal the disorder of the post–cold war world, replacing it with a genuinely new world order of peace and freedom, as envisaged in our Charter.

And the third was to protect the rights and dignity of individuals, particularly women, which were so widely trampled underfoot.

As the second African to serve as Secretary-General, I felt that all three of these challenges—the security challenge; the development challenge; the challenge of human rights and the rule of law—concerned me directly.

Africa was in great danger of being excluded from the benefits of globalization—indeed, of being left to rot on the margins of the world economy.

Africa was also the scene of some of the most protracted and brutal conflicts.

And many of Africa's people felt they were unjustly condemned to be exploited and oppressed, generation after generation, since colonial rule had been replaced by an inequitable economic order on the global level and sometimes by corrupt rulers and warlords at the local level.

In the decade since then, many people have been struggling to confront these three global challenges. Much has been achieved, but events have also presented us with new challenges—or rather, have given the old ones new form, or a sharper bite.

In the *economic* arena, both globalization and growth have continued apace.

Some developing countries, notably in Asia, have played a major role in this growth. Many millions of their people have thereby been released from the prison of perpetual poverty.

Meanwhile, at the level of development policy, the debate has advanced, moving from rival models to agreed targets. And the world has now recognized HIV/AIDS as a major challenge to development and begun to confront it. I am proud of the role the United Nations has played in this. Development, and the Millennium Development Goals, now take pride of place in all our work.

But let's not delude ourselves. The Asian miracle is yet to be replicated in other parts of the world. And even within the most dynamic Asian countries, its benefits are far from equally shared.

By the same token, the Millennium Goals are unlikely to be achieved everywhere by 2015.

True, in many developing countries there is now a much better understanding of what good governance is, and why it's important. But many still fall short of it in practice.

True, there is progress on debt relief, as well as encouraging promises on aid and investment. But the "global partnership for development" is still more phrase than fact—especially in the all-important area of trade.

My friends, globalization is not a tide that lifts all boats. Even among those whom the statistics tell us are benefiting, many are deeply insecure and strongly resent the apparent complacency of those more fortunate than themselves.

So globalization, which in theory brings us all closer together, in practice risks driving us further apart.

Are we any more secure against the second challenge—*the ravages of war?*

Again, some statistics would tell us so. There are fewer inter-State conflicts than there used to be, and many civil wars have ended.

Here, too, I am proud of the United Nations' role in this. And I am proud of what my fellow Africans have achieved in ending many of the conflicts that disfigured our continent.

But here, too, we should be under no illusion.

In far too many parts of the world—especially the developing world—people are still exposed to brutal conflicts, fought with small but deadly weapons.

And people in all parts of the world are threatened—though some are more aware of it than others—by the spread of weapons of mass destruction. It is shameful that last year's Summit Outcome does not contain even one word about non-proliferation and disarmament—basically because States could not agree which of the two should be given priority. It is high time to end this dispute and tackle both tasks with the urgency they demand.

Moreover, just as some who benefit from globalization may feel threatened by it, so many who are statistically safer from conflict do not feel safe.

For that, we have terrorism to thank. It kills and maims relatively few people, compared to other forms of violence and conflict. But it spreads fear and insecurity. And that in turn drives people to huddle together with those who share their beliefs or their way of life, while shunning those who appear "alien."

Thus, at the very time when international migration has brought millions of people of different creed or culture to live as fellow-citizens, the misconceptions and stereotypes underlying the idea of a "clash of civilizations" have come to be more and more widely shared, and insensitivity towards other people's beliefs or sacred symbols—intentional or otherwise—is seized upon by those who seem eager to foment a new war of religion, this time on a global scale.

Moreover, this climate of fear and suspicion is constantly refueled by the violence in the Middle East.

We might like to think of the Arab-Israeli conflict as just one regional conflict among many. But it is not. No other conflict carries such a powerful symbolic and emotional charge among people far removed from the battlefield.

As long as the Palestinians live under occupation, exposed to daily frustration and humiliation, and as long as Israelis are blown up in buses and in dance-halls, so long will passions everywhere be inflamed.

On one side, supporters of Israel feel that it is harshly judged, by standards that are not applied to its enemies—and too often this is true, particularly in some UN bodies.

On the other side, people are outraged by the disproportionate use of force against the Palestinians and by Israel's continued occupation and confiscation of Arab land.

As long as the Security Council is unable to end this conflict and the now nearly 40-year-old occupation, by bringing both sides to accept and implement its resolutions, so long will respect for the United Nations continue to decline. So long, too, will our impartiality be questioned. So long will our best efforts to resolve other conflicts be resisted, including those in Iraq and Afghanistan, whose peoples need our help just as badly and are entitled to it. And so long will our devoted and courageous staff, instead of being protected by the blue flag, find themselves exposed to rage and violence, provoked by policies they neither control nor support.

But what about the third great challenge facing humanity—the challenge of the rule of law and *our rights and dignity as human beings*? Here, too, there has been significant progress.

More rights have been enshrined in international treaties—and this Assembly is now about to codify the rights of a group who particularly need it: people who suffer from handicaps and disabilities.

More governments today are elected by, and are accountable to, those whom they govern.

Humanity has actually brought to justice some of those who committed the most heinous crimes against it.

And this Assembly, meeting last year at the highest level, has solemnly proclaimed the responsibility—of each individual State in the first instance, but ultimately of the whole international community, acting through the United Nations—to "protect populations from genocide, war crimes, ethnic cleansing and crimes against humanity."

And yet. And yet.

Every day, reports reach us of new laws broken, of new bestial crimes to which individuals and minority groups are subjected.

Even the necessary and legitimate struggle around the world against terrorism is used as a pretext to abridge or abrogate fundamental human rights, thereby ceding moral ground to the terrorists and helping them find new recruits.

Sadly, once again the biggest challenge comes from Africa—from Darfur, where the continued spectacle of men, women and children driven from their homes by murder, rape and the burning of their villages makes a mockery of our claim, as an international community, to shield people from the worst abuses.

In short, the events of the last ten years have not resolved, but sharpened, the three great challenges I spoke of—an unjust world economy, world disorder, and widespread contempt for human rights and the rule of law. As a result, we face a world whose divisions threaten the very notion of an international community, upon which this institution stands.

And this is happening at the very time when, more than ever before, human beings throughout the world form a single society. So many of the challenges we face are global. They demand a global response, in which all peoples must play their part.

I deliberately say "all peoples," echoing the preamble of our Charter, and not "all States." It was clear to me ten years ago, and is even clearer now, that international relations are not a matter of States alone. They are relations between peoples, in which so-called non-State actors play a vital role, and can make a vital contribution. All must play their part in a true multilateral world order, with a renewed, dynamic United Nations at its center.

Yes, I remain convinced that the only answer to this divided world must be a truly United Nations. Climate change, HIV/AIDS, fair trade, migration, human rights—all these issues, and many more, bring us back to that point. Addressing each is indispensable for each of us in our village, in our neighborhood, and in our country. Yet each has acquired a global dimension that can only be reached by global action, agreed and coordinated through this most universal of institutions.

What matters is that the strong, as well as the weak, agree to be bound by the same rules, to treat each other with the same respect.

What matters is that all peoples accept the need to listen, to compromise, to take each other's views into account.

What matters is that they come together, not at cross purposes but with a common purpose: to shape their common destiny.

And that can only happen if peoples are bound together by something more than just a global market or even a set of global rules.

Each of us must share the pain of all who suffer and the joy of all who hope, wherever in the world they may live.

Each of us must earn the trust of his fellow men and women, no matter what their race, color or creed, and learn to trust them in turn.

That is what the founders of this Organization believed in. It is what I believe in. It is what the vast majority of people in this world want to believe in....

Madam President, dear friends:

This is the last time I shall have the honor of presenting my annual report to this Assembly. Let me conclude by thanking you all for allowing me to serve as Secretary-General during this remarkable decade.

Together we have pushed some big rocks to the top of the mountain, even if others have slipped from our grasp and rolled back. But this mountain with its bracing winds and global views is the best place on earth to be.

It's been difficult and challenging, but at times thrillingly rewarding. And while I look forward to resting my shoulder from those stubborn rocks in the next phase of my life, I know I shall miss the mountain. Yes, I shall miss what is, when all is said and done, the world's most exalting job. I yield my place to others with an obstinate feeling of hope for our common future.

Five Lessons

Speech at the Harry S. Truman Presidential Library and Museum
Independence, Missouri
11 December 2006

Annan's time in office coincided with the "unipolar moment," during which world affairs were dominated by a single superpower, the United States, which is also the host country of the United Nations. It was therefore necessarily one of his priorities to maintain a working relationship with the United States and to explain to the American public why the United Nations needed American leadership and why a strong United Nations was in America's national interest, even though the United States must take account of other views beside its own. In this speech to an American audience at a site commemorating the president who was one of the founders of the United Nations—Harry S. Truman—Annan bade farewell to the American people and sought to sum up the main lessons of his two terms as Secretary-General.

Today I want to talk to you particularly about five lessons I have learnt in the last ten years, during which I have had the difficult but exhilarating job of Secretary-General.

I think it's especially fitting that I do so here in the house that honors the legacy of Harry S. Truman. If FDR was the architect of the United Nations, then President Truman was the master-builder and the faithful champion of the Organization in its early years, when it had to face quite different problems from the ones FDR had expected. Truman's name will always and forever be associated with the memory of farsighted American leadership in a great global endeavor. And every one of my five lessons brings me to the conclusion that such leadership is no less sorely needed now than it was sixty years ago.

My first lesson is that, in today's world, *the security of every one of us is linked to that of everyone else.*

That was already true in Truman's time. The man who in 1945 gave the order for nuclear weapons to be used—for the first, and let us hope the only, time in history—understood that security for some could never again come or be achieved at the price of insecurity for others. He was determined, as he had told the founding conference of the United Nations in San Francisco, to "prevent, if human mind, heart, and hope can prevent it, the repetition of the disaster [meaning the world war] from which the entire world will suffer for years to come." He believed strongly that henceforth security must be collective and indivisible. That was why, for instance, he insisted, when faced with aggression by North Korea against the South in 1950, on bringing the issue to the United Nations and placing US troops under the UN flag, at the head of a multinational force.

But how much more true it is in our open world today: a world where deadly weapons can be obtained not only by rogue States but by extremist groups; a world where avian flu can be carried across oceans, let alone national borders, in a matter of hours; a world where failed States in the heart of Asia or Africa can become havens for terrorists; a world where even the climate is changing in ways that will affect the lives of everyone on the planet.

Against such threats as these, no nation can make itself secure by seeking supremacy over all others. We all share responsibility for each other's security, and only by working to make each other secure can we hope to achieve lasting security for ourselves.

And I would add that this responsibility is not simply a matter of States being ready to come to each other's aid when attacked—important though that is. It also includes our shared responsibility to protect populations from genocide, war crimes, ethnic cleansing and crimes against humanity—a responsibility solemnly accepted by all nations at last year's UN world summit. That means that respect for national sovereignty can no longer be used as a shield by governments intent on massacring their own people or as an excuse for the rest of us to do nothing when heinous crimes are committed.

But, as Truman said, "If we should pay mere lip service to inspiring ideals, and later do violence to simple justice, we would draw down upon us the bitter wrath of generations yet unborn." And when I look at the murder, rape and starvation to which the people of Darfur are being subjected, I fear that we have not got far beyond "lip service." The lesson here is that high-sounding doctrines like the responsibility to protect will remain pure rhetoric unless and until those with the power to intervene effectively—by exerting political, economic or, in the last resort, military muscle—are prepared to take the lead.

And I believe we have a responsibility not only to our contemporaries but also to future generations—a responsibility to preserve resources that belong to them as well as to us and without which none of us can survive. That means we must do much more, and urgently, to prevent or slow down climate change. Every day that we do nothing, or too little, imposes higher costs on our children and our children's children. Of course, it reminds me of an African proverb—the earth is not ours but something we hold in trust for future generations. I hope my generation will be worthy of that trust.

My second lesson is that we are not only all responsible for each other's security. *We are also,* in some measure, *responsible for each other's welfare.* Global solidarity is both necessary and possible.

It is necessary because without a measure of solidarity no society can be truly stable and no one's prosperity truly secure. That applies to national societies—as all the great industrial democracies learned in the twentieth century—but it also applies to the increasingly integrated global market economy that we live in today. It is not realistic to think that some people can go on deriving great benefits from globalization while billions of their fellow human beings are left in abject poverty or even thrown into it. We have to give our fellow citizens, not only within each nation but in the global community, at least a chance to share in our prosperity.

That is why, six years ago, the UN Millennium Summit adopted a set of goals—the "Millennium Development Goals"—to be reached by 2015: goals such as reducing by 50 percent the proportion of people in the world who don't have clean water to drink; making sure all girls and boys receive at least primary education; slashing infant and maternal mortality; and stopping the spread of HIV/AIDS.

Much of that can only be done by governments and people in the poor countries themselves. But richer countries, too, have a vital role to play. Here, too, Harry Truman proved himself a pioneer, proposing in his 1949 inaugural address a program of what came to be known as development assistance. And our success in mobilizing donor countries to support the Millennium Development Goals, through debt relief and increased foreign aid, convinces me that global solidarity is not only necessary but possible.

Of course, foreign aid by itself is not enough. Today, we realize that market access, fair terms of trade, and a non-discriminatory financial system are equally vital to the chances of poor countries....

My third lesson is that *both security and development ultimately depend on respect for human rights and the rule of law.*

Although increasingly interdependent, our world continues to be divided—not only by economic differences, but also by religion and culture. That is not in itself a problem. Throughout history human life has been enriched by diversity, and different communities have learnt from each other. But if our different communities are to live together in peace we must stress also what unites us: our common humanity and our shared belief that human dignity and rights should be protected by law.

That is vital for development, too. Both foreign investors and a country's own citizens are more likely to engage in productive activity when their basic rights are protected and they can be confident of fair treatment under the law. And policies that genuinely favor economic development are much more likely to be adopted if the people most in need of development can make their voice heard.

In short, human rights and the rule of law are vital to global security and prosperity. As Truman said, "We must, once and for all, prove by our acts conclusively that Right Has Might." That's why this country has historically been in the vanguard of the global human rights movement. But that lead can only be maintained if America remains true to its principles, including in the struggle against terrorism. When it appears to abandon its own ideals and objectives, its friends abroad are naturally troubled and confused.

And States need to play by the rules towards each other, as well as towards their own citizens. That can sometimes be inconvenient, but ultimately what matters is not inconvenience. It is doing the right thing. No State can make its own actions legitimate in the eyes of others. When power, especially military force, is used, the world will consider it legitimate only when convinced that it is being used for the right purpose—for broadly shared aims—in accordance with broadly accepted norms.

No community anywhere suffers from too much rule of law; many do suffer from too little—and the international community is among them. This we must change.

The US has given the world an example of a democracy in which everyone, including the most powerful, is subject to legal restraint. Its current moment of world supremacy gives it a priceless opportunity to entrench the same principles at the global level. As Harry Truman said, "We all have to recognize, no matter how great our strength, that we must deny ourselves the license to do always as we please."

My fourth lesson—closely related to the last one—is that *governments must be accountable for their actions in the international arena,* as well as in the domestic one.

Today the actions of one State can often have a decisive effect on the lives of people in other States. So does it not owe some account to those other States and their citizens, as well as to its own? I believe it does.

As things stand, accountability between States is highly skewed. Poor and weak countries are easily held to account, because they need foreign assistance. But large and powerful States, whose actions have the greatest impact on others, can be constrained only by their own people, working through their domestic institutions.

That gives the people and institutions of such powerful States a special responsibility to take account of global views and interests, as well as national ones. And today they need to take into account also the views of what, in UN jargon, we call "non-State actors." I mean commercial corporations, charities and pressure groups, labor unions, philanthropic foundations, universities and think tanks—all the myriad forms in which people come together voluntarily to think about, or try to change, the world.

None of these should be allowed to substitute itself for the State or for the democratic process by which citizens choose their governments and decide policy. But they all have the capacity to influence political processes, on the international as well as the national level. States that try to ignore this are hiding their heads in the sand.

The fact is that States can no longer—if they ever could—confront global challenges alone. Increasingly, we need to enlist the help of these other actors, both in working out global strategies and in putting those strategies into action once agreed. It has been one of my guiding principles as Secretary-General to get them to help achieve UN aims—for instance through the Global Compact with international business, which I initiated in 1999, or in the worldwide fight against polio, which I hope is now in its final chapter, thanks to a wonderful partnership between the UN family, the US Centers for Disease Control and—crucially—Rotary International.

So that is four lessons. Let me briefly remind you of them:

* First, we are all responsible for each other's security.
* Second, we can and must give everyone the chance to benefit from global prosperity.
* Third, both security and prosperity depend on human rights and the rule of law.
* Fourth, States must be accountable to each other and to a broad range of non-State actors, in their international conduct.

My fifth and final lesson derives inescapably from those other four. We can only do all these things by *working together through a multilateral system* and by making the best possible use of the unique instrument bequeathed to us by Harry Truman and his contemporaries, namely the United Nations.

In fact, it is only through multilateral institutions that States can hold each other to account. And that makes it very important to organize those institutions in a fair and democratic way, giving the poor and the weak some influence over the actions of the rich and the strong.

That applies particularly to the international financial institutions, such as the World Bank and the International Monetary Fund. Developing countries should have a stronger voice in these bodies, whose decisions can have almost a life-or-death impact on their fate. And it also applies to the UN Security Council, whose membership still reflects the reality of 1945, not of today's world.

That's why I have continued to press for Security Council reform. But reform involves two separate issues. One is that new members should be added, on a permanent or long-term basis, to give greater representation to parts of the world which have limited voice today. The other, perhaps even more important, is that all Council members, and especially the major powers who are permanent members, must accept the special responsibility that comes with their privilege. The Security Council is not just another stage on which to act out national interests. It is the management committee, if you will, of our fledgling collective security system.

As President Truman said, "The responsibility of the great States is to serve and not dominate the peoples of the world." He showed what can be done and what can be achieved when the US assumes that responsibility. And still today, none of our global institutions can accomplish much when the US remains aloof. But when it is fully engaged, the sky is the limit.

These five lessons can be summed up as five principles, which I believe are essential for the future conduct of international relations: collective responsibility, global solidarity, the rule of law, mutual accountability, and multilateralism. Let me leave them with you, in solemn trust, as I hand over to a new Secretary-General in three weeks' time.

My friends, we have achieved much since 1945, when the United Nations was established. But much remains to be done to put those five principles into practice.

Standing here, I am reminded of Winston Churchill's last visit to the White House, just before Truman left office in 1953. Churchill recalled their only previous meeting, at the Potsdam Conference in 1945. "I must confess, sir," he said boldly, "I held you in very low regard then. I loathed your taking the place of Franklin Roosevelt." Then he paused for a moment and continued: "I misjudged you badly. Since that time you, more than any other man, have saved Western civilization."

My friends, our challenge today is not to save Western civilization—or Eastern, for that matter. All civilization is at stake, and we can save it only if all peoples join together in the task.

You Americans did so much, in the last century, to build an effective multilateral system, with the United Nations at its heart. Do you need it less today, and does it need you less, than 60 years ago?

Surely not. More than ever today Americans, like the rest of humanity, need a functioning global system through which the world's peoples can face global challenges together. And in order to function more effectively, the system still cries out for farsighted American leadership, in the Truman tradition.

I hope and pray that the American leaders of today, and tomorrow, will provide it.

❋ CHAPTER TWO ❋

DEVELOPMENT AND THE GLOBAL COMMUNITY

The Emerging Power of Civil Society

Statement to the Parliamentary Group Parlatino
São Paulo, Brazil
14 July 1998

During an official visit to Brazil, in July 1998, Annan was invited to address a meeting at the headquarters of the "Parlatino," or Latin American Parliament—an association that brings together the legislatures of the region—in which many civil society organizations took part. He chose as his theme the growing importance of civil society and the private sector in international affairs.

I n the past decade the transformation which Latin America has undergone has provided a source of inspiration to all the world. The region has entered an era of democracy and stability, upheld by the pillars of good governance and the rule of law. It will be as much of an inspiration for the world to see the region build a future where these pillars become unshakeable. And much of the foundation for that future, I would venture, lies in people like you here today. It lies in the development of civil society. Because democracy is ultimately the product, not the creator, of civil society.

A strong civil society promotes responsible citizenship and makes democratic forms of government work. A weak civil society supports authoritarian rule, which keeps society weak.

I know that Brazil has understood this symbiotic partnership well. Your First Lady, Ruth Cardoso, spoke eloquently about that partnership … at the United Nations last year. She spoke of the unique role that the non-governmental, non-profit sector can play as an agent for change and as a partner in development—about the youth literacy programs in this country financed by the private sector, undertaken by universities and supported by UNESCO, that have brought literacy to thousands of people across Brazil. As Ms. Cardoso rightly noted, "We know from experience that the State by itself cannot meet the challenges of equitable, sustainable development and that civil society's participation is essential."

The nature of diplomacy too is changing everywhere, to take in civil society. Traditionally, diplomacy has been an activity conducted exclusively by State actors and a subject debated exclusively by paid experts. In the United Nations a few decades ago, the governments of Member States were virtually the sole players in the international process; nongovernmental organizations (NGOs) were seen as supporters, allies, and mobilizers of public opinion in favor of the goals and values of the United Nations Charter.

There is now a growing awareness among the public that any national project is influenced by international conditions—whether these be the environment, Mercosul,[1] intellectual property negotiations, or reform of the United Nations Security Council. And that awareness has been matched by engagement.

A milestone in civil society's engagement in intergovernmental processes was reached here in Brazil six years ago. The United Nations Conference on Environment and Development at Rio became a focal point for NGOs involved in environment and sustainable development everywhere, who understood that the summit agenda was their agenda. It attracted an unprecedented level of grassroots engagement, from the preparations through the meetings to the follow-up to this day.

And to this day, Rio has become the benchmark against which future conferences and summits are measured in terms of civil society response—whether it be the summit on women in Beijing, the human rights conference in Vienna, Habitat in Istanbul, the population conference in Cairo or the conference on climate change at Kyoto last December.

The global information revolution has transformed civil society before our very eyes. Take the international campaign to ban landmines—the driving force behind last year's Treaty to ban the production, stockpile,

---

1. "Mercosul" is the Portuguese name of Mercosur, the common market of the countries of the South American cone.

export and use of these abominable weapons. The campaign demonstrated that there are no limits to what civil society can achieve in partnership with governments. A growing awareness among ordinary people, a grassroots movement of conviction matched by courage, made governments acknowledge that the cost of landmines far outweighed the need to use them. Propelled by the demands of citizens everywhere, promoted tirelessly by regional and non-governmental organizations, the elimination of landmines became a truly global cause.

How did they do it? One thousand NGOs in 60 countries were linked together by one unbending conviction and a weapon that would ultimately prove more powerful than the landmine: e-mail.

Or more recently, look to the role of civil society in advocating the establishment of an effective and just International Criminal Court. A conference is currently under way in Rome to establish such a court, the missing link in the international legal system. In the run-up, the NGO coalition for an International Criminal Court brought together a broad-based network of hundreds of NGOs and international law experts to develop strategies and foster awareness. Again, the key to their network was e-mail and the World Wide Web.

It stands to reason that the relationship between the United Nations and civil society has changed beyond all recognition. Five years ago, when I was Under-Secretary-General for Peacekeeping, an incident occurred in Somalia that taught us—both in the United Nations and in the NGO community— a lesson about the importance of understanding each other well.

With the United Nations Operation in Somalia came the first mandate of a peacekeeping operation to include the protection of humanitarian workers. On one occasion the NGO representatives—40 of them—decided to have a picnic on the beach at Mogadishu. When the NGO workers were attacked there, they asked for the protection of United Nations peacekeepers. The United Nations commander's first reaction was, "Why didn't they tell me they were going to do this?"

I sometimes tell this story to illustrate a cultural gap between non-governmental organizations and the United Nations that is rapidly and happily disappearing. If the global agenda is to be properly addressed, a true partnership between NGOs and the United Nations is not an option; it is a necessity.

Today, NGOs are often on the ground before the international community gives the United Nations a mandate to act. They are indispensable operators in areas ranging from de-mining to human rights, from health care to refugees. And they are seen not only as disseminators of public information or providers of services, but also as shapers of public policy.

Yet, despite the growing manifestations of an ever more robust global civil society, the United Nations has been inadequately equipped to engage it and make it a true partner in our work. And so when I took up the position of Secretary-General and embarked on a quiet revolution to reform the United Nations, enhanced cooperation with NGOs formed a crucial theme in my proposals. This stemmed from a recognition that our common work will be more successful if it is supported by all concerned actors of the international community.

Under the reforms I introduced last year, all substantive departments of the United Nations are designating an NGO liaison officer to facilitate access to the Organization. At the country level, where appropriate, the United Nations system is creating more opportunities for tripartite cooperation with civil society. Training programs for United Nations staff will include a component dedicated to cooperation with civil society. This will be reflected in the curricula of the United Nations Staff College.

Since taking office, I have similarly placed a high priority on building a stronger relationship with the business community and on rebuilding private-sector confidence in the United Nations. The basis for this new partnership is solid. The Organization is no longer prisoner to conflicting ideologies. We fully recognize that business is the main creator of wealth, jobs and prosperity, without which development cannot occur, nor peace be sustained.

That is why we have engaged in a very constructive dialogue with business groups such as the International Chamber of Commerce. And that is why we have instilled a new awareness, throughout the United Nations family, that working with the business community can bring benefits to all. Indeed, all United Nations agencies are searching for practical ways to translate the potential of cooperation into concrete action.

One of the biggest challenges we face today is to secure an open and rule-based international economy. Markets are global, while governments remain local. National economies are becoming more and more inter-dependent. Our choice today is between regulatory consistency and chaos, and between spreading the benefits of globalization or reserving them for just a few. The United Nations has a keen interest in ensuring that markets remain open and that global engagement prevails over an inward-looking orientation.

As I stand here in the business powerhouse of São Paulo—which, if it were a country, would be the twentieth biggest economy in the world—let me suggest some practical ways in which business can interact with the United Nations:

First, you can make your views heard in United Nations debates, at world conferences and in the drafting of international conventions. Business was an important presence at the Rio Summit. This past April, the Commission on Sustainable Development conducted a groundbreak-ing dialogue among delegates from businesses, trade unions, citizens' groups and governments. The United Nations is not just open to your participation; it needs your expertise.

Second, you can cooperate on projects. This is taking various forms, a sign of great flexibility and creativity.

* Some businesses see great value in advocacy: insurance compa-nies, for example, concerned about the cost of disasters caused by climate change.
* Others, such as banks, are helping to promote investment through micro-finance projects to help poor people, especially women, start their own businesses.
* Still others are focusing on "know-how." Information technology companies are contributing technical assistance to an automated customs system developed by the United Nations Conference on Trade and Development, so as to improve trade efficiency in de-veloping countries.
* And then, of course, there is fund-raising, as we have seen in the generosity of Ted Turner,[2] Rotary Clubs and many others. Such

---

2. In September 1997 Ted Turner, founder of CNN and vice chairman of Time Warner, had announced a donation of $1 billion over the next decade to United Nations programs. This led to the creation of the United Nations Foundation.

generosity is easily matched in the goodwill that accrues to the company or business on the giving end.

This past year, I have been hosting a series of gatherings involving eminent leaders of business and NGOs alike. And, in the year 2000, alongside the Millennium Assembly of the United Nations, civil NGOs will be holding a Millennium Forum that will provide an excellent opportunity to further cement our relationship.

As we move towards the end of the decade, NGOs' agendas are focusing increasingly on ways to implement the goals agreed at the conferences of the 1990s. But I hope you will also continue to share with us your vigilance in identifying future needs and priorities, for in a world where change is an essential condition of life, these will continue to evolve.

This changing world presents us with new challenges. Not all effects of globalization are positive; not all non-State actors are good. There has been an ominous growth in the activities of the drug traffickers, gun-runners, money launderers, exploiters of young people for prostitution. These forces of "uncivil society" can be combated only through global cooperation, with the help of civil society.

Information technology has empowered civil society to be the true guardians of democracy and good governance everywhere. Oppressors cannot hide inside their borders any longer. A strong civil society, bound together across all borders with the help of modern communications, will not let them. In a sense, it has become the new superpower—the peoples determined to promote better standards of life in larger freedom.

Every movement starts somewhere—usually from scratch. There are no limits to what the campaigns of tomorrow can achieve—campaigns not yet born, for causes not yet articulated, championed by hearts and minds still being formed. And it is often those single-minded enough to believe their mission to be the most important who are also likely to make it the most successful.

A Global Compact with Business

Address to the World Economic Forum
Davos, Switzerland
31 January 1999

By the late 1990s the annual meeting of the World Economic Forum in Davos had become a major world event and an opportunity for business and political leaders to exchange views. Annan attended the Forum almost every year during his time as Secretary-General. In 1999 he chose it as the platform to make his proposal for a Global Compact between the United Nations and international business, which in time evolved into the world's largest corporate social-responsibility initiative.

I am delighted to join you again at the World Economic Forum. . . .

I am pleased to acknowledge that, in the past two years, our relationship has taken great strides. We have shown through cooperative ventures—both at the policy level and on the ground—that the goals of the United Nations and those of business can, indeed, be mutually supportive.

This year, I want to challenge you to join me in taking our relationship to a still higher level. I propose that you, the business leaders gathered in Davos, and we, the United Nations, initiate a global compact of shared values and principles, which will give a human face to the global market.

Globalization is a fact of life. But I believe we have underestimated its fragility. The problem is this. The spread of markets outpaces the ability of societies and their political systems to adjust to them, let alone to guide the course they take. History teaches us that such an imbalance between the economic, social and political realms can never be sustained for very long.

The industrialized countries learned that lesson in their bitter and costly encounter with the Great Depression. In order to restore social harmony and political stability, they adopted social safety nets and other measures, designed to limit economic volatility and compensate the victims of market failures. That consensus made possible successive moves towards liberalization, which brought about the long post-war period of expansion.

Our challenge today is to devise a similar compact on the global scale, to underpin the new global economy. If we succeed in that, we would lay the foundation for an age of global prosperity, comparable to that enjoyed by the industrialized countries in the decades after the Second World War. Specifically, I call on you—individually through your firms, and collectively through your business associations—to embrace, support and enact a set of core values in the areas of human rights, labor standards, and environmental practices.

Why those three? In the first place, because they are the areas where you, as businessmen and -women, can make a real difference. Secondly, they are the areas in which universal values have already been defined by international agreements, including the Universal Declaration, the International Labor Organization's Declaration on fundamental principles and rights at work, and the Rio Declaration of the United Nations Conference on Environment and Development in 1992. Finally, I chose these three areas because they are ones where I fear that, if we do not act, there may be a threat to the open global market and especially to the multilateral trade regime.

There is enormous pressure from various interest groups to load the trade regime and investment agreements with restrictions aimed at reaching adequate standards in the three areas I have just mentioned. These are legitimate concerns. But restrictions on trade and impediments to investment flows are not the means to use when tackling them. Instead, we should find a way to achieve our proclaimed standards by other means. And that is precisely what the compact I am proposing to you is meant to do.

Essentially there are two ways we can do this. One is through the international policy arena. You can encourage States to give us, the multilateral institutions of which they are all members, the resources and the authority we need to do our job.

The United Nations as a whole promotes peace and development, which are prerequisites for successfully meeting social and environmental goals alike. And the International Labor Organization, the United Nations High Commissioner for Human Rights and the United Nations Environmental Program strive to improve labor conditions, human rights and environmental quality. We hope, in the future, to count you as our allies in these endeavors.

The second way you can promote these values is by tackling them directly, by taking action in your own corporate sphere. Many of you are big investors, employers and producers in dozens of different countries across the world. That power brings with it great opportunities—and great responsibilities. You can uphold human rights and decent labor and environmental standards directly, by your own conduct of your own business.

Indeed, you can use these universal values as the cement binding together your global corporations, since they are values people all over the world will recognize as their own:

❋ You can make sure that in your own corporate practices you uphold and respect human rights and that you are not yourselves complicit in human rights abuses.
❋ Don't wait for every country to introduce laws protecting freedom of association and the right to collective bargaining. You can at least make sure your own employees, and those of your subcontractors, enjoy those rights. You can at least make sure that you yourselves are not employing underage children or forced labor, either directly or indirectly. And you can make sure that, in your own hiring and firing policies, you do not discriminate on grounds of race, creed, gender or ethnic origin.
❋ You can also support a precautionary approach to environmental challenges. You can undertake initiatives to promote greater environmental responsibility. And you can encourage the development and diffusion of environmentally friendly technologies.

That, ladies and gentlemen, is what I am asking of you. But what, you may be asking yourselves, am I offering in exchange? Indeed, I believe the United Nations system does have something to offer.

The United Nations agencies—the United Nations High Commissioner for Human Rights, the International Labor Organization (ILO), the United Nations Environment Program (UNEP)—all stand ready to assist you, if you need help, in incorporating these agreed values and principles into your mission statements and corporate practices. And we are ready to facilitate a dialogue between you and other social groups, to help find viable solutions to the genuine concerns that they have raised....

More important, perhaps, is what we can do in the political arena, to help make the case for, and maintain, an environment which favors trade and open markets.

I believe what I am proposing to you is a genuine compact, because neither side of it can succeed without the other. Without your active commitment and support, there is a danger that universal values will remain little more than fine words—documents whose anniversaries we can celebrate and make speeches about but with limited impact on the lives of ordinary people. And unless those values are really seen to be taking hold, I fear we may find it increasingly difficult to make a persuasive case for the open global market.

National markets are held together by shared values. In the face of economic transition and insecurity, people know that if the worst comes to the worst, they can rely on the expectation that certain minimum standards will prevail. But in the global market, people do not yet have that confidence. Until they do have it, the global economy will be fragile and vulnerable—vulnerable to backlash from all the "isms" of our post–cold war world: protectionism, populism, nationalism, ethnic chauvinism, fanaticism, and terrorism.

What all those "isms" have in common is that they exploit the insecurity and misery of people who feel threatened or victimized by the global market. The more wretched and insecure people there are, the more those "isms" will continue to gain ground. What we have to do is find a way of embedding the global market in a network of shared values. I hope I have suggested some practical ways for us to set about doing just that.

Let us remember that the global markets and multilateral trading system we have today did not come about by accident. They are the result of enlightened policy choices made by governments since 1945. If we want to maintain them in the new century, all of us—governments, corporations, non-governmental organizations, international organizations—have to make the right choices now.

We have to choose between a global market driven only by calculations of short-term profit and one which has a human face. Between a world which condemns a quarter of the human race to starvation and squalor and one which offers everyone at least a chance of prosperity, in a healthy environment. Between a selfish free-for-all in which we ignore the fate of the losers and a future in which the strong and successful accept their responsibilities, showing global vision and leadership.

I am sure you will make the right choice.

❋

Peace and Development

Address to World Bank Staff
Washington, DC
19 October 1999

One of Annan's achievements as Secretary-General was to forge much closer relations between the United Nations and the Washington-based "Bretton Woods institutions"—the International Monetary Fund and the World Bank. In the case of the World Bank, this was facilitated by his friendship with its president, James Wolfensohn. In 1999 Wolfensohn invited him to speak to the Bank's staff. Annan chose this as an occasion to speak on "Peace and Development—One Struggle, Two Fronts."

The founders of the United Nations clearly recognized the connection between the struggle for peace and security—where victory spells freedom from fear—and the struggle for economic and social progress, where victory spells freedom from want.

Since then there have been five decades of real progress on both fronts. The world as a whole is both more peaceful and more prosperous than it was in 1945. But that progress has not been equally shared.

Nearly half the human race—an estimated 2.8 billion people—is still struggling to survive on less than two dollars a day.

And according to one estimate, five and a half million people have died in war during the 1990s. Many times that number have had their lives ruined—by injury, by the loss of their loved ones, by being driven from their homes or by the destruction of their property.

The vast majority of these conflicts occur in the developing world.

Most of the world's 20 poorest countries have experienced significant violent conflict in the past decades. In Africa, out of 45 countries where the United Nations has development programs, 18 are experiencing civil strife and 11 are in varying stages of political crisis.

Clearly, war is not the only cause of poverty, and poverty by itself does not cause war. If it did, all poor countries would be at war. Thank God, most of them are not.

Nor is inequality in itself a sufficient explanation for conflict. The relationship is much more complex than that.

But one thing is indisputable: development has no worse enemy than war.

Prolonged armed conflicts don't only kill people: they destroy a country's physical infrastructure, divert scarce resources and disrupt economic life, including food supplies. They radically undermine education and health services.

A war of national liberation or self-defense may sometimes bind a nation together—albeit at a cruel and unacceptable human cost. But almost all today's conflicts are civil wars, in which civilian populations are not incidental casualties but direct targets. These wars completely destroy trust between communities, breaking down normal social relations and undermining the legitimacy of government—not to mention investor confidence. They are also harder to end, because the opposing sides have to live together after the peace, rather than withdrawing behind State borders.

Wars between States, fought with expensive modern weaponry, are very destructive but do at least tend to be short-lived: think of the Gulf War in 1991 or the Kosovo conflict this year. But today's more typical wars are fought in poor countries, with weapons that are cheap and easy to obtain. The misery of these wars can be sustained for years, or even decades: think of Afghanistan, Angola, Sudan.

Much of our work at the United Nations is devoted to coping with the immense suffering caused by these conflicts and the search for ways to settle them peacefully.

The search is always long and often thankless—but not as hopeless as the headlines might make you think. During the past nine years, three times as many peace agreements have been signed as in the previous three decades. Some have failed, often amid great publicity, but most have held.

Success, however, brings with it new tasks and problems: what we in the United Nations call "post-conflict peace-building." This has been a major innovation of the 1990s and something of a growth industry.

From Namibia and El Salvador to Kosovo and East Timor, you and we are working side by side, along with local government officials, non-governmental organizations (NGOs) and citizens' groups, to help provide emergency relief, demobilize combatants, clear mines, organize elections, encourage reconciliation, build impartial police forces and reestablish basic services. Most difficult but most important of all, we are trying to rebuild relationships—that precious capital of trust within and between communities which is the first casualty of every war, and the hardest thing to restore. There has been much talk of "bridging the gap" or "managing the transition" between these tasks and longer-term development efforts. But increasingly, I think, we understand that the two are not separate. Crisis management and peace-building have to be part of a development strategy. If countries wait until all their conflicts and crises are settled before embarking on such a strategy they are likely to wait forever.

But how much better it would be if we could prevent these conflicts from arising in the first place!

I shall not waste time trying to persuade you of that with facts and figures, because none of you would disagree. No one doubts that prevention is desirable. What some question is whether it is feasible, or whether decision-makers will ever have long enough time horizons to take it seriously. It is even said that "convincing politicians to invest in conflict prevention is like asking a teenager to start saving for a pension."

I believe such cynicism is misplaced, but there is a need for humility. Even if we did receive all the resources we need for prevention, we should not overestimate our powers.

Unless the government and people of a country are genuinely willing to confront the problems that may cause conflict, there is not much that even the best informed and most benevolent outsiders can do.

This is not a counsel of despair, simply a note of necessary caution.

What is clear is that to succeed in preventing wars we need to understand the forces that create them.

Of course these are complex, and—as usual—there is a lot of disagreement among scholars who have studied them. But on some key points a consensus is beginning to emerge.

First, no one single factor can explain all conflicts—and therefore no simple nostrum can prevent them all. Prevention policies must be tailored to the particular circumstances of the country or region and must address many different issues at the same time.

Secondly, most researchers agree that it is useful to distinguish "structural" or long-term factors, which make violent conflict more likely, from "triggers," which actually ignite it.

The structural factors all have to do with social and economic policy and the way societies govern themselves. It is here that the link between security and development policy is most obvious.

A major study by the United Nations University, to be published later this year, suggests that simple inequality between rich and poor is not enough to cause violent conflict.[1] What is highly explosive is what the authors of the study call "horizontal" inequality: when power and resources are unequally distributed between groups that are also differentiated in other ways—for instance by race, religion or language. So-called "ethnic" conflicts occur between groups which are distinct in one or more of these ways, when one of them feels it is being discriminated against or another enjoys privileges which it fears to lose.

Economic stagnation or decline—sometimes caused by factors quite outside a government's control, such as deterioration in the terms of trade—do make conflict more likely. As resources get scarcer, competition for them gets fiercer, and elites use their power to retain them at everyone else's expense.

And when economic decline is prolonged—especially when it starts from an already low base—the result can be a steady degeneration of the State's capacity to govern, until the point where it can no longer maintain public order.

---

1. See Frances Stewart, *Horizontal Inequality: A Neglected Dimension of Development* (WIDER Annual Lecture, 2001), United Nations University, World Institute for Development Economic Research, 2002. http://www.wider.unu.edu/publications/annual-lectures/en_GB/AL5.

So the fact that political violence occurs more frequently in poor countries has more to do with failures of governance, and particularly with failure to redress "horizontal" inequalities, than with poverty as such. A well-governed poor country can avoid conflict. It also, of course, has a better chance of escaping from poverty.

Even where these long-term factors are present, actual conflict requires a short-term "trigger."

Often this takes the form of a deliberate mobilization of grievances by rival elites, with the careful cultivation of dehumanizing myths within one group about another group, propagated and amplified by hate-media.

At the very edge of war, relatively small events which appear to confirm these myths can provide the spark to ignite full-scale violence. And once it has started, whole communities become gripped by hate and fear. Each action by one tends to reinforce the fears of the other.

Often it is the State, or the group that controls the State, which initiates large-scale violence, as a response to non-violent protests by opposition groups. This is not surprising, because governments are usually better armed than their opponents, at least at the beginning of a conflict. However strong their grievances, people seldom take up arms in sufficient numbers to defeat the State unless they are driven to it by violent repression.

But many wars have more to do with greed than with grievance—as several recent studies have shown, including one done here in the Bank's Research Department. War can be profitable for some, especially where it involves control over valuable export commodities like diamonds, drugs or timber. Where governments are weak and legitimate economic opportunities are few, resort to violent crime may seem a logical alternative to destitution, especially for unemployed youth. And when such criminal violence occurs on a large scale—and is resisted, as it must be, by the State—it can all too easily escalate into civil war.

So what can we do about all this?

First of all, if "horizontal" inequality is indeed a major cause of conflict, then obviously our policies must seek to reduce it. Yet, until very recently, development policy tended to ignore this problem. As a result, some policies which were meant to enhance growth have had the unintended consequence of aggravating this kind of inequality, thus increasing the risk of instability and violence.

That is one reason why I welcome Jim Wolfensohn's call for the Bank and its partners to start asking hard questions about "how we can best integrate a concern for conflict prevention into development operations." And I am interested to hear that the British Government is now actively discussing the idea of "conflict impact assessments." The idea is that before adopting a particular policy or imposing a particular type of conditionality, you would check, through a process of consultation, that that policy will reduce the danger of conflict in a country—or at least not actually increase it.

Like a lot of good ideas, this seems common sense once you have thought of it. But in the past it has not been done.

Secondly, if conflict is often caused by different groups having unequal access to political power, then it follows that a good way to avoid conflict is to encourage democracy—not the winner-takes-all variety, but inclusive democracy, which gives everyone a say in decisions that affect their lives.

During the 1990s, largely as a result of the end of the cold war, there have been two remarkable changes in the international system. First, the number of democratic States in the world almost doubled between 1990 and 1998. And second, the number of armed conflicts in the world declined—from fifty-five in 1992 to thirty-six in 1998.

That second statement may seem surprising, when each of us can reel off a list of horrific conflicts, from Bosnia to Sierra Leone to East Timor.

But the truth—so far entirely missed by the media—is that more old wars have ended than new ones have begun.

Of course the increase in the number of democracies is not the sole cause of the decline in the number of wars. Other factors, not least the ending of cold war ideological conflicts, have also played a role. And in some cases peace may have made democratization possible, rather than the other way round. But a number of studies do show that democracies have very low levels of internal violence compared with non-democracies.

When you think about it, that is what you would expect. Democracy is, in essence, a form of non-violent conflict management. But a note of caution is in order. While the end result is highly desirable, the process of democratization can be highly destabilizing—especially when States introduce "winner-take-all" electoral systems without adequate provision for human rights. At such times different groups can become more conscious of their unequal status and nervous about each other's power. Too often, they resort to preemptive violence.

But that should not discourage us from urging the right sort of democratization as part of our development policies.

Good governance, of course, means much more than democratization in a formal political sense. Another very important aspect of it is the reform of public services—including the security sector, which should be subject to the same standards of efficiency, equity and accountability as any other public service....

Conflict is much less likely to occur in a State if all its inhabitants feel that their lives and property are made safer by the work of the security services. Conflict is more likely when a significant group of citizens feels excluded from the security services and exploited or terrorized by them.

If I could sum up my message this afternoon in one sentence, it is that human security, good governance, equitable development and respect for human rights are interdependent and mutually reinforcing. If war is the worst enemy of development, healthy and balanced development is the best form of conflict prevention.

The case for allocating more time and resources to development policies such as I have outlined is compelling. It is cost-effective, and it can save millions of lives. But it will not be easy.

The costs of prevention have to be paid in the present, while its benefits lie in the distant future. Moreover, the benefits are intangible: they are the wars and disasters that do not happen. Yet there has been a great upsurge of interest in prevention over the past few years, among donor States as well as international organizations. We must build on it....

We must learn how to work better with each other, with the other parts of the United Nations system, with governments and with NGOs.

We must also learn from each other, never thinking that our own particular group or agency is the sole repository of wisdom.

Above all, we must learn from the people of developing countries. Each country, each province, even each village has its own particular problems but also its own insights and inspiration.

I believe the single most valuable quality, for diplomats and development economists alike, is the ability to listen.

And now it's my turn to listen to you.

❄

Global Market, Global Values

Address to the Third Ministerial Meeting of
the World Trade Organization (WTO)
Seattle, Washington
30 November 1999

Though a version of it was published in the Wall Street Journal *on November 29, 1999, this speech was never actually delivered. Annan had traveled to Seattle to put the case for open markets to the WTO ministerial meeting but was unable to make the short journey from his hotel to the conference hall because the streets had been taken over by anti-globalization protesters. In a sense this confirmed the warning he had given to the world business community at Davos earlier in the year, that globalization would be fragile as long as it was not underpinned by solidarity and social justice.*

L et me begin by thanking the city government and people of Seattle for hosting this very important, but evidently very controversial, conference. I wonder if they realized what they were letting themselves in for!

Personally, I am delighted to be here and deeply honored to be invited to address this gathering, which is indeed very important. I hope and believe it will be remembered as the Conference which launched the "development round" and laid the foundations of a world trade system which will be fair as well as free.[1]

In the past, developing countries have been told time and again that they stand to benefit from trade liberalization and that they must open up their economies.

They have done so, often at great cost. For the poorest countries the cost of implementing trade commitments can be more than a whole year's budget.

---

1. In the event, the development round was not launched until two years later, after the 9/11 attacks, at the following ministerial conference in Doha, Qatar. As of 2013 it has still not been concluded.

But, time and again, they have found the results disappointing—not because free trade is bad for them but because they are still not getting enough of it.

In the last great round of liberalization—the Uruguay Round—the developing countries cut their tariffs, as they were told to do. But in absolute terms many of them still maintain high tariff barriers, thereby not only restricting competition but denying crucial imports to their own producers and thus slowing down economic growth.

Even so, they found that rich countries had cut their tariffs less than poor ones. Not surprisingly, many of them feel they were taken for a ride.

Ever more elaborate ways have been found to exclude third world imports, and these protectionist measures bite deepest in areas where developing countries are most competitive, such as textiles, footwear and agriculture.

In some industrialized countries, it seems almost as though emerging economies are assumed to be incapable of competing honestly, so that whenever they do produce something at a competitive price they are accused of dumping—and subjected to anti-dumping duties.

In reality, it is the industrialized countries who are dumping their surplus food on world markets—a surplus generated by subsidies worth $250 billion every year—and thereby threatening the livelihood of millions of poor farmers in the developing world, who cannot compete with subsidized imports.

So it is hardly surprising if developing countries suspect that arguments for using trade policy to advance various good causes are really yet another form of disguised protectionism.

I am sure that in most cases that is not the intention: those who advance such arguments are usually voicing genuine fears and anxieties about the effects of globalization, which do need to be answered.

They are right to be concerned—about jobs, about human rights, about child labor, about the environment, about the commercialization of scientific and medical research. They are right, above all, to be concerned about the desperate poverty in which so many people in developing countries are condemned to live.

But globalization must not be used as a scapegoat for domestic policy failures. The industrialized world must not try to solve its own problems at the expense of the poor. It seldom makes sense to use trade restrictions to tackle problems whose origins lie not in trade, but in other areas of national and international policy. By aggravating poverty and obstructing development, such restrictions often make the problems they are trying to solve even worse.

Practical experience has shown that trade and investment not only bring economic development, but often bring higher standards of human rights and environmental protection as well. All these things come together when countries adopt appropriate policies and institutions. Indeed, a developing civil society will generally insist on higher standards, as soon as it is given the chance to do so.

What is needed is not new shackles for world trade, but greater determination by governments to tackle social and political issues directly—and to give the institutions that exist for that purpose the funds and the authority they need. The United Nations and its specialized agencies are charged with advancing the causes of development, the environment, human rights, and labor. We can be part of the solution.

So too can the private sector. Transnational companies, which are the prime beneficiaries of economic liberalization, must share some of the responsibility for dealing with its social and environmental consequences.

Economic rights and social responsibilities are two sides of the same coin. This is why, earlier this year, I proposed a Global Compact between business and the United Nations, under which we will help the private sector to act in accordance with internationally accepted principles in the areas of human rights, labor standards and the environment. The response so far has been encouraging, and I believe we can achieve a great deal by working together more closely.

But this meeting, and this Organization, must not be distracted from their vital task—which is to make sure that this time a new round of trade negotiations really does extend the benefits of free trade to the developing world. Unless we convince developing countries that globalization really does benefit them, the backlash against it will become irresistible. That would be a tragedy for the developing world, and indeed for the world as a whole.

Trade is better than aid. If industrialized countries do more to open their markets, developing countries can increase their exports by many billions of dollars per year—far more than they now receive in aid. For millions and millions of poor people this could make the difference between their present misery and a decent life. And yet the cost for the rich countries would be minuscule.

In fact, industrialized countries might even be doing themselves a favor. It has been calculated that some of them are currently spending as much as 6 or 7 percent of their gross domestic product on various kinds of trade protection measures. No doubt some of their citizens are benefiting from this, but surely there must be a cheaper and less harmful way for the rest of the population to help them!

This time, tariffs and other restrictions on developing countries' exports must be substantially reduced. For those of the least developed countries, I suggest, duties and quotas should be scrapped altogether.

And developing countries should receive technical assistance, both in the negotiations themselves and in implementing and benefiting from the agreements once reached. At present, some of them do not even have missions in Geneva. But the United Nations Conference on Trade and Development (UNCTAD) is there to help, if given the resources to do so.

In exactly one month we shall leave the twentieth century behind. The first half of it saw the world almost destroyed by war, partly as a result of its division into rival trade blocs.

The second half, by contrast, has seen an unprecedented expansion of global trade, which has also brought unprecedented economic growth and development, even if as yet very unequally distributed.

That expansion did not happen by accident. After the carnage and devastation of the Second World War, farsighted statesmen deliberately constructed a post-war economic and political order governed by rules which would make free trade possible—and thereby, they believed, make future wars less likely. Broadly speaking, they were right.

Several factors combined at that time to make such a liberal world order possible. One of them was a broad consensus on the role of the State in ensuring full employment, price stability and social safety nets. Another was that most big firms were still organized within a single country—so that international economic relations could be negotiated between States, each of which corresponded to a distinct national economy, and could be controlled by raising or lowering barriers at national frontiers.

And that in turn made it relatively easy to put in place a set of international organizations which were based on, and in their turn supported, the economic order: the World Bank, the International Monetary Fund, the General Agreement on Tariffs and Trade and the United Nations.

Today's world is very different. Today, networks of production and finance have broken free from national borders and become truly global. But they have left the rest of the system far behind.

Nation States, and the institutions in which they are represented, can set the rules within which international exchanges take place, but they can no longer dictate the terms of such exchanges exclusively among themselves....

The result is that, on top of the gross imbalance of power and wealth between industrialized countries and developing ones, there is now a second imbalance: the gap between the integration of the world economy and the continued parochialism of political and social institutions. While economics is global, politics remains obstinately local. It is for this reason, I believe, that so many people, even in the industrialized world, feel vulnerable and helpless.

And that is why this is such a historic moment.

It will depend on what we decide here, and in a few other crucial meetings over the next few years, whether the twenty-first century will be like the first half of the twentieth, only worse—or like the second half, only better.

Let's not take the onward march of free trade and the rule of law for granted. Instead, let us resolve to underpin the free global market with genuinely global values and secure it with effective institutions. Let us show the same firm leadership in defense of human rights, labor standards and the environment as we already do in defense of intellectual property.

In short, let us emulate the wisdom, and the willpower, of those who laid the foundations of the liberal world order after the Second World War. They made change work for the people—and we must do the same.

❋

We the Peoples

Address to the General Assembly
New York, New York
3 April 2000

At Annan's suggestion, made soon after he took office as Secretary-General, the General Assembly decided to designate its 55th session, starting on 5 September 2000, as the Millennium Assembly of the United Nations and to hold a Millennium Summit. To provide an agenda for the Summit, in March 2000 Annan produced his Millennium Report, entitled We the Peoples: The Role of the United Nations in the 21ˢᵗ Century.[1] *It contained the first draft of what was to become the Millennium Declaration, including the Millennium Development Goals. In this statement, he presented the report to the General Assembly.*

The Millennium might have been no more than an accident of the calendar. But you, the governments and the peoples of the world, have chosen to make it more than that—an occasion for all humanity to celebrate and to reflect.

The world did celebrate on New Year's Eve, in one time zone after another. And you, the General Assembly, have provided a unique opportunity for us all to reflect on our common destiny, by convening what will surely be the largest gathering of political leaders the world has ever seen.

The object of my Report is to provide that gathering with a basic document to work from. In it, I have attempted to identify the main challenges that we face, as we enter the twenty-first century, and to sketch out an action plan for addressing them.

If one word encapsulates the changes we are living through, it is "globalization." We live in a world that is interconnected as never

---

1. Published by the UN Department of Public Information: DPI/2103—March 2000—I 5 M.

before—one in which groups and individuals interact more and more directly across State frontiers, often without involving the State at all. This has its dangers, of course. Crime, narcotics, terrorism, disease, weapons—all these move back and forth faster, and in greater numbers, than in the past. People feel threatened by events far away.

But the benefits of globalization are obvious too: faster growth; higher living standards; and new opportunities, not only for individuals, but also for better understanding between nations, and for common action.

One problem is that, at present, these opportunities are far from equally distributed. How can we say that the half of the human race, which has yet to make or receive a telephone call, let alone use a computer, is taking part in globalization? We cannot, without insulting their poverty.

A second problem is that, even where the global market does reach, it is not yet underpinned, as national markets are, by rules based on shared social objectives. In the absence of such rules, globalization makes many people feel they are at the mercy of unpredictable forces.

So the overarching challenge of our times is to make globalization mean more than bigger markets. To make a success of this great upheaval, we must learn how to govern better, and—above all—how to govern better together. We need to make our States stronger and more effective at the national level. And we need to get them working together on global issues, all pulling their weight and all having their say.

What are these global issues? I have grouped them under three headings, each of which relates to a fundamental human freedom—freedom from want, freedom from fear, and the freedom of future generations to sustain their lives on this planet.

First, *freedom from want*. How can we call human beings free and equal in dignity when over a billion of them are struggling to survive on less than one dollar a day, without safe drinking water, and when half of all humanity lacks adequate sanitation? Some of us are worrying about whether the stock market will crash or struggling to master our latest computer, while more than half our fellow men and women have much more basic worries, such as where their children's next meal is coming from.

Unless we redouble and concert our efforts, poverty and inequality will get worse still, since world population will grow by a further two billion in the next quarter century, with almost all the increase in the poorest countries.

Many of these problems are worst in sub-Saharan Africa, where extreme poverty affects a higher proportion of the population than anywhere else, and is compounded by a higher incidence of conflict, HIV/AIDS, and other ills. I am asking the world community to make special provision for Africa's needs, and give full support to Africans in their struggle to overcome these problems.

My Report sets a series of targets for reversing these frightening trends throughout the world. Within the next 15 years, I believe we can halve the population of people living in extreme poverty; ensure that all children—girls and boys alike, and particularly, girls—receive a full primary education; and halt the spread of HIV/AIDS. In 20 years, we can also transform the lives of one hundred million slum dwellers around the world. And, I believe, we should be able to offer all young people between 15 and 24 the chance of decent work.

These targets are realistic, if we take full advantage of the opportunities offered by globalization and the revolution in information technology. Much depends on developing countries themselves adopting the right policies, but the industrialized world too has a vital part to play. It must fully open its markets to products from developing countries. It must provide faster and deeper debt relief. And it must give more, and better focused, development assistance.

Needless to say, the role of the private sector is also crucial. It is vital that we form new partnerships to make the most of the new technology. I am announcing several new examples in my Report....

The second main heading in the Report is *freedom from fear.* Wars between States are mercifully less frequent than they used to be. But in the last decade, internal wars have claimed more than 5 million lives, and driven many times that number of people from their homes. Moreover, we still live under the shadow of weapons of mass destruction. Both these threats, I believe, require us to think of security less in terms of merely defending territory, and more in terms of protecting *people.* That means we must tackle the threat of deadly conflict at every stage in the process. We must do more to prevent conflicts from happening at all. Most conflicts happen in poor countries, especially those which are badly governed or where power and wealth are very unfairly distributed between ethnic or religious groups. So, the best way to prevent conflict is to promote political arrangements in which all groups are fairly represented, combined with human rights, minority rights, and broad-based economic development. Also, illicit transfers of weapons, money or natural resources must be forced into the limelight, so that we can control them better.

We must protect vulnerable people by finding better ways to enforce humanitarian and human rights law, and to ensure that gross violations do not go unpunished. National sovereignty offers vital protection to small and weak States, but it should not be a shield for crimes against humanity. In extreme cases, the clash of these two principles confronts us with a real dilemma, and the Security Council may have a moral duty to act on behalf of the international community.

But, in most cases, the international community should be able to preserve peace by measures which do *not* infringe State sovereignty. It can do so, if our capacity to conduct peace operations is strengthened....

Economic sanctions are one weapon available to the Security Council, of which it made extensive use during the 1990s. But, too often these sanctions fail to impress delinquent rulers, while causing much unnecessary suffering to innocent people. We must target them better. Finally, we must pursue our disarmament agenda more vigorously. Since 1995, it has lost momentum in an alarming way. That means controlling the traffic in small arms much more tightly, but also returning to the vexed issue of nuclear weapons....

The third fundamental freedom my Report addresses is one that is not clearly identified in the Charter, because in 1945 our founders could scarcely imagine that it would ever be threatened. I mean the *freedom of future generations to sustain their lives on this planet.* Even now, many of us have not understood how seriously that freedom is threatened. I am told that, in all your deliberations and all your preparatory work for the Millennium Assembly over the last 18 months, the environment was never seriously considered. And in preparing this section of my Report, I found many fewer policy prescriptions ready to be put into practice than I did in the other areas I have mentioned.

Yet, the facts set out in this section are deeply troubling. I beseech you to read it with at least as much attention as the rest of the Report.

If I could sum it up in one sentence, I should say we are plundering our children's heritage to pay for our present unsustainable practices. This must stop. We must reduce emissions of carbon and other "greenhouse gases," to put a stop to global warming. Implementing the Kyoto Protocol is a vital first step.

The "Green Revolution," which brought dramatic increases in agricultural productivity in the 1970s and 1980s, has slowed down. We need to follow it with a "Blue Revolution," focused on increasing productivity per unit of water, and on managing our watersheds and flood plains more carefully.

We must face the implications of a steadily shrinking surface of cultivable land, at a time when every year brings many millions of new mouths to feed. Biotechnology may offer the best hope, but only if we can resolve the controversies and allay the fears surrounding it. I am convening a global policy network to consider these issues urgently, so that the poor and hungry do not lose out. We must preserve our forests, fisheries, and the diversity of living species, all of which are close to collapsing under the pressure of human consumption and destruction.

In short, we need a new ethic of stewardship. We need a much better informed public, and we need to take the environmental costs and benefits fully into account in our economic policy decisions. We need regulations and incentives to discourage pollution and over-consumption of non-renewable resources, and to encourage environment-friendly practices. And we need more accurate scientific data.

Above all, we need to remember the old African wisdom which I learned as a child—that the earth is not ours. It is a treasure we hold in trust for our descendants.

But, you may be asking by now, what about the United Nations? Is not the theme of the Summit, and of the Report, "the role of the United Nations in the twenty-first century"?

Yes it is, and the Report contains a further section on renewing the United Nations, which I hope the Member States will take very seriously. But let us not forget why the United Nations matters. It matters only to the extent that it can make a useful contribution to solving the problems and accomplishing the tasks I have just outlined.

Those are the problems and the tasks which affect the everyday lives of our peoples. It is on how we handle them that the utility of the United Nations will be judged. If we lose sight of that point, the United Nations will have little or no role to play in the twenty-first century.

Let us never forget that our Organization was founded in the name of "We, the Peoples"—the words I have chosen as the title of my Report. We are at the service of the world's peoples, and we must listen to them. They are telling us that our past achievements are not enough. They are telling us that we must do more, and do it better.

※

Leadership Is Coming from Women

*Keynote Address to the Third Annual Gala of the
International Women's Health Coalition
New York, New York
15 January 2004*

I want to pay tribute to the International Women's Health Coalition for the wonderful work it is doing around the globe.

The IWHC and its partners provide indispensable leadership for the health and rights of girls and women worldwide. If there were more pioneers like you, the world would be a better place. And I am not at all surprised—because I have found this to be true in so many places—that leadership like this is coming above all from women.

You are a shining example of the increasingly crucial role that civil society plays in the work to improve the lives of people everywhere. In the past few decades, this role has grown beyond all recognition—as civil society groups have become advocates, shapers of policy, and allies of governments in the work on the ground. Today, for the United Nations to succeed in many of its endeavors, partnership with civil society is not an option—it is a necessity.

Let me remind you that we have just entered the tenth anniversary year of the historic International Conference on Population and Development, held under UN auspices in Cairo in 1994. As you know, that conference forged an extraordinary consensus on actions to ensure that reproductive health is recognized as a human right. It also reached agreement on a wide range of actions to achieve gender equality, development, as well as economic and ssocial justice.

Six years later, the Cairo consensus helped pave the way for the Millennium Development Goals—adopted by all the world's countries as a blueprint for building better lives for people everywhere in the twenty-first century.

The adoption of the MDGs was a seminal event in the history of the United Nations. These eight commitments range from halving extreme poverty to halting the spread of HIV/AIDS, from reducing child mortality to eliminating gender disparity in education—all by the target date of 2015. They represent a set of simple but powerful objectives that every man and woman in the street, from New York to New Delhi, from Lima to Luanda, can easily understand and support.

In other words, the MDGs are a call to which every one of us can and should respond. And the International Women's Health Coalition has responded eloquently. You are an exceptionally active and constructive partner in the work to translate the Millennium Development Goals into reality. You have understood that one of the most effective ways to do that is through the education and empowerment of girls and women.

Study after study has taught us that there is no tool for development more effective than the education of girls and the empowerment of women. No other policy is as likely to raise economic productivity, lower infant and maternal mortality, or improve nutrition and promote health, including the prevention of HIV/AIDS. When women are fully involved, the benefits can be seen immediately: families are healthier; they are better fed; their income, savings, and reinvestment go up. And what is true of families is true of communities and, eventually, whole countries.

And yet, out of more than 860 million illiterate adults in the world today, two-thirds are women. Out of more than 100 million children who are not in school, the majority are girls.

At the same time, more than half a million women still die every year from preventable conditions and injuries related to pregnancy and childbirth. And in many parts of the world, HIV/AIDS is now spreading more rapidly among women than among men. It is a shocking fact, and one of which I as an African man feel ashamed, that a girl in sub-Saharan Africa is six times more likely to be infected than a boy. There are many reasons, ranging from abuse and coercion by older men and men having several partners, to lack of awareness and empowerment among girls and women....

From issues of morality to issues of mortality, girls and women pay a higher price. When poverty and other constraints force parents to choose which children to send to school, girls are more likely to be kept at home. When the family income needs to be supplemented, girls are more likely to be sent out to work. Even when girls do go to school, their attendance and performance suffer because they will often have to do housework at the expense of homework. When girls become pregnant, school policies force them to drop out. And when catastrophe strikes—whether in the form of illness or conflict, displacement or hardship—women and girls, from 65 to five years old, are more likely to shoulder the burden of keeping family and household together.

Nothing illustrates their burden more amply than the impact of HIV/AIDS. Girls are more likely than boys to care for a sick family member and help keep the household running. Deprived of basic schooling, they are denied information about how to protect themselves against the virus. Without the benefits of an education, they risk being forced into early sexual relations, and thereby becoming infected. Thus they pay, many times over, the deadly price of not getting an education.

But by the same token, education is a critical tool in helping us to break the vicious cycle. The key to all the locks that keep this cycle going—from AIDS to poverty to inequality—lies in education for all and the empowerment of women.

It is often said that education empowers girls by building up their confidence and enabling them to make informed decisions about their lives. For those of us who attend events such as this, that statement may seem to be about university degrees, income, or career fulfillment. But for most of the world's girls, it is about something much more fundamental. It is about escaping the trap of child labor, or the perils of going into the labor of childbirth while still a child yourself; about managing pregnancies so that they do not threaten your health, your livelihood or even your life; about ensuring that your children, in their turn, are guaranteed their right to education.

It is about being able to earn an income when women before you earned none; about protecting yourself against violence and enjoying rights which women before you never knew they had; about taking part in economic and political decision-making; finally, it is about educating your children to do the same, and their children after them. It is about ending a spiral of poverty and impotence which previously seemed to have no end. It is about achieving a deep social revolution that will give more power to women, and transform relations between women and men at all levels of society.

That must be our goal for the coming generation. There are now 1.2 billion adolescents in the world—the largest number of young girls and boys the world has ever known. In the developing world, more than 40 percent of the population is under 20. The shape of the future lies in the decisions these young people make. Their faith in themselves, their respect for one another, their access to accurate, comprehensive information and education, including information on sexual health and access to comprehensive health services, will determine not only their own well-being, but that of the world.

This revolution cannot be imposed from outside. But it can be encouraged, through support for leadership figures that are emerging in every type of society. That encouragement must be our mission.

Let me give you an example of the kind of leadership we need. There was a beautiful young woman Nane and I met in Ethiopia who had been diagnosed with HIV one week after her 21st birthday. Two years on, she had made it her full-time mission to go out and talk in schools about prevention. Nane told her that young people would probably listen more to her than to me. She immediately agreed. We will never forget what she told us next: that it was important for young people to see how healthy she looked—meaning you cannot rely on looks to tell you whether a potential partner has AIDS or not.

Look at the women in a district in Tamil Nadu, India, where 15 years ago the literacy rate was well below the national average. While learning how to read and write, these women wanted to teach women in other, more remote villages the same. How to reach them? They learnt to ride bicycles. Within three years, the district was declared fully literate.

Or look at the Girls' Power Initiative in Nigeria, which works towards the political and social empowerment of Nigerian women. With its brother organization, it educates and enlightens adolescent girls—and boys—about health and rights.

As I said at the outset, I am not at all surprised that leadership like that is most often to be found among women. And—as some of you may have heard me say before—when it comes to solving many of the problems of this world, I believe in girl power.

It is among young people like these that the heroes and heroines of our age are to be found. It is our job to furnish them with hope. I am deeply grateful to you ... for doing just that and for being such wonderful partners of the United Nations family.

❋

Climate Change:
An All-Encompassing Threat

Address to the United Nations Climate Change Conference
Nairobi, Kenya
15 November 2006

In his last months in office, Annan sought, in a series of speeches, to sum up his message to the world on several major issues for the new century. Perhaps none of these issues was more important or urgent than climate change.

All of us in this hall are devoted to the betterment of the human condition. All of us want to see a day when everyone, not just a fortunate few, can live in dignity and look to the future with hope. All of us want to create a world of harmony among human beings, and between them and the natural environment on which life depends.

◂ 81 ▸

That vision, which has always faced long odds, is now being placed in deeper jeopardy by climate change. Even the gains registered in recent years risk being undone.

Climate change is not just an environmental issue, as too many people still believe. It is an all-encompassing threat.

It is a threat to health, since a warmer world is one in which infectious diseases such as malaria and yellow fever will spread further and faster.

It could imperil the world's food supply, as rising temperatures and prolonged drought render fertile areas unfit for grazing or crops.

It could endanger the very ground on which nearly half the world's population lives—coastal cities such as Lagos or Cape Town, which face inundation from sea levels rising as a result of melting icecaps and glaciers.

All this and more lies ahead. Billion-dollar weather-related calamities. The destruction of vital ecosystems such as forests and coral reefs. Water supplies disappearing or tainted by saltwater intrusion.

Climate change is also a threat to peace and security. Changing patterns of rainfall, for example, can heighten competition for resources, setting in motion potentially destabilizing tensions and migrations, especially in fragile States or volatile regions. There is evidence that some of this is already occurring....

This is not science fiction. These are plausible scenarios, based on clear and rigorous scientific modeling. A few die-hard sceptics continue to deny global warming is taking place and try to sow doubt. They should be seen for what they are: out of step, out of arguments, and out of time. In fact, the scientific consensus is becoming not only more complete but also more alarming. Many scientists long known for their caution are now saying that global warming trends are perilously close to a point of no return.

A similar shift may also be taking place among economists. Earlier this month, a study by the former chief economist of the World Bank, Sir Nicholas Stern of the United Kingdom, called climate change "the greatest and widest-ranging market failure ever seen." He warned that climate change could shrink the global economy by 20 percent, and cause economic and social disruption on a par with the two world wars and the Great Depression.

The good news is that there is much we can do in response. We have started using fossil fuels more cleanly and efficiently. Renewable energy is increasingly available at competitive prices. With more research and development ... we could be much farther along....

The climate challenge offers real opportunities to advance development and place our societies on a more sustainable path.... So let there be no more denial. Let no one say we cannot afford to act. It is increasingly clear that it will cost far less to cut emissions now than to deal with the consequences later. And let there be no more talk of waiting until we know more. We know already that an economy based on high emissions is an uncontrolled experiment on the global climate.

But even as we seek to cut emissions, we must at the same time do far more to adapt to global warming and its effects. The impact of climate change will fall disproportionately on the world's poorest countries, many of them here in Africa. Poor people already live on the front lines of pollution, disaster and the degradation of resources and land. Their livelihoods and sustenance depend directly on agriculture, forestry and fisheries. Think, for example, of the women and girls forced to forage for fuel and water.... Or of the innumerable African communities that have suffered climate-related disasters in recent years. The floods of Mozambique, the droughts in the Sahel and here in Kenya, are fresh in our memories. For them, adaptation is a matter of sheer survival....

The message is clear. Global climate change must take its place alongside those threats—conflict, poverty, the proliferation of deadly weapons—that have traditionally monopolized first-order political attention. And the United Nations offers the tools the world needs to respond....

UN agencies will continue to bring their expertise to bear. But the primary responsibility for action rests with individual States—and for now, that means those that have been largely responsible for the accumulation of carbon dioxide in the atmosphere. They must do much more to bring their emissions down. While the Kyoto Protocol is a crucial step forward, that step is far too small. And as we consider how to go further still, there remains a frightening lack of leadership.

In developing countries, meanwhile, emissions cannot continue to grow uncontrolled. Many of them have taken impressive action on climate change. Rapidly growing economies, like China, have been increasingly successful in decoupling economic growth from energy use.... But more needs to be done.

Business, too, can do its part. Changes in corporate behavior, and in the way private investment is directed will prove at least as significant in winning the climate battle as direct government action.

And individuals too have roles to play. A single energy-efficient light bulb placed in a kitchen socket may not seem like much but multiplied by millions, the savings are impressive. Voting power could be similarly compelling, if people were to make action on climate change more of an election issue than it is today, and individuals through their purchasing choices can put pressure on corporations to go green.

There is still time for all our societies to change course. Instead of being economically defensive, let us start being more politically courageous.... The question is not whether climate change is happening or not, but whether, in the face of this emergency, we ourselves can change fast enough.

❋ CHAPTER THREE ❋

PEACE AND SECURITY

❇
Preventing Deadly Conflict

Speech at the Presentation of the Carnegie Commission
Report on Preventing Deadly Conflict
New York, New York
5 February 1998

The Carnegie Commission on Preventing Deadly Conflict was established
by the Carnegie Corporation of New York in 1994. It was co-chaired by Dr.
David Hamburg, then president of the corporation, and Cyrus Vance, the
former US secretary of state. Annan made this speech when the Commission
presented its final report, just over a year after he became Secretary-General.

Before sharing with you my vision for the United Nations mission in conflict prevention, I would like to acknowledge the extraordinary accomplishment that we mark today. In an era when violent conflicts too often are ignored and too readily accepted, at a time when people would rather look away than look ahead, the Carnegie Commission has called the world to action. You have reminded us that prevention is always better than cure. And you have detailed, as never before, the means, the uses and the promise of prevention. We are in your debt.

The final report of the Carnegie Commission is guided by three central observations: first, that deadly conflict is not inevitable; second, that the need to prevent such conflict is increasingly urgent; and third, that successful prevention is possible.

It presents a clear challenge to the international community to create a "culture of prevention"—a challenge the world can and must meet.

For the United Nations, there is no higher goal, no deeper commitment and no greater ambition than preventing armed conflict. The prevention of conflict begins and ends with the protection of human life and the promotion of human development. Ensuring human security is, in the broadest sense, the United Nations' cardinal mission. Genuine and lasting prevention is the means to achieve that mission.

Throughout the world today, but particularly in Africa and other parts of the South, intra-State wars are the face of modern conflict.

In these wars, the destruction not just of armies but of civilians and entire ethnic groups, is increasingly the main aim. Preventing these wars is no longer a matter of defending interests or promoting allies. It is a matter of defending humanity itself.

And yet we seem never to learn. Time and again differences are allowed to develop into disputes and disputes allowed to develop into deadly conflicts. Time and again, warning signs are ignored and pleas for help overlooked. Only after the deaths and the destruction do we intervene, at a far higher human and material cost and with far fewer lives to save. Only when it is too late do we value prevention.

There are, in my view, three main reasons for the failure of prevention when prevention so clearly is possible. First, the reluctance of one or more of the parties to a conflict to accept external intervention of any kind. Second, the lack of political will at the highest levels of the international community. Third, a lack of integrated conflict-prevention strategies within the United Nations system and the international community.

Of all these, the will to act is the most important. Without the political will to act when action is needed, without the will to answer the call that must be heeded, no amount of improved coordination or early warning will translate awareness into action.

All Member States facing situations of conflict must recognize that far from infringing upon their sovereignty, early warning and preventive diplomacy seek to support and restore legitimate authority and global order....

In its report, the Carnegie Commission has identified a valuable distinction between "operational prevention" and "structural prevention." The United Nations operational prevention strategy involves four fundamental activities—early warning, preventive diplomacy, preventive deployment and early humanitarian action. The United Nations structural prevention strategy involves three additional activities—preventive disarmament, development and peace-building. Guiding and infusing all these efforts is the promotion of human rights, democratization and good governance as the foundations of peace.

Preventive deployment, in one particular example, has already had a remarkable effect in the explosive region of the Balkans. Such a force is only a "thin blue line."

But the UN Preventive Deployment Force's (UNPREDEP) role so far in the former Yugoslav republic of Macedonia suggests that preventive deployment, adequately mandated and supported, can make the difference between war and peace.

Preventive disarmament is another measure whose importance needs to be recognized and advanced. The United Nations has disarmed combatants in the context of peacekeeping operations from Nicaragua to Mozambique.

In other cases, destroying yesterday's weapons prevents them from being used tomorrow. This is also what the United Nations has been attempting to do in Iraq, where the inspections of the United Nations Special Commission have succeeded in destroying more weapons of mass destruction than did the entire Persian Gulf War.

Urgent action is also needed to curtail the flow of conventional weapons. In particular, we must do more to halt the proliferation of small arms, with which most wars are fought today. As part of my reform agenda, I have therefore established a new Department for Disarmament Affairs with a range of new tasks. High on its agenda will be the challenge of "micro-disarmament," to work with governments in focusing on the illegal trade in small arms.

But we cannot do it alone. The work of prevention—if it is to be lasting—must be supported by all sides and carried to success by the peoples and parties themselves. Their role and responsibility is fundamental. So is the role of arms-producing countries and those that permit the transit of arms.

Long-term prevention can, however, be facilitated by many elements of the international community. There are cases where the United Nations, mandated with unique universal legitimacy, must lead. There will be other cases where a regional or subregional organization's proximity to a conflict and historical experience make it most able to prevent deadly violence. In all cases, the United Nations is poised to support those efforts....

The policies of prevention that I have outlined so far—early warning, preventive diplomacy, preventive deployment and preventive disarmament—will succeed only if the root causes of conflict are addressed with the same will and wisdom.

These causes are often economic and social. Poverty, endemic underdevelopment and weak or non-existent institutions inhibit dialogue and invite the resort to violence. A long, quiet process of sustainable economic development, based on respect for human rights and legitimate government, is essential to preventing conflict.

The United Nations of the twenty-first century must become a global center for visionary and effective preventive action.

A Chinese proverb holds that it is difficult to find money for medicine, but easy to find it for a coffin.

The last decade's intra-State and ethnic wars have made this proverb all too real for our time.

Have we not seen enough coffins—from Rwanda to Bosnia and Herzegovina to Cambodia—to pay the price for prevention? Have we not learned the lesson too painfully and too often that we can, if we will, prevent deadly conflict? Have we not heard General Dallaire[1] say that 5,000 peacekeepers could have saved 500,000 lives in Rwanda?

Indeed, we have no excuses anymore. We have no excuses for inaction and no alibis for ignorance. Often we know even before the very victims of conflict that they will be victimized. We know because our world now is one—in pain and in prosperity. No longer must the promise of prevention be a promise deferred. Too much is at stake; too much is possible; too much is needed.

---

1. Roméo Dallaire, Force Commander of the UN Assistance Mission for Rwanda (UNAMIR) during the genocide of 1994.

❋

The Use of Force

Statement on NATO Action against Yugoslavia
New York, New York
24 March 1999

*On 24 March 1999, after the Federal Republic of Yugoslavia had refused
to accept an external peacekeeping force in Kosovo, NATO began an in-
tensive bombing campaign. This put Annan in a difficult position. He had
repeatedly drawn attention to human rights violations in Kosovo and had
warned that Kosovo might be the "next time" when the Security Council
would have to live up to its responsibilities better than it had done in
Rwanda and Bosnia. (See "On Intervention" in Chapter 8.) Yet NATO
had acted without Security Council approval. In addressing the media,
Annan therefore had to weigh his words even more carefully than usual.*

I speak to you at a grave moment for the international community.
Throughout the last year, I have appealed on many occasions to the
Yugoslav authorities and the Kosovo Albanians to seek peace over
war, compromise over conflict. I deeply regret that, in spite of all the efforts
made by the international community, the Yugoslav authorities have per-
sisted in their rejection of a political settlement, which would have halted the
bloodshed in Kosovo and secured an equitable peace for the population there.

It is indeed tragic that diplomacy has failed, but there are times when
the use of force may be legitimate in the pursuit of peace.

In helping maintain international peace and security, Chapter VIII
of the United Nations Charter assigns an important role to regional
organizations. But as Secretary-General, I have many times pointed
out, not just in relation to Kosovo, that under the Charter the Security
Council has primary responsibility for maintaining international peace
and security—and this is explicitly acknowledged in the North Atlantic
Treaty. Therefore, the Council should be involved in any decision to
resort to the use of force.

✳

Cool and Reasoned Judgment

Statement on the Attacks on New York and Washington
New York, New York
11 September 2001

Annan made this televised statement at his official residence in Sutton Place, New York, on the morning of September 11, soon after the attacks on the World Trade Center and the Pentagon had been confirmed.

We are all traumatized by this terrible tragedy. We do not know yet how many people have been killed or injured, but inevitably the number will be high. Our first thoughts and prayers must be for them, and for their families. I wish to express my profound condolences to them, and to the people and government of the United States.

There can be no doubt that these attacks are deliberate acts of terrorism, carefully planned and coordinated—and as such I condemn them utterly. Terrorism must be fought resolutely wherever it appears.

In such moments, cool and reasoned judgment is more essential than ever. We do not know yet who is behind these acts or what objective they hope to achieve. What we do know is that no just cause can be advanced by terror.

✳

The Importance of Multilateralism

Address to the General Assembly
New York, New York
12 September 2002

By long-standing tradition the president of the United States, the host country, speaks to the General Assembly each September on the first day of the General Debate. His speech is therefore liable to overshadow that of the Secretary-General, who speaks earlier the same morning. In 2002 it was known that President George W. Bush would use his speech to set out the case for war against Iraq. Annan took the unusual step of releasing the text of his speech—a plea for any such decision to be taken multilaterally, by the Security Council—the previous night to ensure that it did not go unnoticed. The French ambassador, Jean-David Levitte, said later that it had been "the speech of the Pope to the Emperor."

We cannot begin today without reflecting on yesterday's anniversary—and on the criminal challenge so brutally thrown in our faces on 11 September 2001.

The terrorist attacks of that day were not an isolated event. They were an extreme example of a global scourge, which requires a broad, sustained and global response.

Broad, because terrorism can be defeated only if all nations unite against it.

Sustained, because the battle against terrorism will not be won easily or overnight. It requires patience and persistence.

And global, because terrorism is a widespread and complex phenomenon, with many deep roots and exacerbating factors.

I believe that such a response can only succeed if we make full use of multilateral institutions.

I stand before you today as a multilateralist—by precedent, by principle, by Charter and by duty.

I also believe that every government that is committed to the rule of law at home, must be committed also to the rule of law abroad. And all States have a clear interest, as well as clear responsibility, to uphold international law and maintain international order.

Our founding fathers, the statesmen of 1945, had learnt that lesson from the bitter experience of two world wars and a great depression.

They recognized that international security is not a zero-sum game. Peace, security and freedom are not finite commodities—like land, oil or gold—which one State can acquire at another's expense. On the contrary, the more peace, security and freedom any one State has, the more its neighbors are likely to have.

And they recognized that, by agreeing to exercise sovereignty together, they could gain a hold over problems that would defeat any one of them acting separately.

If those lessons were clear in 1945, should they not be much more so today, in the age of globalization?

On almost no item on our agenda does anyone seriously contend that each nation can fend for itself. Even the most powerful countries know that they need to work with others, in multilateral institutions, to achieve their aims.

Only by multilateral action can we ensure that open markets offer benefits and opportunities to all.

Only by multilateral action can we give people in the least developed countries the chance to escape the ugly misery of poverty, ignorance and disease.

Only by multilateral action can we protect ourselves from acid rain, or global warming, from the spread of HIV/AIDS, the illicit trade in drugs, or the odious traffic in human beings.

That applies even more to the prevention of terrorism. Individual States may defend themselves, by striking back at terrorist groups and at the countries that harbor or support them. But only concerted vigilance and cooperation among all States, with constant, systematic exchange of information, offers any real hope of denying the terrorists their opportunities.

On all these matters, for any one State—large or small—choosing to follow or reject the multilateral path must not be a simple matter of political convenience. It has consequences far beyond the immediate context.

When countries work together in multilateral institutions—developing, respecting, and when necessary enforcing international law—they also develop mutual trust and more effective cooperation on other issues.

The more a country makes use of multilateral institutions—thereby respecting shared values and accepting the obligations and restraints inherent in those values—the more others will trust and respect it and the stronger its chance to exercise true leadership.

And among multilateral institutions, this universal Organization has a special place.

Any State, if attacked, retains the inherent right of self-defense under Article 51 of the Charter. But beyond that, when States decide to use force to deal with broader threats to international peace and security, there is no substitute for the unique legitimacy provided by the United Nations.

Member States attach importance, great importance in fact, to such legitimacy and to the international rule of law. They have shown— notably in the action to liberate Kuwait twelve years ago—that they are willing to take actions under the authority of the Security Council, which they would not be willing to take without it.

The existence of an effective international security system depends on the Council's authority—and therefore on the Council having the political will to act, even in the most difficult cases, when agreement seems elusive at the outset. The primary criterion for putting an issue on the Council's agenda should not be the receptiveness of the parties but the existence of a grave threat to world peace.

Let me now turn to four current threats to world peace, where true leadership and effective action are badly needed.

First, *the Israeli-Palestinian conflict....*

As we agreed at the Quartet meeting in Washington last May, an international peace conference is needed without delay, to set out a roadmap of parallel steps: steps to strengthen Israel's security, steps to strengthen Palestinian economic and political institutions, and steps to settle the details of the final peace agreement. Meanwhile, humanitarian steps to relieve Palestinian suffering must be intensified. The need is urgent.

Second, the leadership of *Iraq* continues to defy mandatory resolutions adopted by the Security Council under Chapter VII of the Charter.

I have engaged Iraq in an in-depth discussion on a range of issues, including the need for arms inspectors to return, in accordance with the relevant Security Council resolutions.

Efforts to obtain Iraq's compliance with the Council's resolutions must continue. I appeal to all those who have influence with Iraq's leaders to impress on them the vital importance of accepting the weapons inspections. This is the indispensable first step towards assuring the world that all Iraq's weapons of mass destruction have indeed been eliminated, and—let me stress—towards the suspension and eventual ending of the sanctions that are causing so many hardships for the Iraqi people.

I urge Iraq to comply with its obligations—for the sake of its own people and for the sake of world order. If Iraq's defiance continues, the Security Council must face its responsibilities.

Third, permit me to press all of you, as leaders of the international community, to maintain your commitment to *Afghanistan*....

And finally, in *South Asia* the world has recently come closer than for many years past to a direct conflict between two countries with nuclear capability.[1] The situation may now have calmed a little, but it remains perilous. The underlying cause must be addressed....

Excellencies, let me conclude by reminding you of your pledge two years ago, at the Millennium Summit, to make the United Nations a more effective instrument in the service of the peoples of the world.

Today I ask all of you to honor that pledge.

Let us all recognize, from now on—in each capital, in every nation, large and small—that the global interest *is* our national interest.

❈

A Fork in the Road

Address to the General Assembly
New York, New York
23 September 2003

This speech was Annan's considered reaction to the invasion of Iraq by the United States, the United Kingdom, and their allies without Security Council agreement, which had led to a deeper and more bitter division of the international community than at any time since the end of the cold war. He pleaded for a clearer understanding about when it was legitimate to use force and announced the formation of a High-Level Panel on global-security issues, which was to report the following year.

---

1. In 1998 both India and Pakistan had tested nuclear devices. In 2002 both countries massed troops along their international border and on the Line of Control in Kashmir, and Pakistan's President Pervez Musharraf refused to rule out nuclear retaliation if his country was attacked.

T he last twelve months have been very painful for those of us who believe in collective answers to our common problems and challenges.

In many countries, terrorism has once again brought death and suffering to innocent people.

In the Middle East and in certain parts of Africa, violence has continued to escalate.

In the Korean peninsula and elsewhere, the threat of nuclear proliferation casts an ominous shadow across the landscape.

And barely one month ago, in Baghdad, the United Nations itself suffered a brutal and deliberate assault, in which the international community lost some of its most talented servants.[1] Yesterday it was attacked again. Another major disaster was averted only by the prompt action of the Iraqi police, one of whom paid with his life....

Excellencies, you *are* the United Nations. The staff who were killed and injured in the attack on our Baghdad headquarters were your staff. You had given them a mandate to assist the suffering Iraqi people and to help Iraq recover their sovereignty.

In future, not only in Iraq but wherever the United Nations is engaged, we must take more effective measures to protect the security of our staff. I count on your full support—legal, political and financial.

Meanwhile, let me reaffirm the great importance I attach to a successful outcome in Iraq. Whatever view each of us may take of the events of recent months, it is vital to all of us that the outcome is a stable and democratic Iraq—at peace with itself and with its neighbors, and contributing to stability in the region.

Subject to security considerations, the United Nations system is prepared to play its full role in working for a satisfactory outcome in Iraq and to do so as part of an international effort, an effort by the whole international community, pulling together on the basis of a sound and viable policy. If it takes extra time and patience to forge that policy, a policy that is collective, coherent and workable, then I for one would regard that time as well spent. Indeed, this is how we must approach all the many pressing crises that confront us today.

---

1. See "Unhealable Wounds" in Chapter 1.

Excellencies,

Three years ago, when you came here for the Millennium Summit, we shared a vision, a vision of global solidarity and collective security, expressed in the Millennium Declaration.

But recent events have called that consensus in question.

All of us know there are new threats that must be faced—or, perhaps, old threats in new and dangerous combinations: new forms of terrorism and the proliferation of weapons of mass destruction.

But, while some consider these threats as self-evidently the main challenge to world peace and security, others feel more immediately menaced by small arms employed in civil conflict, or by so-called soft threats such as the persistence of extreme poverty, the disparity of income between and within societies, and the spread of infectious diseases, or climate change and environmental degradation.

In truth, we do not have to choose. The United Nations must confront all these threats and challenges—new and old, "hard" and "soft." It must be fully engaged in the struggle for development and poverty eradication, starting with the achievement of the Millennium Development Goals; in the common struggle to protect our common environment; and in the struggle for human rights, democracy and good governance.

In fact, all these struggles are linked. We now see, with chilling clarity, that a world where many millions of people endure brutal oppression and extreme misery will never be fully secure, even for its most privileged inhabitants.

Yet the "hard" threats, such as terrorism and weapons of mass destruction, are real and cannot be ignored.

Terrorism is not a problem only for rich countries. Ask the people of Bali or Bombay, Nairobi or Casablanca.[2]

Weapons of mass destruction do not threaten only the western or northern world. Ask the people of Iran or of Halabja in Iraq.[3]

Where we disagree, it seems, is on how to respond to these threats.

Since this Organization was founded, States have generally sought to deal with threats to the peace through containment and deterrence, by a system based on collective security and the United Nations Charter.

2. All these cities had suffered major terrorist attacks in the course of 2003.
3. Saddam Hussein had used chemical weapons against Iranian troops and against the Kurdish city of Halabja during the Iran-Iraq war of 1980 to 1988.

Article 51 of the Charter prescribes that all States, if attacked, retain the inherent right of self-defense. But until now it has been understood that when States go beyond that and decide to use force to deal with broader threats to international peace and security, they need the unique legitimacy provided by the United Nations.

Now, some say this understanding is no longer tenable, since an "armed attack" with weapons of mass destruction could be launched at any time, without warning, or by a clandestine group.

Rather than wait for that to happen, they argue, States have the right and obligation to use force preemptively, even on the territory of other States and even while weapons systems that might be used to attack them are still being developed.

According to this argument, States are not obliged to wait until there is agreement in the Security Council. Instead, they reserve the right to act unilaterally or in ad hoc coalitions.

This logic represents a fundamental challenge to the principles on which, however imperfectly, world peace and stability have rested for the last fifty-eight years.

My concern is that, if it were to be adopted, it could set precedents that resulted in a proliferation of the unilateral and lawless use of force, with or without justification.

But it is not enough to denounce unilateralism, unless we also face up squarely to the concerns that make some States feel uniquely vulnerable, since it is those concerns that drive them to take unilateral action. We must show that those concerns can, and will, be addressed effectively through collective action.

We have come to a fork in the road. This may be a moment no less decisive than 1945 itself, when the United Nations was founded.

At that time, a group of farsighted leaders, led and inspired by President Franklin D. Roosevelt, were determined to make the second half of the twentieth century different from the first half. They saw that the human race has only one world to live in and that unless it manages its affairs prudently, all human beings may perish.

So they drew up rules to govern international behavior and founded a network of institutions, with the United Nations at its center, in which the peoples of the world could work together for the common good.

Now we must decide whether it is possible to continue on the basis agreed then, or whether radical changes are needed.

And we must not shy away from questions about the adequacy and effectiveness of the rules and instruments at our disposal.

Among those instruments, none is more important than the Security Council itself.

In my recent report on the implementation of the Millennium Declaration, I drew attention to the urgent need for the Council to regain the confidence of States and of world public opinion—both by demonstrating its ability to deal effectively with the most difficult issues and by becoming more broadly representative of the international community as a whole, as well as the geopolitical realities of today.[4]

The Council needs to consider how it will deal with the possibility that individual States may use force "preemptively" against perceived threats.

Its members may need to begin a discussion on the criteria for an early authorization of coercive measures to address certain types of threats—for instance, terrorist groups armed with weapons of mass destruction.

And they still need to engage in serious discussions of the best way to respond to threats of genocide or other comparable massive violations of human rights—an issue which I raised myself from this podium in 1999.[5] Once again this year, our collective response to events of this type—in the Democratic Republic of the Congo and in Liberia—has been hesitant and tardy.

As for the composition of the Council, that has been on the agenda of this Assembly for over a decade. Virtually all Member States agree that the Council should be enlarged, but there is no agreement on the details.

I respectfully suggest to you that in the eyes of your peoples, the difficulty of reaching agreement does not excuse your failure to do so. If you want the Council's decisions to command greater respect, particularly in the developing world, you need to address the issue of its composition with greater urgency.

---

4. Here Annan was responding to the widespread feeling, especially among developing countries, that the Security Council was too much weighted in favor of the global North and that the five permanent members (China, France, Russia, the United Kingdom, and the United States) were the great powers of 1945, not necessarily those of the twenty-first century.
5. See "Two Concepts of Sovereignty" in Chapter 8.

But the Security Council is not the only institution that needs strengthening. As you know, I am doing my best to make the Secretariat more effective—and I look to this Assembly to support my efforts.

Indeed, in my report I also suggested that this Assembly itself needs to be strengthened and that the role of the Economic and Social Council—and the role of the United Nations as a whole in economic and social affairs, including its relationship to the Bretton Woods institutions[6]—needs to be rethought and reinvigorated.

I even suggested that the role of the Trusteeship Council[7] could be reviewed, in light of new kinds of responsibility that you have given to the United Nations in recent years.

In short, Excellencies, I believe the time is ripe for a hard look at fundamental policy issues and at the structural changes that may be needed in order to strengthen them.

History is a harsh judge: it will not forgive us if we let this moment pass.

For my part, I intend to establish a High-Level Panel of eminent personalities, to which I will assign four tasks:

* First, to examine the current challenges to peace and security;
* Second, to consider the contribution which collective action can make in addressing these challenges;
* Third, to review the functioning of the major organs of the United Nations and the relationship between them; and
* Fourth, to recommend ways of strengthening the United Nations, through reform of its institutions and processes.

The Panel will focus primarily on threats to peace and security. But it will also need to examine other global challenges, in so far as these may influence or connect with those threats.

I will ask the Panel to report back to me before the beginning of the next session of this General Assembly, so that I can make

---

6. The International Monetary Fund and the World Bank, both founded at the Bretton Woods Conference of 1944.
7. One of the principal organs of the United Nations, which has had no real function since the former Trust territories (mainly former German colonies that had been entrusted to other colonial powers by the League of Nations after the First World War) became independent. Annan had suggested that the Council might have a role in supervising territories such as East Timor that came under temporary UN administration, but Member States did not take up the suggestion.

recommendations to you at that session.[8] But only you can take the firm and clear decisions that will be needed.

Those decisions might include far-reaching institutional reforms. Indeed, I hope they will.

But institutional reforms alone will not suffice. Even the most perfect instrument will fail, unless people put it to good use.

The United Nations is by no means a perfect instrument, but it is a precious one. I urge you to seek agreement on ways of improving it, but above all of using it as its founders intended—to save succeeding generations from the scourge of war, to reaffirm faith in fundamental human rights, to reestablish the basic conditions for justice and the rule of law, and to promote social progress and better standards of life in larger freedom.

The world may have changed, but those aims are as valid and urgent as ever. We must keep them firmly in our sights.

❋

Democracy, Terrorism, and Security

Speech to the International Summit on
Democracy, Terrorism, and Security
Madrid, Spain
11 March 2005

On March 11, 2004, during Madrid's morning rush hour, ten bombs exploded on four trains at the Atocha station, killing more than 190 people and injuring nearly 2,000. One year later, Madrid was the setting for a conference whose proclaimed purpose was "to build a common agenda on how the community of democratic nations can most effectively confront terrorism, in memory of its victims from across the world." Annan was invited to give the keynote speech at a special plenary, speaking immediately after King Juan Carlos.

---

8. In fact the High-Level Panel on Threats, Challenges and Change presented its report only in December 2004. Annan then incorporated many of its recommendations in his *In Larger Freedom* report, which formed the agenda for the 2005 World Summit.

Why have you invited me to speak here? Because terrorism is a threat to all States, to all peoples, which can strike anytime, anywhere.

It is a direct attack on the core values the United Nations stands for: the rule of law; the protection of civilians; mutual respect between people of different faiths and cultures; and peaceful resolution of conflicts.

So of course the United Nations must be at the forefront in fighting against it, and first of all in proclaiming, loud and clear, that terrorism can never be accepted or justified, in any cause whatsoever.

By the same token, the United Nations must continue to insist that, in the fight against terrorism, we cannot compromise the core values I have listed. In particular, human rights and the rule of law must always be respected. As I see it, terrorism is in itself a direct attack on human rights and the rule of law. If we sacrifice them in our response, we will be handing victory to the terrorists.

Since terrorism is clearly one of the major threats that we face in this century, it is only right that it received close attention in the report *A More Secure World—Our Shared Responsibility,* produced by the High-Level Panel[1] that I set up to study global threats and recommend changes in the international system....

The Panel asked me to promote a principled, comprehensive strategy. I intend to do that. This seems to me a fitting occasion to set out the [five] main elements of that strategy and the role of the United Nations in it....

Let me start with the first D: *Dissuading disaffected groups from choosing terrorism as a tactic.*

Groups use terrorist tactics because they think those tactics are effective and that people, or at least those in whose name they claim to act, will approve. Such beliefs are at the "root cause" of terrorism. Our job is to show unequivocally that they are wrong.

We cannot, and need not, redress all the grievances that terrorists claim to be advancing. But we must convince all those who may be tempted to support terrorism that it is neither an acceptable nor an effective way to advance their cause. It should be clearly stated, by all

---

1. See previous speech, "A Fork in the Road."

possible moral and political authorities, that terrorism is unacceptable under any circumstances and in any culture.

The United Nations and its Specialized Agencies played a central role in negotiating and adopting twelve international anti-terrorism treaties. Now the time has come to complete a comprehensive convention outlawing terrorism in all its forms.

For far too long the moral authority of the United Nations in confronting terrorism has been weakened by the spectacle of protracted negotiations.[2] But the report of the High-Level Panel offers us a way to end these arguments. We do not need to argue whether States can be guilty of terrorism, because deliberate use of armed force by States against civilians is already clearly prohibited under international law. As for the right to resist occupation, it must be understood in its true meaning. It cannot include the right to deliberately kill or maim civilians.

The Panel calls for a definition of terrorism which would make it clear that any action constitutes terrorism if it is intended to cause death or serious bodily harm to civilians and non-combatants, with the purpose of intimidating a population or compelling a government or an international organization to do or abstain from any act. I believe this proposal has clear moral force, and I strongly urge world leaders to unite behind it.

Not only political leaders, but civil society and religious leaders should clearly denounce terrorist tactics as criminal and inexcusable. Civil society has already conducted magnificent campaigns against landmines, against the recruitment of children as soldiers, and against allowing war crimes to go unpunished. I should like to see an equally strong global campaign against terrorism.

Finally, we must pay more attention to the victims of terrorism, and make sure that their voices can be heard. We at the UN especially are conscious of this, having lost beloved colleagues to a terrorist attack in Baghdad two years ago. Last October the Security Council itself, in its Resolution 1566, suggested an international fund to compensate victims and their families, to be financed in part from assets seized from terrorist

---

2. Member States were unable to agree on a definition of terrorism, and particularly on whether it could include actions by states or their regular security forces, on the one hand, or by people resisting foreign occupation of their homeland, on the other.

organizations, their members and sponsors. This suggestion should be urgently followed up.

I will now turn to the second D: *Denying terrorists the means to carry out their attacks.* That means making it difficult for them to travel, to receive financial support, or to acquire nuclear or radiological material.

Here the United Nations has made important contributions. The UN Convention on the Suppression of Financing of Terrorism has been in force for three years. And the Security Council has long since imposed travel and financial sanctions against members of Al Qaida and associated entities. But we must do more to ensure that those sanctions are fully enforced.

We also need effective action against money laundering. Here the United Nations could adopt and promote the eight Special Recommendations on Terrorist Financing produced by the OECD's[3] Financial Action Task Force.

Perhaps the thing that it is most vital to deny to terrorists is access to nuclear materials. Nuclear terrorism is still often treated as science fiction. I wish it were. But unfortunately we live in a world of excess hazardous materials and abundant technological know-how, in which some terrorists clearly state their intention to inflict catastrophic casualties. Were such an attack to occur, it would not only cause widespread death and destruction, but would stagger the world economy and thrust tens of millions of people into dire poverty. Given what we know of the relationship between poverty and infant mortality, any nuclear terrorist attack would have a second death toll throughout the developing world.

That such an attack has not yet happened is not an excuse for complacency. Rather, it gives us a last chance to take effective preventive action.

That means consolidating, securing, and when possible eliminating potentially hazardous materials and implementing effective export controls. Both the G8 and the UN Security Council have taken important steps to do this and to plug gaps in the non-proliferation regime. We need to make sure these measures are fully enforced and that they reinforce each other. I urge the Member States of the United Nations to complete and adopt, without delay, the international convention on nuclear terrorism....

---

3. Organization for Economic Cooperation and Development: the association of industrialized countries.

My third D is the need to *Deter states from supporting terrorist groups.*

In the past the United Nations has not shrunk from confronting States that harbor and assist terrorists, and the Security Council has repeatedly applied sanctions. Indeed, it is largely thanks to such sanctions that several States which used to sponsor terrorists no longer do so.

This firm line must be maintained and strengthened. All States must know that, if they give any kind of support to terrorists, the Council will not hesitate to use coercive measures against them.

The fourth D is to *Develop state capacity to prevent terrorism.*

Terrorists exploit weak States as havens where they can hide from arrest and train their recruits. Making all States more capable and responsible must therefore be the cornerstone of our global counter-terrorism effort. This means promoting good governance and above all the rule of law, with professional police and security forces who respect human rights.

The United Nations has already done a lot in this area. The Security Council, in its Resolution 1373, required every State to take important steps in preventing terrorism. The Counterterrorism Committee follows how well States are implementing that resolution.

But many poor countries genuinely cannot afford to build the capacity they need. They need help. The new Counter-Terrorism Directorate will assess their needs and develop a comprehensive approach to technical assistance.

Every State must be able to develop and maintain an efficient criminal justice system. The UN Office on Drugs and Crime Prevention is experienced at this work and is prepared to do more....

Terrorist groups find it easiest to recruit among people with a narrow or distorted view of the world. We must therefore help States to give all their citizens a modern education that encourages scientific inquiry and free thought. UNESCO has done much good work in this area but, I hope, can do more.

Few threats more vividly illustrate the imperative of building State capacity than biological terrorism, which could spread deadly infectious disease across the world in a matter of days. Neither States nor international organizations have yet adapted to a new world of biotechnology, full of promise and peril. There will soon be tens of thousands of laboratories around the world capable of producing designer bugs with awesome lethal potential.

All experts agree that the best defense against this danger lies in strengthening public health. The World Health Organization's Global Outbreak and Response Network, working on a shoestring budget, has done an impressive job in monitoring and responding to outbreaks of deadly infectious disease. But in the case of an overwhelming outbreak—natural or man-made—it is local health systems that will be in the front line, and in many poor countries they are inadequate or non-existent. We need a major initiative to build such systems.

The last D is *Defend human rights.*

I regret to say that international human rights experts, including those of the UN system, are unanimous in finding that many measures which States are currently adopting to counter terrorism infringe on human rights and fundamental freedoms.

Human rights law makes ample provision for counter-terrorist action, even in the most exceptional circumstances. But compromising human rights cannot serve the struggle against terrorism. On the contrary, it facilitates achievement of the terrorist's objective—by ceding to him the moral high ground and provoking tension, hatred, and mistrust of government among precisely those parts of the population where he is most likely to find recruits.

Upholding human rights is not merely compatible with successful counter-terrorism strategy. It is an essential element....

That completes my brief summary of the most important elements of a comprehensive strategy to fight terrorism.

All Departments and Agencies of the United Nations can and must contribute to carrying out this strategy. I am creating an implementation task force, under my office, which will meet regularly to review the handling of terrorism and related issues throughout the UN system and make sure that all parts of it play their proper role.

Tomorrow morning we shall commemorate, in deep sorrow and in common with the whole of Europe—indeed, the whole world—the 192 innocent people who were so brutally, inexcusably murdered in the last terrorist attack here in Madrid one year ago. We shall affirm our solidarity with their families and friends; with almost two thousand other, equally innocent, people who were injured by the explosions; and with the Spanish people, who have suffered so much from terrorism over the past 30 years but have remained true to their democratic convictions.

At the same time, we will remember the victims of 11 September 2001 and those of other terrorist attacks in Dar-es-Salaam, Nairobi, Tel Aviv, Bali, Istanbul, Riyadh, Casablanca, Baghdad, Bombay, Beslan—indeed, all victims of terrorism everywhere, no matter what their nationality, race or creed.

Some injuries can be healed with the passage of time. Others can never heal fully—and that applies especially to the mental anguish suffered by the survivors, whether wounded in body or, by the loss of their loved ones, in spirit.

To all victims around the world, our words of sympathy can bring only hollow comfort. They know that no one who is not so directly affected can truly share their grief. At least let us not exploit it. We must respect them. We must listen to them. We must do what we can to help them.

We must resolve to do everything in our power to spare others from meeting their fate.

Above all, we must not forget them.

❈

Non-Proliferation and Disarmament: Two Sides of a Coin

Lecture at Princeton University
Princeton, New Jersey
28 November 2006

The 2005 review conference of the Treaty on the Non-Proliferation of Nuclear Weapons (NPT) ended without a consensus document, essentially because the nuclear-weapon states (China, France, Russia, United Kingdom, and United States) were unable to agree with the other signatories on whether to give priority to preventing further proliferation or to working towards "general and complete disarmament," as prescribed by Article VI of the treaty. Annan was deeply frustrated by this stalemate and decided to make one last appeal for compromise before leaving office at the end of 2006.

A lmost everyone in today's world feels insecure, but not everyone feels insecure about the same thing. Different threats seem more urgent to people in different parts of the world. Probably the largest number would give priority to economic and social threats, including poverty, environmental degradation and infectious disease.

Others might stress inter-State conflict; yet others internal conflict, including civil war. Many people—especially but not only in the developed world—would now put terrorism at the top of their list.

In truth, all these threats are interconnected, and all cut across national frontiers. We need common global strategies to deal with all of them—and indeed governments are coming together to work out and implement such strategies, in the UN and elsewhere. The one area where there is a total lack of any common strategy is the one that may well present the greatest danger of all: the area of nuclear weapons.

Why do I consider it the greatest danger? For three reasons:

* First, nuclear weapons present a unique existential threat to all humanity.
* Secondly, the nuclear non-proliferation regime now faces a major crisis of confidence. North Korea has withdrawn from the Nuclear Non-Proliferation Treaty (NPT), while India, Israel, and Pakistan have never joined it. There are, at least, serious questions about the nature of Iran's nuclear program....
* Thirdly, the rise of terrorism, with the danger that nuclear weapons might be acquired by terrorists, greatly increases the danger that they will be used.

Yet, despite the grave, all-encompassing nature of this threat, the governments of the world are addressing it selectively, not comprehensively.

In one way, that's understandable. The very idea of global self-annihilation is unbearable to think about. But that is no excuse. We must try to imagine the human and environmental consequences of a nuclear bomb exploding in one, or even in several, major world cities—or indeed of an all-out confrontation between two nuclear-armed States.

In focusing on nuclear weapons, I am not seeking to minimize the problem of chemical and biological ones, which are also weapons of mass destruction and are banned under international treaties. Indeed, perhaps the most important, under-addressed threat relating to terrorism—one which acutely requires new thinking—is the threat of terrorists using a biological weapon.

But nuclear weapons are the *most* dangerous. Even a single bomb can destroy an entire city, as we know from the terrible example of Hiroshima and Nagasaki, and today there are bombs many times as powerful as those. These weapons pose a unique threat to humanity as a whole.

Forty years ago, understanding that this danger must be avoided at all costs, nearly all States in the world came together and forged a grand bargain, embodied in the NPT.

In essence, that treaty was a contract between the recognized nuclear-weapon States at that time and the rest of the international community. The nuclear-weapon States undertook to negotiate in good faith on nuclear disarmament, to prevent proliferation, and to facilitate the peaceful use of nuclear energy, while separately declaring that they would refrain from threatening non-nuclear-weapon States with nuclear weapons. In return, the rest committed themselves not to acquire or manufacture nuclear weapons and to place all their nuclear activities under the verification of the International Atomic Energy Agency (IAEA).[1] Thus the treaty was designed both to prevent proliferation and to advance disarmament, while assuring the right of all States, under specified conditions, to use nuclear energy for peaceful purposes.

From 1970—when it entered into force—until quite recently, the NPT was widely seen as a cornerstone of global security. It had confounded the dire predictions of its critics. Nuclear weapons did not—and still have not—spread to dozens of States, as John F. Kennedy and others predicted in the 1960s. In fact, more States have given up their ambitions for nuclear weapons than have acquired them.

---

1. The International Atomic Energy Agency: the body charged with ensuring that non-nuclear-weapon states have access to nuclear energy for peaceful purposes but cannot use it as a cover for developing nuclear weapons.

And yet in recent years the NPT has come under withering criticism—because the international community has been unable to agree how to apply it to specific crises in South Asia, the Korean peninsula and the Middle East and because a few States party to the treaty are allegedly pursuing their own nuclear-weapons capabilities.

Twice in 2005, governments had a chance to strengthen the treaty's foundations—first at the review conference in May, then at the World Summit in September. Both times they failed—essentially because they couldn't agree whether non-proliferation or disarmament should come first.

The advocates of "non-proliferation first"—mainly nuclear-weapon States and their supporters—believe the main danger arises not from nuclear weapons as such, but from the character of those who possess them and therefore from the spread of nuclear weapons to new States and to non-State actors (so-called horizontal proliferation). The nuclear-weapon States say they have carried out significant disarmament since the end of the cold war but that their responsibility for international peace and security requires them to maintain a nuclear deterrent.

"Disarmament first" advocates, on the other hand, say that the world is most imperiled by existing nuclear arsenals and their continual improvement (so-called vertical proliferation). Many non-nuclear-weapon States accuse the nuclear-weapon States of retreating from commitments they made in 1995 (when the NPT was extended indefinitely) and reiterated as recently as the year 2000. For these countries, the NPT "grand bargain" has become a swindle. They note that the UN Security Council has often described the proliferation of weapons of mass destruction as a threat to international peace and security but has never declared that nuclear weapons in and of themselves are such a threat. They see no serious movement towards nuclear disarmament and claim that the lack of such movement presages a permanent "apartheid" between nuclear "haves" and "have-nots."

Both sides in this debate feel that the existence of four additional States with nuclear weapons, outside the NPT, serves only to sharpen their argument.

The debate echoes a much older argument: Are weapons a cause or a symptom of conflict? I believe both debates are sterile, counterproductive, and based on false dichotomies.

Arms buildups can give rise to threats leading to conflict, and political conflicts can motivate the acquisition of arms. Efforts are needed both to reduce arms and to reduce conflict. Likewise, efforts are needed to achieve both disarmament and non-proliferation.

Yet each side waits for the other to move. The result is that "mutually assured destruction"[2] has been replaced by mutually assured paralysis. This sends a terrible signal of disunity and waning respect for the treaty's authority. It creates a vacuum that can be exploited.

I said earlier this year that we are "sleepwalking towards disaster." In truth, it is worse than that—we are asleep at the controls of a fast-moving aircraft. Unless we wake up and take control, the outcome is all too predictable.

An aircraft, of course, can remain airborne only if both wings are in working order. We cannot choose between non-proliferation and disarmament. We must tackle both tasks with the urgency they demand.

Allow me to offer my thoughts to each side in turn.

To those who insist on disarmament first, I say this:

* Proliferation is not a threat only, or even mainly, to those who already have nuclear weapons. The more fingers there are on nuclear triggers, and the more those fingers belong to leaders of unstable States—or, even worse, non-State actors—the greater the threat to all humankind.

* Lack of progress on disarmament is no excuse for not addressing the dangers of proliferation. No State should imagine that, by pushing ahead with a nuclear-weapon program, it can pose as a defender of the NPT; still less that it will persuade others to disarm.

* I know some influential States, which themselves have scrupulously respected the treaty, feel strongly that the nuclear-weapon States have not lived up to their disarmament obligations. But they must be careful not to let their resentment put them on the side of the proliferators. They should state clearly that acquiring prohibited weapons never serves the cause of their elimination. Proliferation only makes disarmament even harder to achieve.

---

2. This was the name given to the balance of terror that preserved a precarious peace between the two superpowers during the cold war.

❃ I urge all States to give credit where it is due. Acknowledge disarmament whenever it does occur. Applaud the moves which nuclear-weapon States have made, whether unilaterally or through negotiation, to reduce nuclear arsenals or prevent their expansion. Recognize that the nuclear-weapon States have virtually stopped producing new fissile material for weapons and are maintaining moratoria on nuclear tests.

❃ Likewise, support even small steps to contain proliferation, such as efforts to improve export controls on goods needed to make weapons of mass destruction, as mandated by Security Council Resolution 1540.

❃ And please support the efforts of the Director-General of the IAEA and others to find ways of guaranteeing that all States have access to fuel and services for their civilian nuclear programs without spreading sensitive technology. Countries must be able to meet their growing energy needs through such programs, but we cannot afford a world where more and more countries develop the most sensitive phases of the nuclear fuel cycle themselves.

❃ Finally, do not encourage or allow any State to make its compliance with initiatives to eliminate nuclear weapons or halt their proliferation conditional on concessions from other States on other issues. The preservation of human life on this planet is too important to be used as a hostage.

To those who insist on non-proliferation first, I say this:

❃ True, there has been some progress on nuclear disarmament since the end of the cold war. Some States have removed many nuclear weapons from deployment and eliminated whole classes of nuclear delivery systems. The US and Russia have agreed to limit the number of strategic nuclear weapons they deploy and have removed non-strategic ones from ships and submarines; the US Congress refused to fund the so-called bunker-buster bomb; most nuclear test sites have been closed; and there are national moratoria on nuclear tests, while three nuclear-weapon States—France, Russia and the UK—have ratified the Comprehensive Nuclear-Test-Ban Treaty.

❃ Yet stockpiles remain alarmingly high: 27,000 nuclear weapons reportedly remain in service, of which about 12,000 are actively deployed.

❊ Some States seem to believe they need fewer weapons, but smaller and more useable ones—and even to have embraced the notion of using such weapons in conflict. All of the NPT nuclear-weapon States are modernizing their nuclear arsenals or their delivery systems. They should not imagine that this will be accepted as compatible with the NPT. Everyone will see it for what it is: a euphemism for nuclear rearmament.

❊ Nor is it clear how these States propose to deal with the four nuclear-weapon-capable States outside the NPT.[3] They warn against a nuclear domino effect if this or that country is allowed to acquire a nuclear capability, but they do not seem to know how to prevent it or how to respond to it once it has happened. Surely they should at least consider attempting a "reverse domino effect," in which systematic and sustained reductions in nuclear arsenals would devalue the currency of nuclear weapons and encourage others to follow suit.

❊ Instead, by clinging to and modernizing their own arsenals, even when there is no obvious threat to their national security that nuclear weapons could deter, nuclear-weapon States encourage others—particularly those that do face real threats in their own region—to regard nuclear weapons as essential, both to their security and to their status. It would be much easier to confront pro-liferators if the very existence of nuclear weapons were universally acknowledged as dangerous and ultimately illegitimate.

❊ Similarly, States that wish to discourage others from undertaking nuclear or missile tests could argue their case much more convincingly if they themselves moved quickly to bring the Comprehensive Nuclear-Test-Ban Treaty into force,[4] halt their own missile testing, and negotiate a robust multilateral instrument regulating missiles. Such steps would do more than anything else to advance the cause of non-proliferation.

---

3. India, Israel, North Korea, and Pakistan.
4. The treaty will enter into force 180 days after the forty-four States listed in Annex 2 of the treaty have ratified it. As of 2013, eight Annex 2 states have not ratified the treaty: China, Egypt, Iran, Israel, and the United States have signed but not ratified the treaty; India, North Korea, and Pakistan have not signed it.

✴ Important powers such as Argentina, Brazil, Germany and Japan have shown, by refusing to develop them, that nuclear weapons are not essential to either security or status. South Africa destroyed its arsenal and joined the NPT. Belarus, Ukraine and Kazakhstan gave up nuclear weapons from the former Soviet nuclear arsenal. And Libya has abandoned its nuclear and chemical weapons programs. The nuclear weapon States have applauded all these examples. They should follow them.

✴ Finally, governments and civil society in many countries are increasingly questioning the relevance of the cold war doctrine of nuclear deterrence—the rationale used by all States that possess nuclear weapons—in an age of growing threats from non-State actors. Do we not need, instead, to develop agreed strategies for preventing proliferation?

✴ For all these reasons, I call on all the States with nuclear weapons to develop concrete plans—with specific timetables—for implementing their disarmament commitments. And I urge them to make a joint declaration of intent to achieve the progressive elimination of all nuclear weapons, under strict and effective international control.

In short, my friends, the only way forward is to make progress on both fronts—non-proliferation and disarmament—at once. And we will not achieve this unless at the same time we deal effectively with the threat of terrorism, as well as the threats, both real and rhetorical, which drive particular States or regimes to seek security, however misguidedly, by developing or acquiring nuclear weapons.

It is a complex and daunting task, which calls for leadership, for the establishment of trust, for dialogue and negotiation. But first of all, we need a renewed debate, which must be inclusive, must respect the norms of international negotiations, and must reaffirm the multilateral approach....

Let me conclude by appealing to young people everywhere....

My dear young friends, you are already admirably engaged in the struggle for global development, for human rights, and to protect the environment. Please bring your energy and imagination to this debate. Help us to seize control of the rogue aircraft on which humanity has embarked and bring it to a safe landing before it is too late.

❉ CHAPTER FOUR ❉

HUMAN RIGHTS

Against Racism

*Opening Address to the World Conference against Racism,
Racial Discrimination, Xenophobia, and Related Intolerance
Durban, South Africa
31 August 2001*

*The Durban Conference is remembered mainly for the attempt by
non-governmental organizations and some Member States to use it
as a platform for denunciation of Israel and Zionism, which led to the
withdrawal of the US and Israeli delegations—although the language
they objected to was deleted from the conference's final Declaration
and Program of Action after they left. Unfortunately the final text
was not officially published until sometime later, after world attention
had shifted to the terrorist attacks of 11 September (which happened
three days after the conference closed). Annan's opening speech to the
conference, which had made a strong impression on those present, was
likewise largely forgotten.*

E very one of us must feel the symbolism of this moment—the
conjunction of theme, of time and of place.

For decades the name of this country was synonymous with
racism in its vilest form. But today, Mr. President,[1] you and your fellow
citizens have transformed its meaning—from a byword for injustice
and oppression into a beacon of enlightenment and hope, not only for
a troubled continent, but for the entire world.

Where else, my friends, could we hold this conference? Who could
teach us how to overcome racism, discrimination and intolerance, if not
the people of this country? We salute you. We salute your leadership,
Mr. President. We salute the heroic movement that you represent.

---

1. President Thabo Mbeki of South Africa, who hosted the conference.

We salute Madiba,[2] whose absence today we all regret, but whose presence, in a more profound sense, we all feel.

We salute the memory of all who struggled for justice and freedom in this country—from Mohandas Gandhi to Oliver Tambo, from Steve Biko to Ruth First—and, of course, Govan Mbeki,[3] for whom we are all in mourning today.

And we also recognize the courage of F. W. de Klerk, who faced up to the inevitable and persuaded his own people to accept it.[4]

But we are here to learn, not to celebrate. We are here to share experiences, perspectives and assessments—of how far we have come, and how much further we must go, if racism is to be defeated.

One thing we *can* celebrate is the fact that racism is now universally condemned. Few people in the world today openly deny that human beings are born with equal rights.

But far too many people are still victimized because they belong to a particular group—whether national, ethnic, religious, defined by gender or by descent.

Often this discrimination veils itself behind spurious pretexts. People are denied jobs ostensibly because they lack educational qualifications, or they are refused housing because there is a high crime rate in their community.

Yet these very facts, even when true, are often the result of discrimination. Injustice traps people in poverty, poverty becomes the pretext for injustice—and so new wrongs are piled on the old.

In many places people are maltreated and denied protection on the grounds that they are not citizens but unwanted immigrants. Yet often they have come to a new country to do work that is badly needed or are present not by choice but as refugees from persecution in their own country. Such people have a special need for protection and are entitled to it.

In other cases indigenous peoples and national minorities are oppressed because their culture and self-expression are seen as threats to national unity—and when they protest, this is taken as proof of their guilt.

---

2. Nelson Mandela.
3. Govan Mbeki, father of the president and a hero of the anti-apartheid struggle, had died the previous day.
4. F. W. de Klerk, state president of South Africa from 1989 to 1994, took the historic decision to release Nelson Mandela and negotiate an end to the apartheid regime.

In extreme cases—which, alas, are all too common—people belonging to such groups are forced from their homes, or even massacred, because it is claimed that their very presence threatens another people's security.

Sometimes these problems are in part the legacy of terrible wrongs in the past—such as the exploitation and extermination of indigenous peoples by colonial powers or the treatment of millions of human beings as mere merchandise, to be transported and disposed of by other human beings for commercial gain.

The further those events recede into the past, the harder it becomes to trace lines of accountability. Yet the effects remain. The pain and anger are still felt. The dead, through their descendants, cry out for justice.

Tracing a connection with past crimes may not always be the most constructive way to redress present inequalities, in material terms. But man does not live by bread alone. The sense of continuity with the past is an integral part of each man's or each woman's identity.

Some historical wrongs are traceable to individuals who are still alive or corporations that are still in business. They must expect to be held to account. The society they have wronged may forgive them, as part of the process of reconciliation, but they cannot demand forgiveness, as of right.

Far more difficult are the cases where individual profit and loss have been obscured by a myriad of other, more recent transactions—yet there is still continuity between the societies and States of today and those that committed the original crimes.

Each of us has an obligation to consider where he or she belongs in this complex historical chain. It is always easier to think of the wrongs one's own society has suffered. It is less comfortable to think in what ways our own good fortune might relate to the sufferings of others, in the past or present. But if we are sincere in our desire to overcome the conflicts of the past, all of us should make that mental effort.

A special responsibility falls on political leaders, who have accepted the task of representing a whole society. They are accountable to their fellow citizens, but also—in a sense—accountable *for* them and for the actions of their predecessors. We have seen, in recent decades, some striking examples of national leaders assuming this responsibility, acknowledging past wrongs and asking pardon from—or offering an apology to—the victims and their heirs.

Such gestures cannot right the wrongs of the past. They can sometimes help to free the present—and the future—from the shackles of the past.

But in any case, past wrongs must not distract us from present evils. Our aim must be to banish from this new century the hatred and prejudice that have disfigured previous centuries.

The struggle to do that is at the very heart of our work at the United Nations....

Only if we tackle these evils at the source can we hope to prevent conflicts before they break out. And that means taking firm action to root them out in every society—for, alas, no society is immune.

Last year, the leaders of our Member States resolved, in their Millennium Declaration, "to take measures to ensure respect for and protection of the human rights of migrants, migrant workers and their families, to eliminate the increasing acts of racism and xenophobia in many societies, and to promote greater harmony and tolerance in all societies."

With those words, they gave this conference its true agenda. We must not leave this city without agreeing on practical measures which all States should take to fulfill that pledge. It must be reflected in our budgets and development plans, in our laws and institutions—and, above all, in our school curricula.

Let us remember that no one is born a racist. Children learn racism as they grow up, from the society around them—and too often the stereotypes are reinforced, deliberately or inadvertently, by the mass media. We must not sacrifice freedom of the press, but we must actively refute pseudo-scientific arguments and oppose negative images with positive ones—teaching our children and our fellow citizens not to fear diversity, but to cherish it.

This conference has been exceptionally difficult to prepare, because the issues are not ones where consensus is easily found.

Yes, we can all agree to condemn racism. But that very fact makes the accusation of racism, against any particular individual or group, particularly hurtful. It is hurtful to one's pride, because few of us see ourselves as racists. And it arouses fear, because once a group is accused of racism it becomes a potential target for retaliation, perhaps for persecution in its turn.

Nowhere is that truer today than in the Middle East. The Jewish people have been victims of anti-Semitism in many parts of the world, and in Europe they were the target of the Holocaust—the ultimate abomination. This fact must never be forgotten or diminished. It is understandable, therefore, that many Jews deeply resent any accusation of racism directed against the State of Israel—and all the more so when it coincides with indiscriminate and totally unacceptable attacks on innocent civilians.

Yet we cannot expect Palestinians to accept this as a reason why the wrongs done to them—displacement, occupation, blockade, and now extra-judicial killings—should be ignored, whatever label one uses to describe them.

But, my friends, mutual accusations are not the purpose of this conference. Our main objective must be to improve the lot of the victims.

Let us admit that all countries have issues of racism and discrimination to address. Rather than pick on any one country or region, let us aim to leave here with a commitment from every country to draw up and implement its own national plan to combat racism, in accordance with general principles that we will have agreed....

Friends, this conference is a test of our international community—of its will to unite on a topic of central importance in people's lives. Let us not fail this test. The buildup to this conference has prompted an extraordinary mobilization of civil society in many different countries. It has raised expectations which we must not disappoint.

If we leave here without agreement, we shall give comfort to the worst elements in every society. But if, after all the difficulties, we can leave with a call to action supported by all, we shall send a signal of hope to brave people struggling against racism all over the world. Let us rise above our disagreements. The wrangling has gone on for too long. Let us echo the slogan that resounded throughout this country during the elections of 1994, at the end of the long struggle against apartheid:

SEKUNJALO. The time has come.

✳

The Very Heart of the UN's Mission

Address at an Event to Mark International Human Rights Day
New York, New York
8 December 2006

Annan had a closer relationship with the international human rights
movement than did any of his predecessors as Secretary-General. In his last
month in office, Human Rights Watch, one of the leading non-governmental
organizations in that field, sponsored a special event in his honor, at which
Annan summed up the progress made during his tenure and the main chal-
lenges the United Nations still had to confront in its human rights work.

I could not ask for better company, on the last International Human Rights Day of my time in office, than this group of courageous human rights leaders from around the world.

I don't need to tell you, of all people, that the United Nations has a special stake, and a special responsibility, in promoting respect for human rights worldwide. But equally, and less happily, I don't need to tell you that the UN has often failed to live up to that responsibility. I know that ten years ago many of you were close to giving up on any hope that an organization of governments, many of which are themselves gross violators of human rights, could ever function as an effective human rights defender.

One of my priorities as Secretary-General has been to try and restore that hope, by making human rights central to all the UN's work. But I'm not sure how far I have succeeded or how much nearer we are to bringing the reality of the UN in line with my vision of human rights as its "third pillar," on a par with development and peace and security.

Development, security and human rights go hand in hand; no one of them can advance very far without the other two. Indeed, anyone who speaks forcefully for human rights but does nothing about security and development, including the desperate need to fight extreme poverty, undermines both his credibility and his cause. Poverty in particular remains both a source and a consequence of rights violations. Yet, if we are serious about human deprivation, we must also demonstrate that we are serious about human dignity, and vice versa.

Are you any more confident today than you were ten years ago that an intergovernmental organization can really do this job? I fear the answer may be no and that the first steps of the Human Rights Council, which we all fought so hard to establish,[1] may not have given you much encouragement. So this morning I suggest that we try and think through, together, what is really needed.

First, we must give real meaning to the principle of *responsibility to protect.*

As you know, last year's World Summit formally endorsed that momentous doctrine, which means, in essence, that respect for national sovereignty can no longer be used as an excuse for inaction in the face of genocide, war crimes, ethnic cleansing and crimes against humanity. Yet one year later, to judge by what is happening in Darfur, our performance has not improved much since the disasters of Bosnia and Rwanda. Sixty years after the liberation of the Nazi death camps and thirty years after the Cambodian killing fields, the promise of "never again" is ringing hollow.

The tragedy of Darfur has raged for over three years now, and still reports pour in of villages being destroyed by the hundred and of the brutal treatment of civilians spreading into neighboring countries. How can an international community which claims to uphold human rights allow this horror to continue?

There is more than enough blame to go around. It can be shared among those who value abstract notions of sovereignty more than the lives of real families, those whose reflex of solidarity puts them on the side of governments and not of peoples, and those who fear that action to stop the slaughter would jeopardize their commercial interests.

The truth is, none of these arguments amount even to excuses, let alone justifications, for the shameful passivity of most governments.

---

1. One reform Annan had proposed in his *In Larger Freedom* report that was taken up by the 2005 World Summit was the replacement of the UN's Commission on Human Rights with a stronger Human Rights Council. This had been established by the General Assembly in the spring of 2006, and on the day of this speech, it had just completed its third regular session.

We have still not summoned up the collective sense of urgency that this issue requires.

Some governments have tried to win support in the global South by caricaturing "responsibility to protect" as a conspiracy by imperialist powers to take back the hard-won national sovereignty of formerly colonized peoples. This is utterly false.

We must do better. We must develop the responsibility to protect into a powerful international norm that is not only quoted but put into practice, whenever and wherever it is needed.

Above all we must not wait to take action until genocide is actually happening, by which time it is often too late to do anything effective about it. Two years ago I announced an action plan for the prevention of genocide[2] and appointed a Special Adviser to help me implement it. While his work has been extremely valuable, much more needs to be done. I hope my successor will take up this banner and that Member States will support him.

Second, we must put *an end to impunity*.

We have made progress in holding people accountable for the world's worst crimes. The establishment of the International Criminal Court, the work of the UN tribunals for Yugoslavia and Rwanda, the hybrid ones in Sierra Leone and Cambodia, and the various Commissions of Experts and Inquiry have proclaimed the will of the international community that such crimes should no longer go unpunished.

And yet they still do. Mladic[3] and Karadzic[4] and the leaders of the Lord's Resistance Army,[5] to name but a few, are still at large. Unless these indicted war criminals are brought to court, others tempted to emulate them will not be deterred.

---

2. See Chapter 8.
3. Ratko Mladic, chief of staff of the Army of the Republika Srpska (the Bosnian Serb Army) in the Bosnian war of 1992 to 1995. In 1995, he was indicted by the International Criminal Tribunal for the Former Yugoslavia (ICTY) for genocide, war crimes, and crimes against humanity. But it was not until 2011 that he was arrested (in northern Serbia) and extradited to The Hague, where his trial began in May 2012.
4. Radovan Karadzic, president of the Republika Srpska in Bosnia during the breakup of Yugoslavia. Indicted by the ICTY in 1995, along with Mladic, for crimes against humanity and war crimes, he was arrested and extradited to The Hague in 2008. His trial began in 2009 and is still in progress as of August 2013.
5. In 2005 the International Criminal Court issued arrest warrants against Joseph Kony and four other leaders of the Lord's Resistance Army, a dissident movement that had started in northern Uganda and then spread to neighboring countries. They were charged with crimes against humanity and war crimes, including murder, rape, sexual slavery, and enlisting children as combatants. As of August 2013 none of them had been arrested, although three have been reported killed.

Some say that justice must sometimes be sacrificed in the interests of peace. I question that. We have seen in Sierra Leone and in the Balkans that, on the contrary, justice is a fundamental component of peace. Indeed, justice has often bolstered lasting peace by delegitimizing and driving underground those individuals who pose the gravest threat to it. That is why there should never be amnesty for genocide, crimes against humanity and massive violations of human rights. That would only encourage today's mass murderers and tomorrow's would-be mass murderers to continue their vicious work.

Third, we need an *anti-terrorism strategy* that does not merely pay lip service to the defense of human rights but is built on it.

All States agreed last year that terrorism in all its forms and manifestations, committed by whomever, wherever and for whatever purposes, is one of the most serious threats to international peace and security. They were right. Terrorism in itself is an assault on the most basic human rights, starting with the right to life.

But States cannot fulfill that obligation by themselves violating human rights in the process. To do so means abandoning the moral high ground and playing into the hands of the terrorists. That is why secret prisons have no place in our struggle against terrorism, and why all places where terrorism suspects are detained must be accessible to the International Committee of the Red Cross. Leading promoters of human rights undermine their own influence when they fail to live up to these principles.

We must fight terrorism in conformity with international law, those parts of it that prohibit torture and inhuman treatment and those that give anyone detained against his or her will the right to due process and the judgment of a court. Once we adopt a policy of making exceptions to these rules or excusing breaches of them, no matter how narrow, we are on a slippery slope. The line cannot be held halfway down. We must defend it at the top.

Fourth, let's not content ourselves with grand statements of principle. We must work to *make human rights a reality in each country.*

Of course, protecting and promoting human rights is first and foremost a national responsibility. Every Member State of the UN can draw on its own history to develop its own ways of upholding universal rights. But many States need help in doing this, and the UN system has a vital role to play.

Over the past decade, the UN has rapidly expanded its operational capacity for peacekeeping and for development and humanitarian aid. Our capacity to protect and promote human rights now needs to catch up.

World leaders recognized this at last year's Summit. They agreed to double the budget of the Office of the High Commissioner for Human Rights over the next five years, and as a result the Office is now rapidly expanding. It is helping States build their capacity, giving them technical assistance where necessary, and bringing urgent situations to the attention of the international community. In some countries, such as Colombia and Nepal, its monitoring missions are making a very important contribution to the resolution of conflict.

But the Office's capacity is still far short of the needs it has to meet. I hope the quality of its work will persuade Member States to authorize further increases in the years ahead.

Meanwhile, we must realize the promise of the Human Rights Council, which so far has clearly not justified all the hopes that so many of us placed in it.

Of course it's encouraging that the Council has now decided to hold a special session on Darfur next week. I hope against hope that it will find an effective way to deal with this burning issue.

But I am worried by its disproportionate focus on violations by Israel. Not that Israel should be given a free pass. Absolutely not. But the Council should give the same attention to grave violations committed by other States as well.

And I am also worried by the efforts of some Council members to weaken or abolish the system of Special Procedures, the independent mechanisms for reporting on violations of particular kinds or in specific countries.

The Special Procedures are the crown jewel of the system. They, together with the High Commissioner and her staff, provide the independent expertise and judgment which is essential to effective human rights protection. They must not be politicized or subjected to governmental control.

Instead, the Council's agenda should be broadened to reflect the actual abuses that occur in every part of the world.... Human rights abuses do not occur on paper. They are committed by real people, against real victims, in specific countries.

The world needs an intergovernmental body that deals with human rights. And it needs an intergovernmental body that works. That can only be achieved by a broader leadership. All States that truly believe in human rights, in every part of the world, must work together to transcend narrow interests and make the Human Rights Council live up to its promise. It is a historic opportunity, and history will not be kind if we let it pass.

The truth is, it's not enough just to have the right principles and say what we think should happen. We also have to ask who is going to make it happen. Whom can we look to for support? Who is going to insist that these principles are acted on?

First, *I look to Africa to take the lead.*

Africa's many conflicts are, almost invariably, accompanied by massive human rights violations. Unless Africa wholeheartedly embraces the inviolability of human rights, its struggle for security and development will not succeed.

As I said when I first addressed African heads of State, at Harare in 1997,[6] to treat human rights as an imposition by the industrialized West or a luxury of the rich countries for which Africa is not ready demeans the yearning for human dignity that resides in every African heart. Human rights are, by definition, also African rights. It should be every African government's first priority to ensure that Africans can enjoy them.

South African heroes, like Nelson Mandela and Desmond Tutu, have shown the way. The African Union led the way among international organizations on the responsibility to protect, by proclaiming in its Constitutive Act the right of the Union to intervene in a Member State in respect of grave circumstances, namely war crimes, genocide and crimes against humanity. It has also tried harder than anyone else to act on that doctrine in Darfur and to bring the former Chadian dictator Hissene Habre to justice.

---

6. See "Africa's Third Wave" in Chapter 6.

This is encouraging, but much more needs to be done. In practice, many African governments are still resisting the responsibility to protect. Many, even among the most democratic, are still reluctant to play their role in the Human Rights Council by speaking out impartially against all abuses. They can, and must, do more.

Secondly, *I look to the growing power of women,* which means we must give priority to women's rights.

The equal rights of men and women, promised by the UN Charter 61 years ago, are still far from being a reality. The UN can and must play a greater role in empowering women....

And thirdly, *I look to civil society,* which means you!

We need dedicated individuals and dynamic human rights defenders to hold governments to account. States' performance must be judged against their commitments, and they must be accountable both to their own people and to their peers in the international community. Thank God, then, for the growth in human rights NGOs we have witnessed in the last decade. There are now an estimated 26,000 of them worldwide, specializing in issues from trafficking to torture, from HIV/AIDS to the rights of children and migrants.

This community is the UN and its Member States' essential partner in the struggle for human rights. Without the information you collect, the treaty bodies[7] would be helpless. Without the spotlight you shine, abuses would go unnoticed. In return, we must do everything to protect you from harassment, intimidation and reprisal, so you can carry on your vital work.

Dear friends,

Throughout my time in office my biggest concern has been to make the UN an organization that serves people and treats them as people, that is, individual human beings, not abstractions or mere components of a State.

Of course I know that individuals don't exist in a vacuum. Man is a political and social animal, and individual men and women define their identity by their membership of groups. That's why human rights must always include rights to collective self-expression, which are especially important for minorities.

---

7. Committees of independent experts who monitor implementation of the core international human rights treaties.

But no one's identity can be reduced to membership of a single group, be it ethnic, national, religious, or whatever. Each one of us is defined by a unique combination of characteristics that make up our personality. And it is that individual person whose rights must be preserved and respected.

The task of ensuring that that happens lies at the very heart of the UN's mission. And of all our tasks it is the one that can least safely be left in the hands of governments or of a purely intergovernmental organization. In this task more than any other, the UN needs free spirits like yours to fill the leadership vacuum and hold world leaders and the United Nations to account.

So it's no mere figure of speech, dear friends, when I say that I leave the future of the UN's human rights work in your hands.

✿

The Battle Is Never Finally Won

Special Address to Both Houses of Parliament to Commemorate the Bicentenary of the Abolition of the Slave Trade
London, England
8 May 2007

The Act for the Abolition of the Slave Trade was passed by the British House of Commons in February 1807 and became law a month later. To commemorate the bicentenary, both houses of Parliament invited Annan to give a special address, shortly after he left office.

Two hundred years ago this Parliament voted to abolish the slave trade in the countries—including parts of my own—which were then British colonies. Today we gather, as free men and women, to commemorate that historic event and to recall centuries of struggle against mankind's least human practice.

Let me begin by saying how deeply moved I am by your invitation to share this momentous bicentenary with you. The opportunity to address these Houses, at any time and on any subject, would be a singular honor. But to find appropriate words to say in this place, on this occasion, is also a singular challenge.

Because, of course, the achievement that we commemorate today should never have been necessary. In the long history of human wrongs, the trade in human beings will go down as one of the greatest crimes ever committed.

Numerous forts dot the coastline of my country. The view from their upper levels is as picturesque as their history is dark. One of them, Christiansborg Castle in Accra, was finished in 1661 by the Danes, close to the time the first Asante king Osei Tutu, rose to power. It is still viewed as the symbol of an era in our history that we need to understand better.

It was from these forts and trading posts—through the "door of no return"—that African slaves began their terrible journey across the Atlantic. Many perished in the fetid, dark, overcrowded dungeons even before they could be herded onto ships for the living hell of the "Middle Passage." The New World for them held only the promise of a life of unremitting toil on the plantations, as the disposable chattels of fellow human beings. There were good reasons why these forts became feared as places of no return—and good reasons why every one of us should resolve that humanity must never return … to the cruelty that was practiced there.

Let us not forget that slavery had an earlier history, going back many centuries. It existed in Neolithic Europe, in all the ancient civilizations of Egypt, of the Middle East—and of Greece…. Many generations of Europeans were brought up on Aristotle's *Politics,* in which they could read that certain people were slaves "by nature," being deficient in the capacities for rational deliberation required to manage their own lives.

The Roman Empire enslaved so many people that its armies required trained specialists to deal with the huge number of captives. The English word "slave" itself derives from the Slavs who were captured and sold westward during Europe's Dark Ages.

Hardly any part of the world is exempt from this stain on human history. Most of the great Asian empires developed sophisticated slave routes. Slavery was also part of the indigenous power structures in the Americas, and it was certainly not unknown in Africa before the European traders arrived.

In some parts of the world the slave trade was the first trade of any kind to be carried on over long distances on a large scale—and the means by which whole regions, such as Brazil, were first integrated into the world economy. The first wave of globalization, one could say.

The very distance that the slaves were transported had a commercial value: the further they were taken from their homes, the harder it was for them to escape, and so the more secure the slave owner could feel—and the higher the price he would be prepared to pay.

In short, the trade whose abolition we commemorate today was an abominable practice taken to its most abominable extreme. At the time of its abolition, the transatlantic slave trade involved the forcible transportation of 100,000 people every year. And today we should ask ourselves not only why Britain abolished it 200 years ago, but why it was tolerated for so long.

The economic value of slaves is obvious enough. The plantations in the New World created a huge demand for labor, and the "triangular trade"—in which the same ships carried European goods to Africa, African slaves to the Americas, and American sugar, cotton and tobacco to Europe—was hugely profitable. But that is hardly a sufficient explanation for its prevalence. After all, slavery ran counter to some of the most fundamental Enlightenment values.

Slavery throve partly because its horrors remained largely hidden from the eyes of British and European consumers. They enjoyed the sugar that the slave ships brought back but did not see the cruelty and suffering that lay behind it. Out of sight meant truly out of mind.

It was by making the British people aware of the cruelty and suffering of plantation slavery that the abolitionists eventually prevailed. They publicized the violence, the whippings, the mutilations, and the unpunished murder of slaves; the broken families, children wrenched from their mothers, wives from their husbands, and sold for profit. These powerful images awoke the humanitarian impulse of the British public.

Thomas Clarkson, the moving spirit behind the founding of the Society for Effecting the Abolition of Slavery in 1787, concentrated on highlighting the horrors of the slave trade. His lectures, and the physical evidence of the trade's brutality that he collected, presented a damning indictment.

Twenty years later, when the law abolishing the trade was passed, William Wilberforce, MP, its main sponsor, had this to say:

> I mean not to accuse any one, but to take the shame upon myself, in common, indeed, with the whole Parliament of Great Britain, for having suffered this horrid trade to be carried under their authority. We are all guilty—we ought to plead guilty and not to exculpate ourselves by throwing the blame on others.

Wilberforce was right, for in earlier years this same Parliament had approved more than 100 laws accommodating the slave trade. And even afterwards, this Parliament voted 23 million pounds' worth of compensation—equivalent to 100 times that amount today—for the "victims." Not the victims of slavery or the trade itself, but the victims of its elimination; in other words, the slave owners.

Nor should we think of the slaves themselves as passive recipients of British generosity. The slave trade would not have collapsed without their repeated, often desperate, revolts—not least the great rebellion led by Toussaint L'Ouverture in the French colony of Saint-Domingue, which eventually established the Republic of Haiti and liberated half a million slaves, and the protests led by Sam Sharpe in Jamaica, which paved the way for the abolition of slavery throughout the British Empire.

Ladies and gentlemen,

Abolition, like today's human rights causes, is not a matter for attribution. It is about personal responsibility and the need for each one of us to think what we can do, rather than seeking to shift the blame to someone else. It is a universal fight.

The same way we can celebrate Clarkson and Wilberforce, with the support of the Quakers, as the precursors of today's human rights movement—one could say the first modern NGO—we can also trace examples such as the brave Africans who brought about, in no small way, the *Amistad* Affair, the first American civil rights cause.[1]

---

1. In 1839 a group of African slaves seized control of the *Amistad*, a Spanish schooner that was transporting them to Cuba. The ship was later apprehended off Long Island and taken into custody by the United States. In 1841 the US Supreme Court ruled that the Africans had acted lawfully and authorized their return to their homeland.

The abolitionist movement was the first campaign to bring together a coalition in a struggle against gross violations of human dignity. It showed how effective the mobilization of public opinion can be. The abolitionists of eighteenth-century Britain represented a moral truth that seemed remote from the ways of the world, a moral passion that must at first have seemed utterly impracticable. Yet, by persistence, by resolve, by eloquence, and by imagination, they changed history. They showed that moral suasion could prevail over narrow self-interest. They demonstrated that public opinion could change the law. In the half century following the Slave Trade Act, the Royal Navy freed almost 150,000 human beings. Ideals that once seemed quixotic were backed with battleships. And so we revisit the history of the slave trade not only with horror but with hope.

However, victory in this kind of struggle is never total or final. Even in the British Empire, slavery remained legal for another 26 years after the slave trade was abolished—and, of course, the trade went on through most of the nineteenth century despite British efforts to stop it. We should beware the sigh of relief—there is always more work to be done.

Long after slavery was abolished, many people clung to the premise on which it was based—the notion that certain groups of human beings are hereditarily inferior to others. That was an attitude that helped sponsor a deeper and more widespread colonial occupation of the African continent later in the nineteenth century. That is why I feel it is important today to remember another great anniversary that falls this year. Fifty years ago, my country, Ghana, inaugurated a new era of African independence.

Neither emancipation nor independence can guarantee freedom simply by being proclaimed. In most countries, racial discrimination is now officially frowned on, and laws have been passed against it. But the work of emancipation does not stop there. It must continue until we have removed the stigma, the patterns of deference and the denial of respect which lie at the heart of racism.

We must remember that racism in another guise inflicted a terrible wound on humanity right in the heart of Europe: the Holocaust that was carried out against the Jewish people—and against the Roma and other groups arbitrarily proclaimed "subhuman" by the Nazis. So perhaps it is appropriate that we hold this commemoration on the eighth of May, the day that marks Europe's liberation from Nazism. That enables us to associate these two great self-inflicted tragedies of the human race and the two great, if very different, liberation struggles that brought them to an end. And it reminds us of the greater, un-concluded struggle of which they were both part—the struggle against man's inhumanity to man, so painfully visible in recent years, from the Balkans to Rwanda to Darfur.

Despite the fact that all human beings are born free and equal in human dignity, every day thousands of women and children are sold so that their bodies and their labor can be exploited. Despite international labor standards and a UN Protocol against human trafficking, millions of victims, particularly children—made vulnerable by poverty and exploited by criminals—are working in mines, sweatshops, brothels and plantations—trapped by debt and violence. In a perverse commercialization of humanity, they are used like products and then thrown away.

Slavery cannot be relegated to the annals of history so long as men, women and children are still being coerced, drugged, tricked, and sold to do dangerous and degrading work against their will....

Let us take action to prevent any more victims from having their dreams of a better future turn into nightmares of exploitation and servitude.

Many Africans believe history has not yet repaired past wounds at all. The movement for reparations is fuelled by the desire for recognition. This is a battle better fought in the development domain. In the year 2000, when all Member States of the United Nations approved the Millennium Declaration, including the Millennium Development Goals, they acknowledged that all human beings must face a common future and must do so in a spirit of solidarity based on shared democratic ideals.

In order to build on our common rights and values, we must be conscious of our intertwined fate. And we have to face the possibility, if not the likelihood, that Africa may be the only region of the world that does not attain the majority of the MDGs by 2015. A bold investment in addressing poverty in Africa, as promised by the G8 in Gleneagles,[2] would be the best way to repair the wounds of the past and turn the page.

2. Meeting at Gleneagles, Scotland, in July 2005, leaders of the Group of Eight leading industrialized countries (Canada, France, Germany, Italy, Japan, Russia, the United Kingdom, and the United States) recognized that their national interests were aligned with their responsibility to support Africa's development and agreed on a set of concrete actions—cancelling debt and doubling aid.

My friends,

Let us remember that the officers of the slave ships were for the most part educated people, like you and me. Yet they were apparently at ease in their role. Instead of recognizing the slaves as fellow human beings, they looked on them as simple merchandise. This reminds us how easy it is to blind ourselves to the suffering of fellow creatures, so long as our own comfort and security are not threatened. We should all look carefully at our own lives and ask what abominations we may even now be tolerating, or joining in, or benefiting from. The slave trade as practiced 200 years ago may be history. But moral blindness is ever present. Let us not close our eyes to crimes that shame us all.

The slave trade was eventually abolished because many thousands of people examined their own consciences and took personal responsibility for what was happening around them. We must approach today's abuses in the same spirit—each of us seeking not to blame someone else but to think what we can do to hasten the abuses' end. And we must do so sustained by the knowledge that change—to the point of profound transformation—is possible. This is not the least of the abolitionists' legacy. There is no evil so entrenched that it cannot be eradicated.

Inspired by the abolitionists of two centuries ago, let us fight against exploitation and oppression and stand up for freedom and human dignity.

The battle for freedom and justice is never hopeless, but it is never finally won. Every morning, we must wake up ready to fight it again.

❋ CHAPTER FIVE ❋

PEACEKEEPING AND PEACE-BUILDING

❄

Swords into Ploughshares

Address to a Special Commemorative Meeting
of the General Assembly to Mark the 50th
Anniversary of United Nations Peacekeeping
New York, New York
6 October 1998

On May 29, 1948, the Security Council called for a cessation of hostilities
in Palestine and decided that the truce should be supervised by the UN
Mediator, with the assistance of a group of military observers. The first
group of military observers, which has come to be recognized as the first
UN peacekeeping mission, arrived in the region in June 1948.

Today, it is my great honor to commemorate with you the fiftieth anniversary of the year when soldiers were sent on to the battlefield under a new flag and with a new mission: a mission of peace.

It would be no exaggeration to say that that mission was without precedent in human history. It was an attempt to confront and defeat the worst in man with the best in man; to counter violence with tolerance, might with moderation, and war with peace.

That mission has earned its place in history as the first example of what has come to be known as "peacekeeping." Ever since then, day after day, year after year, United Nations peacekeepers have been meeting the threat and reality of conflict, without losing faith, without giving in, without giving up.

Since 1948, there have been 49 United Nations peacekeeping operations. Thirty-six of those were created since 1988, the year in which United Nations peacekeeping was awarded the Nobel Peace Prize. Well over 750,000 military and civilian police personnel and thousands of other civilians, from 118 different countries, have served in United

Nations peacekeeping operations. Fourteen thousand peacekeepers are serving this very day.

No figures, however, can do justice to the ultimate sacrifice that more than 1,500 peacekeepers have made over this half century. Today we pay tribute, above all, to the brave "blue helmets" who gave their lives in the cause of peace. Whatever success we have had is owed to their sacrifice, their dedication, their heroism.

Later today I shall bestow on three of our fallen peacekeepers, in the presence of their families, a new medal named after one of them: Secretary-General Dag Hammarskjöld.

The United Nations, forged from the battles of two world wars, was dedicated, above all, to the pursuit of peace and, in the enduring words of the Charter, to saving "succeeding generations from the scourge of war." Undoubtedly, peacekeeping falls fairly and squarely within the spirit of that pledge. Yet you will search the Charter in vain for any specific provision for such operations.

"Peacekeeping," from the start, has been an improvisation. To my mind, that is one of its great merits. It proved, and continues to prove, that the United Nations is not a static or hidebound Organization, but a dynamic and innovative one. Indeed, peacekeeping has been one of many activities through which our Organization has shown its ability to adapt to circumstances, to find its way round obstacles, and to make itself relevant to the actual problems at hand.

Not that the evolution of United Nations peacekeeping—from patrolling clearly marked buffer zones and cease-fire lines to the far more complex, multi-dimensional operations of the 1990s—has been either smooth or simple.

Often the expectations placed on peacekeepers have outstripped the resources given to them. Often the demands made of them have cruelly ignored realities on the ground.

Over the decades, we have had some unmistakable successes, such as Namibia, Mozambique and El Salvador. But we have also found ourselves maintaining calm in some seemingly intractable stalemates, such as Cyprus and the Middle East.

And in some places—Rwanda and the former Yugoslavia—we have found ourselves standing by, in impotent horror, while the most appalling crimes were committed. There, the limits of peacekeeping were graphically demonstrated: we learned, the hard way, that lightly armed troops in white vehicles and blue helmets are not the solution to every conflict. Sometimes peace has to be made—or enforced—before it can be kept.

We yield to no one in our regret and our pain over those calamities: the loss of life; the wanton destruction of towns and villages; the shredding of the very fabric of humanity which, in normal times and places, allows men and women of different ethnic origin to live peacefully side by side.…

But that does not mean we succumb to the fatalism of those who would rather stay at home when conflict rages and fellow human beings are suffering in a distant land. That is the cynic's answer and the coward's solution. It is not ours.

We are not here today to declare victory. We cannot claim that peacekeeping has been the answer to every conflict; still less, alas, that it has prevented the recurrence of genocide. What we can and do claim proudly is that, in the first half century of their existence, United Nations "blue helmets" have saved tens of thousands of lives.

In recent times the pendulum may appear to have swung away from support for United Nations peacekeeping. But I have no doubt that history will see it as one of the Organization's most important and lasting contributions to international peace and security.

The mission of United Nations peacekeeping must continue. Too much remains to be done, too many innocents are dying even as we speak, for us to think of leaving the field now. Peacekeeping's promise, after all, was never to end war. Peacekeeping is not the same as peacemaking. It can help prevent, or at least delay, a recurrence of conflict.

It can even be used, as we have shown in the former Yugoslav republic of Macedonia, to help prevent conflict from breaking out in the first place. Above all, it gives time and space for conflict resolution: it gives peace a chance. If the chance is not taken, the peacekeepers are not to blame.

Isaiah's words—"they shall beat their swords into ploughshares, and their spears into pruning-hooks; nation shall not lift up sword against nation; neither shall they learn war any more"—will never be more than an ideal for humanity. If, in our service as United Nations peacekeepers, we can help make that ideal more true than false, more promising than distant, more able to protect the innocent than embolden the guilty, we will have done our part.

The will to peace must exist among the peoples and the parties, but the path to peace is one that we—the United Nations—can help pave. We have done so for the last half century, and I am confident we can continue in the century to come.

❊

What We Have Learnt

Tip O'Neill Lecture, "Learning the Lessons of Peace-Building"
Delivered at Magee Campus, University of Ulster
Londonderry, Northern Ireland
18 October 2004

The conflict in Northern Ireland was never on the United Nations agenda, being dealt with by the United Kingdom and the Republic of Ireland, with some help from the United States. But by 2004 the 1998 Good Friday Agreement had been in place long enough for it to be possible for the UN Secretary-General to visit the province without appearing to interfere. He took the opportunity to reflect on the UN's experience of peacekeeping and peace-building in other places and on how far lessons learnt in one conflict can be applied to another.

My talk today is about learning—not teaching. The question I want to examine with you is, How can outsiders best contribute to the process of building peace in war-torn societies? Such a process must, by its very nature, be deeply rooted in local communities and local identities. Outsiders, however well intentioned, do not know best. The people of the country or region concerned must feel that it is their process, if it is to have any hope of success. Yet I believe that outsiders can help, particularly if they learn the right lessons from their own experience and apply them with sensitivity....

Please do not take my general observations about peace-building as oblique comments on your own problems. You have been managing those without the help of the United Nations. You have well-established mechanisms to do so. And we have an equally well-established policy of not seeking to duplicate such mechanisms.

I don't mean to imply that you have solved all your problems.... But it does seem to me that you are managing them better and more hopefully than in the past. For some years now you have been spared the large-scale violence and terror that used to disfigure your beautiful part of the country and seemed to blight its future. Your efforts to create a better world for your children have been a source of inspiration and hope to people in many other countries. If the world is to learn lessons about how to manage a transition from troubles and violence to peace, surely it can learn some of them from you—from your commitment, courage and imagination in seeking solutions and fostering trust between communities which had been at loggerheads for decades.

Which brings me back to my theme. Since the end of the cold war, our Member States have set the United Nations to work in many fractured and war-torn societies. We are no longer asked, as we used to be, just to "keep the peace" by helping maintain a cease-fire. Now, increasingly, we are tasked with going beyond that, to engage in conflict resolution. This means tackling root causes. It means trying to help the people in those fractured societies to work together to build a lasting peace. And I believe we have learnt some valuable lessons, if only by the painful method of trial and error.

For one thing, we have learnt to approach this whole topic with considerable caution. A great Northern Irish poet [Louis MacNeice] once wrote:

World is crazier and, more of it than we think,
Incorrigibly plural.

And that is certainly true of war-torn societies. Each has its own particularity, born of its own—often very local—history, culture, and, quite often, religion and ethnicity. There is no "one size fits all."

So there are no easy answers and very few uncontested ones. There is now a huge literature about post-conflict peace-building. It deals, for instance, with secession and partition; with spoilers; with transitional justice, truth commissions, and reconciliation; with elections and power sharing; with the rule of law; with economic liberalization, reconstruction and development; even with international administration or trusteeship. All these issues have spawned intense debate. Some would put the emphasis on eliminating root causes and dealing with spoilers. Others would give primacy to the need for swift economic growth and reconstruction, arguing that lapses back into conflict are much more common in very poor societies. The debate remains unresolved, because we are all still learning, and it may take some time before the various approaches can be reconciled.

In the last fifteen years or so, the United Nations has developed a considerable body of experience managing and resolving conflict, as well as peace-building. But we should acknowledge that our record has been mixed. Among the successes I would mention particularly Namibia, South Africa, Mozambique, El Salvador, eastern Slavonia, Guatemala and East Timor. The failures, alas, often receive more publicity—especially those of the early and mid-1990s, Somalia, Bosnia, Rwanda and Angola. I do not think it coincidental that, in the case of the failures, either there was no peace to keep or peace agreements proved fragile because the underlying causes of conflict had not been resolved. We have learnt useful lessons from both successes and failures, and are doing our best to put those lessons into practice.

What are these lessons? Let me suggest nine that are well worth considering.

First, we should say no when we need to.

We must know the limits of what is achievable by the United Nations. We should be especially careful not to allow ourselves to be used as a fig leaf for lack of political will by the international community to deal effectively with an issue. If the Security Council seeks to give the Secretary-General a mandate which he believes to be unachievable, especially if coupled with means which he knows to be inadequate, he should say so, clearly and in advance. I believe that we have learnt that lesson, uncomfortable though it may be.

Second, know where you are going.

Our most successful experiences have started from a clear and achievable mandate. In post-conflict work, this means the clearest vision of the end state—or at least, a clear understanding, accepted by all parties, of how and when the end state will eventually be decided....

Third lesson, know the context.

Here I return to Louis MacNeice and his "drunkenness of things being various." The specificity of a conflict will determine what can be done when. In Nicaragua and South Africa, we were able to help with elections in countries that were ripe for elections. But in the Democratic Republic of Congo, where three-and-a-half-million have died in six years of war, careful and thorough preparations are needed before elections can go ahead. In post-conflict situations, elections work best when they are the result of a political consensus as to their objectives. In the absence of such consensus, the parties often feel under no obligation to honor commitments they have entered into. They don't respect the rules of the game because they haven't really acquired the rules of the game.

I wish I could tell you that the United Nations, and in particular the Security Council, was always attuned to the context—to the hard questions of what drove the killing and what drove the end to the killing. Too often it has not been so attuned, and people in the countries concerned have paid the price. The bottom line, I am convinced, is that we need to be closer to those whose peace it is to make or to break.

Fourth, never neglect security.

This is the point closest to achieving consensus among experienced peace-builders: most of the tasks that we call peace-building can only be carried out where there is already a reasonable level of physical security.

Of course that begs the question of what level any given society will consider "reasonable"—and also of how you get there. In some cases security can be achieved purely by negotiation or dialogue between the warring parties; in others you need a stabilization force, with robust rules of engagement.

But it is nonetheless true: without security almost everything else is impossible: no effective government; no reconstruction; no return of refugees; no return to school; no elections.

The fifth lesson, manage expectations.

There is a moment, when the killing stops, when everything seems possible. Expectations run high.

That can be dangerous, because the road to peace often proves long and hard. The various elements of peace-building—transforming suspicion into trust, re-crafting State institutions, reconstructing war-torn economies—can take years or decades to accomplish. During that time people's hope and their faith in the process need to be sustained.

So expectations need to be managed from the beginning and throughout the process—which requires a major effort of public information and education by the peace-builders.

In particular, it is vital to explain what the United Nations is there to do and what it cannot do. Otherwise expectations are unrealistic, and they are inevitably disappointed. When disillusion sets in, the people can easily turn against the very peace agreement they had at first welcomed.

Sixth, stay the course—peace-building is a long-term commitment.

This lesson follows from the previous one. Nearly half of all peace agreements collapse within five years. Others fall into a sort of limbo of no war, no peace. In the life of almost every peace process, there comes a time—usually three to seven years out—when disillusionment is high, when the wheels seem to be turning without any real forward movement. Fatally, this often coincides with the waning of outside interest. Political engagement and financial support are drawn down just when the process needs a second wind.

Hard-won agreements on human rights and the reform of justice are often eroded once domestic and international attention diminishes. In Guatemala, securing such reforms, which were crucial to moving the country beyond the mere absence of warfare towards consolidated peace, was the hardest part.

In Haiti, we had a peacekeeping mission in the mid-1990s and trained a new police force. And then we left—along with other international institutions—before a viable peace had taken root. Now we are back, with much of what we did before swept away—almost literally, as the recent floods have laid bare the legacy of years of misrule.

The lesson—a very important one—is that everyone needs to stay engaged: the Security Council; Member States; international NGOs; and, of course, the former parties to the conflict and the people themselves, who are the most essential actors in any peace-building process....

Now I turn to the *seventh lesson, get the sequencing right.*

One of the things we have learnt, from painful experience, is the peril of trying to do things in the wrong order. For instance:

Before there can be meaningful elections, there must be respect for the law and some shared understanding of what the result will mean and how power will be distributed. We learned that lesson the hard way in Angola.

Before there can be full economic liberalization, there must be some social stability. We have learned how disastrous it can be to introduce policies, however sound in the long term, which cause high short-term unemployment while large numbers of people still have weapons and little or no stake in the peacetime economy. In such circumstances, surely what we need is not stringent structural adjustment but poor-friendly and peace-friendly policies on the part of the international financial institutions.

And before the international community disengages, there must be a growing economy. It should be no surprise that in the poorest countries, with little or no economic growth, like Haiti and Liberia, peace processes failed and conflicts lapsed back into violence.

Eighth, keep everyone on the same page.

We have had massive interventions in the past which failed, or came close to it, because they were too fragmented. The system is now working in a more coherent way. We are reaching out to our colleagues in the United Nations family, to NGOs, to the broader international community and also to the local populations in the countries where we work, to make sure that we are all on the same page, both in setting our priorities and in the way we carry them out.

Finally, local populations should take responsibility—it is they who must live with the peace.

There are many situations in which it seems easier, for everyone, to let outsiders take the lead—to draft the laws; to run the elections or the courts; to make the hard economic choices. But unless those who will live with the effects of decisions have a real part in taking them, the decisions will sooner or later be put aside.

No conflict can be overcome by the goodwill of outsiders alone. Those who live with it understand the dynamics better than any international player. Those who live with it must be involved in the effort to end it and must see benefits that justify the compromises and sacrifices involved.

This is a list that could go on. There are lessons, for example, about greed as well as grievance. Whatever the origins of a conflict, it often cannot be ended without cutting off the resources that sustain it—and providing the fighters with an alternative, peaceful means of earning their living. Nowadays we no longer contemplate demobilization and disarmament—the two "Ds"—without adding an "R," which stands for reintegration into the civilian economy. Without this, it is a virtual certainty that new weapons will be acquired and violence will resume. And there is also, of course, the need for reconciliation, which cannot work unless the victims of atrocities feel that they have obtained justice, or at least a full acknowledgment of past wrongs. Absent such a reckoning, there is a lingering sense of unfinished business, and in the long run this can be destabilizing.

Let me end by saying that the most important lesson of all—for me personally, and for the United Nations as an organization—is that we must always be listening and looking out for new knowledge.

Let us learn those lessons. And let us employ them in our future peace operations, as we work together to try to make the world a better and a safer place, for our own sakes and for our children.

❋ CHAPTER SIX ❋

AFRICA

❋
Africa's Third Wave

Address to the Annual Assembly of Heads of State and the Government of the Organization of African Unity (OAU) Harare, Zimbabwe 2 June 1997

This was the first time that Annan spoke as UN Secretary-General specifically to the leaders of his own continent.

Africa has, in the past five decades, been through a series of momentous changes. First came decolonization and the struggle against apartheid. Then came a second wave, too often marked by civil wars, the tyranny of military rule, and economic stagnation. I believe that a new era is now in prospect, Africa's third wave.

Let us make this third wave one of lasting peace, based on democracy, human rights, and sustainable development.

Portents of this third wave are all around us. We salute the democratic transitions in Namibia, in Mozambique, and, most recently, in South Africa....

How do we build on these positive elements throughout our continent to unleash Africa's third wave in full force?

My friends, I speak to you as a fellow African, and I speak to you from the heart: we will succeed to the extent that we embrace the primacy of democratic rule, the inviolability of human rights, and the imperatives of sustainable development.

The success of the third wave begins with a single and simple proposition—the will of the people. *The will of the people must be the basis of governmental authority* in Africa, and governments, duly elected, should not be overthrown by force.

Last week, military elements in Sierra Leone toppled a democratically elected government. The Secretary-General of the OAU, the government of Zimbabwe,[1] and other African leaders spoke for all of us when they expressed their revulsion.

Africa can no longer tolerate, and accept as *faits accomplis,* coups against elected governments and the illegal seizure of power by military cliques, who sometimes act for sectional interests, sometimes simply for their own. Armies exist to protect national sovereignty, not to train their guns on their own people.

Some may argue that military regimes bring stability and predictability, that they are helpful to economic development. That is a delusion. Look at the example of South America....

Accordingly, let us dedicate ourselves to a new doctrine for African politics: where democracy has been usurped, let us do whatever is in our power to restore it to its rightful owners, the people.

Verbal condemnation, though necessary and desirable, is not sufficient. We must also ostracize and isolate putschists. Neighboring States, regional groupings, and the international community all must play their part.

The success of Africa's third wave depends equally on *respect for fundamental human rights.* The conflicts which have disfigured our continent have, all too often, been accompanied by massive human rights violations.

I am aware of the fact that some view this concern as a luxury of the rich countries for which Africa is not ready. I know that others treat it as an imposition, if not a plot, by the industrialized West.

I find these thoughts truly demeaning, demeaning of the yearning for human dignity that resides in every African heart.

Do not African mothers weep when their sons or daughters are killed or maimed by agents of repressive rule? Are not African fathers saddened when their children are unjustly jailed or tortured? Is not Africa as a whole impoverished when even one of its brilliant voices is silenced?

We cannot afford to lose one life, spare one idea, relinquish one hope, if we are to succeed on our chosen course. So I say this to you, my brothers and sisters: human rights are African rights, and I call upon you to ensure that all Africans are able fully to enjoy them.

Let us work together and with the United Nations to develop good governance and respect for the rule of law. When we succeed, Africa will have taken a great step forward.

---

1. Zimbabwe held the rotating OAU chairmanship at the time.

Finally, the success of the third wave hinges on instituting *sustainable development* throughout Africa....

Imagine a day when assistance from the United Nations is no longer needed for humanitarian emergencies or post-conflict reconstruction but can be redirected at long-term development needs.

Imagine a day when the outflow of capital from Africa to service debt is dwarfed by an inflow of capital-seeking job-creating investments. No—you do not need to imagine. For experience elsewhere in the world has shown that it can happen, and that it can happen quickly.

I pledge the full support of the United Nations, its agencies and the Bretton Woods institutions. We will continue our long-standing efforts to help create an enabling environment for economic growth and prosperity. We will continue to assist your efforts to devise new investment strategies and trade practices....

To take root, sustainable development also requires major policy initiatives at the national level. Democratization and the rule of law, including respect for human rights, are indispensable. Getting economic fundamentals right is axiomatic, but sustainable development requires more.

It needs to provide access by all members of society to development opportunities. It must ensure that the property of the farmer, the shop owner and the manufacturer is secure. It requires that education be prized, health care provided. It implies that renewable resources be managed, not depleted.

Civil society can and must play its part. Once every citizen has a real and lasting stake in the future—politically, economically, and culturally—there will be no limits to what our peoples, the peoples of Africa, can achieve.

My friends, the promise of Africa's third wave beckons. Our turn has come. We can eradicate poverty, settle our scattered people, restore hope, and achieve dynamism. Africa needs external assistance, and Africa deserves it; but in the final analysis, what stands between us and the future is ourselves.

Democratic rule, respect for human rights, and sustainable development are the means that will get us there. Let us embrace them—for Africa and for Africa's children.

✸

AIDS and Africa's Future

Speech to the African Summit on HIV/AIDS
Abuja, Nigeria
26 April 2001

The Organization of Africam Unity's decision to hold a special summit on HIV/AIDS, tuberculosis, and related infectious diseases reflected African leaders' recognition that—as Annan had been arguing for several years— AIDS was not just a health issue but a threat to development in many parts of Africa. Annan seized the occasion to appeal to them to break "the wall of silence and embarrassment" surrounding AIDS in Africa, and he appealed to the world to fund a "war chest" for the war against AIDS—what was to become the Global Fund to Fight AIDS, Tuberculosis and Malaria.

T his is a conference about Africa's future.

The incidence of HIV/AIDS, tuberculosis and other infectious diseases is higher on this continent than on any other. Of course, this fact is connected to Africa's other problems. Africans are vulnerable to these diseases because they are poor, undernourished, and too often uninformed of basic precautions or unwilling to take them. Many are vulnerable because they have neither safe drinking water nor access to basic health care.

They are vulnerable, in short, because their countries are underdeveloped. And therefore, the best cure for all these diseases is economic growth and broad-based development.

We all know that.

But we also know that, in the best of cases, development is going to take time. And we know that disease, like war, is not only a product of underdevelopment. It is also one of the biggest obstacles preventing our societies from developing as they should.

That is especially true of HIV/AIDS, which takes its biggest toll among young adults—the age group that normally produces most and has the main responsibility for rearing the next generation. That is why AIDS has become not only the primary cause of death on this continent, but our biggest development challenge. And that is why I have made the battle against it my personal priority.

In short, my friends, we are here to face a continent-wide emergency. We cannot afford to treat it as just one aspect of the battle for development, because it will not wait for us to win that battle. The cost—whether measured in human misery today or in loss of hope for tomorrow—is simply too high. We have to turn and face it head on.

First, let us be clear what our objectives are. I believe they can be put very simply, under five headings:

Number one: *prevention* ... to halt and reverse the spread of the virus—as all world leaders resolved to do at last year's Millennium Summit—and so to save succeeding generations from this scourge. Prevention can save many millions of lives, and in several African countries it has been shown to work.

Everyone who is not yet infected must know what they need to do to avoid infection. We must give young people the knowledge and power to protect themselves. We need to inform, inspire, and mobilize them through an awareness campaign such as the world has never seen....

That campaign must reach girls as well as boys. At present, in sub-Saharan Africa, adolescent girls are six times more likely to be infected than boys. That is something which should make all of us African men deeply ashamed and angry.

And once they know what they need to do, young people must have the means to do it. That means they must have support from their families and communities, as well as access to voluntary counseling and testing and—when appropriate—to condoms.

Number two: we must prevent the cruelest, most unjust infections of all—those that pass *from mother to child.* All mothers must be able to find out whether they are HIV-positive or not. And those who are must have access to short-term anti-retroviral therapy, which has been shown to halve the risk of transmission.

In some cases, the risk can also be reduced by alternatives to breast feeding. But these must be approached with caution, since breast feeding is the best protection against many other diseases.

Number three: we must put *care and treatment* within everyone's reach. Even a year ago few people thought that effective treatment could be brought within reach of poor people in developing countries. Those already infected with HIV were condemned to be treated like lepers in earlier times—as people from whom the healthy had to be protected but *for* whom nothing could be done.

Now, however, there has been a worldwide revolt of public opinion. People no longer accept that the sick and dying, simply because they are poor, should be denied drugs which have transformed the lives of others who are better off.

Earlier this month I met the leaders of six of the world's biggest pharmaceutical companies. They now accept the need to combine incentives for research with access to medication for the poor. They are ready to sell drugs to those countries at greatly reduced prices.

This crisis is so grave that developing countries must face it by exploiting all options to the full—including the production and importation of "generic" drugs under license, within the terms of international trade agreements.

Everyone who is infected should have access to medicine and medical care. Now we know that that is possible, it is surely an ethical imperative. It is also essential to any successful prevention strategy—because, so long as testing positive is a death sentence without hope, many people will not even want to know their HIV status.

In short, we cannot and should not choose between prevention and treatment. We must do both.

Number four: we must deliver *scientific breakthroughs*. We are still a long way from finding a cure for HIV/AIDS and a long way from finding a vaccine against it. We must make sure that the search is given the highest priority in scientific budgets and be ready, as soon as it produces results, to make them available where they are most needed—not only to those who can afford them.

And finally, we must *protect those made most vulnerable* by the epidemic, *especially orphans*. Millions of children, because they have lost one or both parents to AIDS, are growing up malnourished, under-educated, marginalized, and at risk of being infected themselves. We must break this cycle of death. And we must not wait for parents to die before we intervene. We must help them secure their children's future while they are still fit enough to do so.

Agreeing on those five objectives should not be difficult. But what are the means we need to achieve those ends?

First of all, we need *leadership*. And, my friends, that must start with you, the leaders of Africa. Only you can mobilize your fellow citizens for this great battle. Only you can give it the priority it deserves in your national budgets. Above all, you must take the lead in breaking the wall of silence and embarrassment that still surrounds this issue in too many African societies and in removing the abuse, discrimination, and stigma that still attach to those infected. The epidemic can be stopped, if people are not afraid to talk about it.

Secondly, we need to *involve local communities*. . . . It is only with the fullest support of their families and communities that young people will be able to change their behavior and protect themselves. Above all, we must involve those already living with HIV/AIDS in the struggle against it. They, after all, are the ultimate experts.

Thirdly, we need a deep social revolution that will give *more power to women* and transform relations between women and men at all levels of society. It is only when women can speak up and have a full say in decisions affecting their lives that they will be able to truly protect themselves—and their children—against HIV.

Fourth, we need *stronger health-care systems*. . . . If our aim is to make care and treatment available to all those infected, we need a far more efficient and extensive system of public health than most African countries even begin to provide at present.

Cheaper anti-retroviral drugs, however vital, will not by themselves provide the answer. Without proper health care, they may even do more harm than good—for example, if potentially life-threatening side effects are not addressed or if the therapy is interrupted, leading to drug-resistant forms of HIV. And too many patients still do not have access even to relatively cheap antibiotics and other effective drugs for the many illnesses that prey on their weakened immune systems.

Finally, we need *money*. The war on AIDS will not be won without a war chest of a size far beyond what is available so far. . . .

At a minimum, we need to be able to spend an additional seven to ten billion dollars a year on the struggle against HIV/AIDS in the world as a whole, over an extended period of time.

It sounds a lot, and it is a lot. Somehow we have to bring about a quantum leap in the scale of resources available. But it is not at all impossible, given the amount of wealth in the world. In fact it is little more than 1 percent of the world's annual military spending. We just have to convince those with the power to spend—public and private donors alike—that this would be money well spent.

We need to mobilize the widest possible range of donors ... and we need to win their commitment for the long haul....

I propose the creation of a Global Fund, dedicated to the battle against HIV/AIDS and other infectious diseases. This Fund must be structured in such a way as to ensure that it responds to the needs of the affected countries and people. And it must be able to count on the advice of the best experts in the world—whether they are found in the United Nations system, in governments, in civil society organizations, or among those who live with HIV/AIDS or are directly affected by it.

I intend to pursue this idea with all concerned over the next few weeks, and I hope that in the very near future the Fund will be up and running....

Everyone has his or her part to play. Let us now lay aside all turf battles and doctrinal disputes. The battle against HIV/AIDS is far more important than any one institution or project. Our success will not be measured by resolutions passed, appointments made, or even funds raised. It will be measured in the lives of succeeding generations.

In the last year or so, the world has begun to realize that HIV/AIDS is indeed a world-scale pandemic, which has spread fastest and furthest in Africa.

So this is a moment of hope and potentially a turning point. Africa is no longer being left to face this disaster alone. Its plight has caught the attention, and the conscience, of the whole world.

I believe the world is ready to come to our aid. But it will do so only if we convince the world that we ourselves are making the war against AIDS our personal priority and have a clear strategy for waging it....

Working together, my friends, we can defeat the scourge of HIV/AIDS. For the sake of Africa's future, we must.

※

From OAU to African Union

Address to the Final Summit of the Organization of African Unity and the Inaugural Summit of the African Union Durban, South Africa 8 July 2002

W e have reached this stage and moment by a long and winding road.

Thirty-nine years ago, when your visionary predecessors met in Addis Ababa to found the Organization of African Unity, they could not, even if they wished, have met here in Durban.

South Africa was then only beginning the most acute and painful phase of its struggle against apartheid, and many other African countries were still under the yoke of colonialism.

The road to freedom, for many of our brothers and sisters, was to prove longer and harder than most of us dared imagine in 1963.

The road to prosperity, alas, has proved even more elusive.

And the road to union has been strewn with many obstacles.

Yet apartheid and colonialism have been defeated. And the OAU, which was the unwavering voice of Africa on both those issues, deserves a greater share of the credit than it has been given so far.

It has other achievements, too.

It has established important pan-African doctrines—such as respect for existing frontiers and, more recently, the unique validity of free and fair elections as a means of bringing about political change.

It has also secured peace agreements among several of its members, it has set up a conflict prevention mechanism, and it has begun to develop a peacekeeping capacity.

The fact that you can proclaim the birth of the African Union tomorrow is a tribute to the OAU's success. It is an occasion to celebrate and, more important, an occasion for hope.

The idea of a Union—of Africans helping one another and working together to reach common solutions to their common problems—is noble and inspiring. And in several parts of Africa, it has already yielded results at the subregional level.

The experience of other parts of the world—notably Europe—has also shown that regional unity can bring practical benefits.

Europe in 1945 was utterly devastated by conflict—much more generally so than Africa today. Its present peace and prosperity make a striking contrast, and few would deny that that is due, at least in part, to regional integration.

But let us be careful not to mistake hope for achievement.

Let us not risk jeopardizing what we have already achieved.

And let us not imagine that, once proclaimed, our Union will become a reality without further effort.

A study of the European experience would quickly disabuse us of any such notion. Every step of Europe's road has been fraught with difficulty, and even now Europeans face many doubts and disputes as they prepare to enlarge eastwards.

Yet we Africans have undertaken to build a Union in conditions that are objectively much less favorable:

* We have a much larger geographical space to cover, with far fewer resources. We start at a much earlier stage of industrial development.
* And many of our economies are saddled with unsustainable debt or crippled by the legacy of wars in which, over generations, outside powers exploited and prolonged African quarrels.

To build a successful Union in such conditions will require great stamina and iron political will, combined with the readiness to accept a seemingly endless series of negotiations and compromises.

I believe we Africans have those qualities, or at least that we can develop them.

We have African traditions we can draw on—traditions that teach us the value of democracy based on consensus.

Too often, in recent times, the name of democracy has been misused to describe situations where a vote is taken without free and fair debate beforehand, and where those who have won 51 percent of the votes claim the right to ride roughshod over the other 49 percent.

But that, I suggest, is not true African democracy. In African democracy, the rulers listen to the ruled, and the majority to the minority.

Our traditions teach us to respect each other; to share power; to give every man his say and every woman hers.

Consent and consensus, achieved through long and patient discussion, are at the heart of many of those traditions. Let us keep that in mind and resist the temptation of short cuts or solutions imposed by force.

The empires of the past, built by military conquest, were a simple matter compared with what you are attempting now. But they were also more brittle than our Union will be, if it is built on voluntary agreements between democratic countries, negotiated by leaders and ratified by free vote of the peoples or their representatives.

That is the kind of Union we must build—a Union that will last.

Such a Union cannot replace the sovereign States of which it is composed. On the contrary, it must strengthen them, by allowing each to draw strength from the others.

In the last resort, only a Union of strong States can be strong itself. And the States must derive their strength not from military force, but from the support of their people, mediated through civil society.

I know you understand this—and that is why, in your New Partnership for Africa's Development (NEPAD), you have laid so much emphasis on issues of governance.

We know that States are strongest when they are based firmly on the rule of law and on the free consent of the citizens.

That is what NEPAD is all about: an African model for development based on an investment-friendly climate.

Yes, Africans need help from outside—from those who of late have been more successful or more fortunate than us.

Those outsiders have become very cynical over the decades. Sometimes they use Africa's shortcomings to excuse their own inertia.

But I believe that is beginning to change.

Some of you were with me in Canada the week before last, when we met with the leaders of the Group of Eight,[1] and they announced their Action Plan for Africa.

Did we get all we asked for? No, we did not. But I think we did sense a new respect among those leaders.

And I believe they will respect us even more when they see us actually resolve the conflicts that disfigure our continent. And I do mean resolve them. Managing them is not enough and will not be enough.

Africa's persistent image as a continent in crisis tends to discourage domestic and foreign investors from recognizing or taking advantage of the opportunities that Africa offers them. It imposes almost as high a risk premium on countries that are not in conflict as on those that are.

What this means is that all countries in the region have a stake in promoting peace—and that includes joining the international struggle against terrorism.

People in other parts of the world tend to forget that terrorism has claimed many African victims.

But let us not remind them of that. Let us not portray ourselves as victims, but as men and women determined, in the words of President Mandela, "that Africa's Renaissance will strike deep roots and blossom forever, without regard to the changing seasons."

"Renaissance" is a French word that is current in English. That makes it a fitting word for an African project that must overcome the divisions left on our continent by rival colonial empires—and a regional project that is closely linked to the universal project of the United Nations.

The African Union and our United Nations are striving for the same goals: peaceful settlement of disputes, economic and social development, and the full realization of human rights.

The United Nations Charter, like yours, recognizes that strong regional organizations can complement, and contribute to, the strength of the United Nations.

A year ago the world gathered in this city and resolved to confront racism, xenophobia and intolerance.[2] Next month it has an opportunity

---

1. The G8 summit at Kananaskis, Alberta, June 26–27, 2002.
2. See "Against Racism" in Chapter 4.

to gather again, in Johannesburg,[3] at the renewed invitation of this generous country. I hope it can do so in closer harmony and with even greater conviction.

This time the stakes will even be higher: we have to trace a path for development that will not only be shared by all nations, but can be sustained and enjoyed by future generations. In this part of Africa, already stricken by drought and menaced by famine, we need no reminder of the urgency of that task.

So let us apply ourselves, as Africans, to persuading the rest of the world to join us next month and start implementing the measures we all know are needed, if development is to be truly sustainable.

So doing, Africa will not only confront its own troubles. It will also provide much-needed leadership for the rest of the world!

❋

An Exciting Time to Be an African

*Inaugural Golden Jubilee Lecture as Part of
Ghana's 50th Anniversary Celebrations
Accra, Ghana
25 January 2007*

Less than a month after leaving office, Annan was able to attend the celebration, in his own country, of the 50th anniversary of its independence.

I t is good to be home again. Let me start by saying how deeply moved and gratified I am to be giving the inaugural Golden Jubilee Lecture. I could have expected no better homecoming, and I certainly could desire no greater honor than to speak to you, my fellow citizens, on this historic occasion. As some of you know, this is my first speaking engagement since I stepped down as UN Secretary-General at the end of December.

---

3. The World Summit on Sustainable Development, August 26 to September 4, 2002.

Indeed, until President Kufuor asked me to deliver this lecture, I had every intention of enjoying a quiet few months of civilian life before making any public appearances. But when it is your President who calls, and your own country that beckons, "I would be honored" is the only proper answer.

Let me take this opportunity to thank you, my fellow Ghanaians, for your solid, consistent support and encouragement. Your support and that of millions of people around the world gave me the strength and courage I needed.

Today, I speak as a private Ghanaian citizen after a long, long time. I joined the United Nations in 1962, barely five years after our country's independence. In those days, Kwame Nkrumah was President. My alma mater, the Kwame Nkrumah University of Science and Technology, was then the Kumasi College of Science and Technology. But what I remember most of that era was that—led by Ghana's own example—African hopes for self-determination were brimming over.

It was a time of change and excitement. Africa's wave of decolonization was cresting. Our continent seemed on the cusp of a promising new future. Finally, we Africans were to be masters of our own destiny. Long ruled by foreign crowns, we were to lead ourselves not only to freedom, but to progress and prosperity as well.

Yet, it did not quite unfold that way. Newly independent African States inherited artificial borders, often with social groupings rent asunder by straight lines penciled on a map. Suddenly, African ethnic groups and communities with shared histories often found themselves on opposite sides of new and arbitrary borders.

In response, postcolonial governments sought national unity through the centralization of political and economic power, employing vestigial colonial laws and institutions to stifle and suppress pluralism.

And all too quickly, much of the unifying strength of the independence movement was transformed into one-party rule.

Independent Africa stumbled in other ways as well. Its development policy emphasized the production of primary commodities for export, often at the expense of adequate support for subsistence agriculture. We became subject to the whims of the market without having any say in its functioning.

Over succeeding decades, our continent devolved into a land of big men and broken dreams. Some African liberators became oppressors and/or looters. Many conflicts festered, and economies stagnated.

Thus, by 1997, when I became the second Secretary-General from Africa, I felt my continent was the place least equipped to tackle the three overarching challenges of our age—the need for more security, the demand for better development, and the rising cry for human rights and rule of law.

Africa stood sidelined in the world economy. Africa was also the scene of some of the most protracted and brutal conflicts. And many of the continent's people felt they were unjustly condemned to be exploited and oppressed, generation after generation, since colonial rule had been replaced by an inequitable economic world order and sometimes by bad governance.

Yet, at the same time, I also felt the winds of change—a feeling similar to, if more circumspect than, those heady early days of Ghana's independence.

I believed that a new era was in prospect—Africa's third wave, to succeed earlier swells of decolonization and the ensuing years of wars and conflict.

I called on Africa to make this third wave one of enduring development, peace and respect for human rights.

Over the ensuing decade, I have been privileged to see this third wave unfold. Not always as forcefully as we might have wished, nor so consistently. But, inexorably and unstoppably, it has continued to flow across this rich, vast and varied continent.

The bedrock of this wave—of our African renaissance—is real and measurable progress on *peace and security*.

About half the world's armed conflicts and some three-quarters of the UN's peacekeepers are in Africa. But, compared to a decade ago, there are fewer inter-State conflicts than there used to be, and many civil wars have ended.

In Burundi, the peaceful and democratic conclusion of the transitional process was a milestone for that country and, hopefully, for the Great Lakes region. Wars have stopped in Angola, Ethiopia-Eritrea, Liberia, Mozambique, Sierra Leone and southern Sudan. Let me also urge the political leaders of Côte d'Ivoire to put their nation first, settle their differences and bring peace to the country. That is what the people demand; that is what they deserve.

Lesotho, Guinea-Bissau, Togo, Madagascar and Mauritania have all been through peaceful restoration of constitutional order. The deadly conflict in northern Uganda has entered a negotiating stage. And the Democratic Republic of the Congo has successfully concluded democratic elections for the first time in 40 years.

I am proud that the United Nations was an important actor in these events. And I am proud of what my fellow Africans have achieved in ending many of the conflicts that disfigured our continent.

But we should be under no illusion.

In far too many reaches of the continent, people are still exposed to brutal conflicts, fought with small, but deadly, weapons.

Every day, in Darfur, more men, women and children are being driven from their homes by murder, rape and the burning of their villages. And Somalia is once again engulfed in war. Beyond Sudan and Somalia, less visible but no less deadly conflicts cry out for African resolve and international attention. Peace may be spreading on the continent, but a continent at peace, which is what we all want, remains an idea in search of realization. Most Africans realize today that they need to work together to pacify the continent, and I often say that no one invests in a bad neighborhood. And, when a continent is seen by many as a continent at war, we do scare away foreign partners and investors.

Fortunately, we seem to have understood the high cost of persistent conflict: the years of squandered development, the enormous loss of life and displacement of people, the untold suffering.

Thus we are doing whatever we can to settle these conflicts and to take ownership of the peace and security agenda. Through the African Union we are learning to better manage and resolve conflicts and, most important, to prevent new ones from breaking out. As conflicts subside, governments across Africa have also turned to the essential tasks of economic and social development. Because, ultimately, peace requires more than the mere absence of war. It is sustainable only if accompanied by real progress in *development*, the second pillar of an African renaissance.

Here, again, there is reason for cautious optimism. Today, most African economies are better run: inflation, averaging 8 percent a year, is at historic lows in many countries, while 27 African countries are projected to grow more than 5 percent in terms of GDP this year. Direct investment inflows to African economies have increased by more than 200 percent in the past five years. Exports are also rising, with some countries experiencing double-digit export growth.

There have been spectacular advances on debt relief, as well as encouraging initiatives on aid and investment. The largest debtor on the continent—Nigeria—has bought back all its foreign debt.

And Africa has also recorded encouraging progress on some of the individual Millennium Development Goals.

Take the goal of achieving universal primary education. Over the past five years, more than ten African countries have increased enrolment ratios by over 15 percentage points. And, in several such countries, this improvement came about mainly because of a rise in the enrollment of girls.

Or take the goal of fighting AIDS. Today, the world has recognized HIV/AIDS as a major challenge and a brake on development, and begun to confront it. Prevalence is dropping in several African countries, because more young people are using condoms, reducing the number of sexual partners and waiting longer before they start having sex.

In reducing maternal mortality, several African countries are on target. And most are making progress. In providing safe drinking water, six African countries have already reached the goal, while more than half are on track.

And not all progress is equally difficult. Fighting malaria with bed nets or empowering farmers with improved seed varieties can bring dramatic change relative to the cost.

Today, one thing is clear to all of us here: Africa's development disproves the distorted and widespread image of our continent as a sea of undifferentiated poverty.

Yet the magnitude of African needs leaves little room for complacency.

Despite the fact that our continent has the largest growth rate of mobile phone subscribers in the world—5,000 percent between 1998 and 2003—about 50 percent of all Africans have yet to make or receive a phone call. A small proportion have ever logged on to the Internet. And the global green revolution has bypassed African farmers.

Ours is the only continent that cannot feed itself today, much less ensure food security for its people.

Nowhere is it more important, therefore, to ensure lasting peace and continuous development. Only then can we make up for lost years and bring prosperity to all. To realize this vision, we must embrace *human rights and rule of law* as the third leg of African progress.

Ten years ago, I said some African leaders viewed human rights as a rich country's luxury, for which Africa was not ready; that others treated it as an imposition, if not a plot. I said I found these thoughts demeaning of the yearning for human dignity that resides in every African heart. And I called on Africa to ostracize and isolate those who seize power through coups against elected governments.

Since then, I believe Africans have demonstrated that human rights are African rights. Most African States—more than ever—now have democratically elected governments. And these governments, through the New Partnership for Africa's Development, have explicitly agreed to uphold human rights and democracy, to fight corruption and promote good governance.

Today, Ellen Johnson Sirleaf, the President of Liberia, is the first woman ever to be elected President of an African State. And that speaks more eloquently than words ever could about advances in the rights of women. So does the fact that, in sub-Saharan African countries, the share of women in single or lower houses of parliament is higher than in the developing countries of southern or western Asia.

Throughout Africa, ordinary citizens also are engaged as never before. A vibrant and growing civil society movement has helped energize the African agenda. Africans are standing up for their rights, and governments are beginning to listen. Indeed, by demanding honest and accountable leadership, civil society actors are proving a critical check on our continent's sad history of misrule.

Civil society is also highlighting the need for creative responses to Africa's rapidly changing realities. For twenty-first-century Africa differs in fundamental ways from the continent of old. For instance, half of the population of sub-Saharan Africa is between the ages of 5 and

24, urbanization is changing the very face of our demography, and technological change is slowly putting essential information in the hands of everyone, from farmers to slum dwellers.

These conditions demand that we all think faster and act quicker to serve the needs of our people. They demand more inclusive, more accountable and more responsive governments, and leaders who are in tune with this new Africa and its myriad complexities.

As a Ghanaian, I am proud that—50 years after my country led a wave of African independence—Ghana is at the forefront of Africa's promising third wave as well. What we need now is to keep building on the progress we have achieved so far. To do so we must build a comprehensive strategy for the future—one which gives equal weight and attention to the three pillars of security, development and human rights.

They all reinforce each other; they all depend on each other.

These three pillars must prove the basis of our African renaissance, so that all Africans may enjoy the prosperity that seemed so palpable 50 years ago.

That year, 1957, was when I graduated from Mfantsipim, full of hope for the future and for my country. This year, I have graduated again, this time from the leadership of the United Nations. And once again, I find myself full of hope for Ghana and for Africa. So let me reiterate that it is good to be back home. This is an exciting, if challenging, time to be an African. We all have much work to do, and I look forward to joining hands with all my fellow citizens to lift our nation and our great continent towards the bright future that can and must be ours.

✾ CHAPTER SEVEN ✾

THE MIDDLE EAST

Israel and the United Nations

Speech to the Israel Council on Foreign Relations
Jerusalem, Israel
25 March 1998

On his first visit to Israel as Secretary-General, Annan was anxious to convince Israelis that the United Nations was not structurally biased against their country but able and willing to help them achieve peace with their Arab neighbors. The speech was well received and led to a period of improved relations between Israel and the UN Secretariat.

I t gives me great pleasure to be visiting Israel and especially to be here with you at the Knesset,[1] the seat of one of the world's most vibrant democracies.

Parliamentarians such as yourselves are increasingly active and influential players on the world stage. As elected representatives, you, more than anyone else, are in direct contact with the wishes and sentiments of the global public. And while your responsibilities lie first at the national level, more and more parliamentarians are understanding that there is an international dimension to most of the central issues of our times....

The Israeli parliament, for its part, represents a remarkable range of views and traditions. I know that, at times, the various parties can seem terribly splintered, while, on other occasions, consensus is the order of the day. Throughout your deliberations, I know you never lose sight of the well-being of the Israeli people and your own commitment to dialogue and compromise.

Israeli security and regional security in general are also abiding concerns of the international community. The troubled peace process between Israel and the Palestinians, ongoing hostilities in southern Lebanon, and the crisis in Iraq each, in very dramatic ways, illustrates

---

1. The Israeli parliament.

the maxim that when peace processes are not moving forward, they are sliding backward.

Horrifying acts of violence against innocent civilians have occurred. The day-to-day reality of too many people in the region continues to be one of insecurity and destitution. I have come to the Middle East to listen, but also to deliver a message: that it is long past time for Israelis and Palestinians to make the difficult decisions needed to move the Oslo process[2] forward to a successful outcome. Progress on all other fronts is likewise long overdue. We must move from an era of confrontation to one of cooperation, from despair to development, from enmity to amity.

I have appealed to the parties on several occasions not to let themselves be swayed by the actions of those on either side who work against the peace process, but rather to intensify efforts to overcome all obstacles that stand in the way. I will be reiterating that appeal in the talks that I will have with Israeli and Palestinian officials in the days ahead.

What better serves Israel's interest: a mutually agreed peace with your neighbors that gives both peoples the chance to realize their aspirations for peaceful, prosperous lives? Or unilateral acts and declarations by both sides that could throw the process completely off course? At this time of profound uncertainty, I urge you not to lose sight of the gains you have made thus far. Let us not lose the momentum that has been built up so painstakingly....

I would like to appeal to the Israeli public to look anew at the United Nations. I know that "oom-shmoom,"[3] David Ben-Gurion's catchy rhyme, is used from time to time by Israelis to dismiss a world Organization that some see as either irrelevant or hostile to Israel.

I would hope that Israelis could instead make "room" for "oom," that they could open their minds to the prospect of a new era in relations between Israel and the United Nations. I know that Israel attaches great importance to the spirit and practice of international cooperation. Israel has much to offer, and to gain, through the United Nations. We have put behind us some of the worst chapters in our history, and Israel is

---

2. The peace process resulting from the accord negotiated between Israelis and Palestinians in Oslo, Norway, in 1993.
3. "Oom" is the Hebrew acronym for United Nations. Israel's first prime minister, David Ben-Gurion, famously dismissed the organization by saying "Oom-shmoom," implying that the United Nations was not worth bothering with.

on its way to normalizing its presence at the United Nations.[4] In the end, I think you will agree that in today's interdependent world, without "oom," we shall have "kloom."[5]

In that spirit, I would like to propose a toast: to our host, the Speaker of the Knesset, and this fine democratic institution; to Israel on the occasion of its fiftieth anniversary; to improved ties between Israel and the United Nations; and, most of all, to peace.

※

Following Sadat's Example

Anwar Sadat Lecture at the University of Maryland
College Park, Maryland
13 November 2002

An invitation from Professor Shibley Telhami at the University of Maryland gave Annan the opportunity to review the state of the Arab-Israeli conflict and to set out some basic principles of the UN approach to it. The lecture was named in honor of Egypt's President Anwar Sadat, the first Arab leader to sign a peace treaty with Israel (1979), who was assassinated in 1981.

In just one week's time, we shall reach the twenty-fifth anniversary of Sadat's visit to Jerusalem in 1977.

Seldom has a political move deserved so richly to be called "historic."

It caught the imagination of the world. It transformed the political landscape of the Middle East. And it defined Anwar Sadat as a historical figure.

---

4. Israel at that time had not been accepted as a member of any of the regional groups in the UN General Assembly, but discussions were under way, partly as a result of Annan's pressure, on its possible admission to the West European and Others Group (WEOG). In 2000 this was to go ahead on a temporary basis, and in 2004 it was made permanent. However, it applies only at UN headquarters in New York. At the UN offices in Geneva, Nairobi, Rome, and Vienna, Israel still has only observer status in WEOG.
5. "Kloom" is Hebrew for "nothing."

President Sadat showed courage, decisiveness and extraordinary political insight when he did what until then had seemed unthinkable for any Arab leader: he went to Jerusalem and declared, directly to the Israeli parliament and people, that "we welcome you among us with full security and safety."

His visit represented an extraordinary leap of faith and imagination. He understood that the Arabs could not recover the land that Israel had occupied unless, in return, they offered full and genuine peace.

And he had the intelligence and imagination to make a gesture that sparked a response in the hearts of the Israeli people.

As a result, he was able to convince them that they really could enjoy peace with Egypt if—but only if—they gave up their occupation of Egyptian land. As he said, "There is no peace that could be built on the occupation of the land of others."

And thus his gesture started a process leading to a peace treaty between the two countries based on normal relations and full Israeli withdrawal from Egyptian territory. In other words, land for peace.

Alas, Sadat's journey also led, or at least contributed, to his untimely death. He himself must have known the risk he was taking, and that is the measure of his courage. Like Yitzhak Rabin fourteen years later, he paid the price of peace with his own life.

Looking at the Middle East peace process today, I wish I could say that those two sacrifices had brought a just, lasting and comprehensive peace to the Middle East, or at least that the leaders of today had shown a similar level of courage, vision and statesmanship.

Sadly, I cannot. As we speak, Israelis and Palestinians are still locked in bitter conflict.

Nor is there yet peace between Israel and its northern neighbors. The truce on that front remains fragile and precarious.

An atmosphere of gloom and defeatism has descended on the region. There is the same "utter suspicion and absolute lack of confidence" between the two sides of which Sadat spoke in the Knesset. How right he was to warn that "in the absence of a just solution of the Palestinian problem, never will there be that durable and just peace upon which the entire world insists"!

On both sides—Palestinian and Israeli—only those who believe their enemy can be defeated by force and violence show a grim confidence in the ultimate success of their chosen path.

Yet, on both sides, that confidence is surely misplaced.

No matter what price they are forced to pay, Israelis will not abandon the State they have built.

Nor indeed, I venture to affirm, would the United Nations ever allow one of its Member States to be destroyed by external force. It was to prevent such things from happening that the United Nations was founded, and twelve years ago, in Kuwait, it showed itself capable of rising to the challenge.[1]

But it should also be clear by now that Palestinians will never reconcile themselves to the continued occupation and expropriation of their land, nor renounce their claim to statehood and national independence.

They are just as firmly attached to their land as Israelis are to theirs and just as strong in their national aspirations. They, too, have a right to their own State, supported by the United Nations and by public opinion worldwide.

The only way to settle this conflict remains the solution envisioned by the United Nations Security Council[2] and, indeed, by Anwar Sadat in that historic speech to the Knesset twenty-five years ago: two States, Israel and Palestine, living side by side within secure and recognized borders.

And while the precise location of those borders is to be negotiated between the parties, surely no one doubts that they must be based, as Sadat said, on "ending the occupation of the Arab territories occupied in 1967."

In that very year, 1967, shortly after Israel occupied the remaining parts of mandatory Palestine, along with Egyptian Sinai and Syrian Golan, the Security Council emphasized the inadmissibility of the acquisition of territory by war and affirmed that just and lasting peace in the Middle East must be based on Israeli withdrawal from "territories occupied in the recent conflict," as well as the right of every State in the area "to live in peace within secure and recognized boundaries free from threats or acts of force."

That is the principle of "land for peace"—and that resolution, number 242, has long been accepted by all parties as the basis of a peaceful settlement.

---

1. In the winter of 1990–1991, an international force, authorized by the UN Security Council, restored the independence and territorial integrity of Kuwait after its occupation and annexation by Iraq.
2. In its Resolution 1397 of March 12, 2002.

Such a settlement is envisaged in the Saudi peace initiative, endorsed by the Arab States at their summit last March—and it remains the preferred solution of both Israelis and Palestinians—and President Bush in his speech to the General Assembly also endorsed this solution.

On this point, all opinion polls concur.

The majority of Palestinians accept the continued existence of Israel and are ready to live alongside it in their own State.

And the majority of Israelis accept that peace requires the establishment of a Palestinian State in nearly all of the territory occupied in 1967.

What is missing, on each side, is trust in the other—and without that trust, the hope of peace becomes hard to sustain.

Israelis, bludgeoned by repeated terrorist attacks which take a horrible toll of civilian life, have lost faith in the Palestinian will to peace.

They ask themselves if the partner they thought they had found in the Oslo Accords really exists. They wonder if the Palestinian intention is really, after all, to drive them into the sea. Their doubts are fed by the words, as well as the deeds, of Palestinian extremists and by the joy that sometimes erupts in the Palestinian streets after a particularly bloody terrorist outrage.

This leads to increasing public support for the draconian security measures that have pushed more than a million Palestinians below the poverty line, and the majority of Israelis who favor trading land for peace are reluctant, with no peace in sight, to confront the powerful minority who wish to keep the occupied land for ever.

Yet, tragically, those same draconian measures, combined with the continued and intensifying process of Israeli settlement in the occupied territory, have the effect of pushing the prospect of peace and lasting security further and further away.

Palestinians, on their side, have lost faith in the Israeli will to peace. They point to the unacceptable policy of assassinations of militants—some of them carried out in densely populated areas and causing large-scale civilian casualties. They note that Israel piles precondition on precondition for a return to the negotiating table and destroys the governing institutions of the Palestinian Authority even while calling for their reform.

Confined by roadblocks to their towns and villages, and much of the time by curfews in their homes, the Palestinians watch hilltop after hilltop covered by new Israeli buildings and valley after valley crisscrossed by roads reserved for Israeli settlers.

In some places, Palestinian farmers have even been shot dead by extremist settlers intent on robbing them of their olive harvest. As one Israeli journalist has put it, this sends a message that "it's not a war on terror in the territories but a campaign to deepen the poverty and hunger of the Palestinian population,"[3] and so to drive them off their land.

There are Palestinians who have courageously raised their voices against the wicked and counterproductive tactics of terror and suicide bombing. But in the present atmosphere, they find it hard to make themselves heard.

Given the events of the past two years, it was perhaps inevitable that both peoples would come to doubt, fundamentally, each other's real commitment to peace. With every passing day such doubts become more deeply embedded, and the task of renewing political negotiations gets even harder.

Somehow, we have to restore hope to both peoples by patiently rebuilding their trust in each other. And that is what the Quartet of interested external parties—the United Nations, United States, European Union and Russian Federation—is seeking to do, by setting out a credible road map: a road map of synchronized steps that can lead, within three years, from the grim situation we are in now to the peaceful two-State solution that the majority on both sides desire....

We in the Quartet fully realize that the credibility of this road map will depend on performance. But performance in turn depends on hope. Without a clear promise of the end result and visible political progress towards it, neither side is likely to summon the will to take the risks that each must take, right from the start, to improve the security and living conditions of the other. That is why we say that the process must be "hope driven," as well as performance driven.

And that, surely, is where all parties can learn from the example of Anwar Sadat.

By all conventional wisdom, he should not have done what he did. Going to Jerusalem, with no assurance in advance of any concessions

---

3. Ze'ev Schiff, in *Haaretz*, October 30, 2002.

from the other side, seemed to almost all Arabs at the time an act of folly, if not outright treason.

Yet President Sadat understood the vital importance of psychology in war and peace.

He understood that political behavior is deeply influenced by the mental image that each side has of the other—and that sometimes this image can only be changed by an act of breathtakingly radical daring.

By a leap of imagination Sadat understood that, while Arabs felt oppressed by Israel's seemingly overwhelming strength, Israel felt threatened by the uniform hostility of the surrounding Arab world.

More than anything, the Israeli people needed—and still need—the sense of being accepted by their neighbors in order to find the courage to renew negotiations in good faith, despite all the traumas of the last two years, and to make the necessary concessions.

In the stage the conflict has now reached, I believe both sides are aching for that sense of acceptance.

Many Palestinians, seeing the devastation Israel is able to inflict on their society, find it hard to imagine that Israelis also live in fear and that only by removing that fear can they hope to reach a new and more balanced relationship. Yet it is true.

And many Israelis believe they have already done enough to prove their willingness to accept Palestinians as neighbors and allow them space in which to develop their national life.

Unhappily the life experience of many Palestinians has been very different, and Israel needs to do much more to win their trust. As long as the settlement building and land confiscation continue, as long as a political horizon is missing, as long as there is no real commitment to negotiate the remaining final status issues, Palestinians will never be convinced of Israel's desire for peace.

That may be hard for Israelis to believe. Yet it is true.

The international community stands ready to help. Indeed, we must help both Israelis and Palestinians to break through the barrier of which Sadat spoke: "a barrier of suspicion, a barrier of rejection; a barrier of fear, of deception, a barrier of hallucination … a barrier of distorted interpretation of every event and statement."

But we can only help those who are willing to be helped.

What is needed on both sides is true leadership, such as Anwar Sadat provided in his time. Let us pray that they find it before it is too late.

❋

The Tragedy of Lebanon

Statement to the Security Council on the
Adoption of Resolution 1701
New York, New York
11 August 2006

On July 12, 2006, a unit of Hezbollah, the Lebanese Shi'ite resistance group, crossed into northern Israel and attacked an Israeli patrol, killing eight soldiers and kidnapping two. In retaliation Israel launched an all-out attack on Lebanon. The ensuing conflict lasted thirty-four days, during which Annan, while strongly condemning the Hezbollah attack, repeatedly called for a cessation of hostilities. But only when it became clear that Israel could not achieve its objectives by force was the UN Security Council able to adopt (unanimously) a resolution calling for a permanent cease-fire, based on the creation of a buffer zone in which only UN and Lebanese government forces could be deployed. Annan exercised his right to address the Council before the vote was taken.

I welcome wholeheartedly the resolution you are about to adopt, and I am greatly relieved that it provides for a full and immediate cessation of hostilities. It is absolutely vital that the fighting now stop. Provided it does, I believe this resolution will make it possible to conclude a sustainable and lasting cease-fire agreement in the days ahead. And I hope that this could be the beginning of a process to solve the underlying political problems in the region through peaceful means.

But I would be remiss if I did not tell you how profoundly disappointed I am that the Council did not reach this point much, much earlier. And I am convinced that my disappointment and sense of frustration are shared by hundreds of millions of people around the world. For weeks now, I and many others have been calling repeatedly for an immediate cessation of hostilities, for the sake of the civilian population on both sides who have suffered such terrible, unnecessary pain and loss. All members of this Council must be aware that its inability to act sooner has badly shaken the world's faith in its authority and integrity.

Since 12 July, when Hezbollah launched an unprovoked attack on Israel, killing eight Israeli soldiers and kidnapping two, both Lebanon and Israel have been thrown back into the turmoil of war, death and destruction.

According to the government of Lebanon, over a thousand Lebanese have been killed, and over 3,600 injured. Around a quarter of all Lebanon's inhabitants—close to a million people—have been displaced.

Too many of the victims have been children. In fact, more children than fighters have been killed in this conflict. Israeli bombing has turned thousands of homes to rubble. It has also destroyed dozens of bridges and roads, with the result that more than 100,000 people cannot reach safety; nor can relief supplies reach them. Such devastation would be tragic at any time. That it has been inflicted on Lebanon's people just when they were making real progress towards political reform and economic recovery makes it all the more so.

Israelis, for their part, have been newly awakened to a threat which they hoped, with good reason, to have escaped when—as this Council certified on my recommendation—they withdrew from Lebanon six years ago. Some 41 Israeli civilians have been killed, and hundreds of thousands have had their lives disrupted—being forced into shelters or to flee their homes—by rocket attacks from Hezbollah, which has launched its fire indiscriminately, to sow the widest possible terror, making no effort to distinguish between civilian and military targets, and also endangering civilians on its own side by firing from the midst of heavily populated areas.

Nor has the damage been limited to Lebanon and Israel. A region that could ill afford another chapter of violence and another source of instability has been inflamed further still. Extremists have been given new ammunition. The UN itself has been a target of protest and violence, despite the Organization's humanitarian efforts, including those of our valiant peacekeepers in UNIFIL,[1] to reach people trapped in the cross fire. UNIFIL has had to cope with a situation for which it was neither mandated nor equipped.

I am full of pride and admiration for the courage that the men and women who serve under the UN flag, and indeed all the humanitarian workers, have shown, since 12 July, in carrying out their duties in the midst of intense fighting, which has injured sixteen UN personnel and, tragically, caused the deaths of five.

Indeed, UNIFIL's tenacity has made possible the diplomatic solution you have just forged. Without it, you would have had to face the difficult prospect of UNIFIL's withdrawal. Indeed, you may yet have to face it in the hours and days ahead, if the immediate cessation of hostilities called for in this resolution does not hold.

So this resolution comes none too soon, and it marks a vital step forward. I am glad that Council members have been able to resolve their differences, accommodating many points of view, and I hope they will adopt this text unanimously. Having done so, they must work with equal determination to make what they have agreed fully effective on the ground.

First of all, humanitarian convoys and relief workers must be given a real guarantee of safe passage and access to those who need help. As soon as the fighting stops, the daunting challenge of helping people to return to their homes safely and rebuild their lives begins.

Secondly, the resolution rightly has at its core Lebanon's sovereignty and territorial integrity.... The international community must give the Lebanese government all possible support, so that it can make that sovereignty effective. The government, acting through its regular armed forces and police, must be able to assert its authority throughout the country and on all its borders, particularly to prevent illegal and destabilizing flows of arms. Only when there is one authority, and one gun, will there be a chance of lasting stability. The Lebanese State, like any other sovereign State, must have a monopoly of the use of force on its own territory.

That implies, of course, a full and swift Israeli withdrawal from Lebanese territory. We now have a clear scenario for achieving that.

---

1. The United Nations Interim Force in Lebanon, deployed in the south of the country since 1978.

The decision of the Lebanese government to deploy 15,000 of the country's armed forces to the south is a significant development. But, ready and willing as the Army may be to undertake this task, the government itself has acknowledged the need for help. This makes the Council's decision to strengthen the mandate and the numbers of UNIFIL a vital ingredient of the package.

Now, UNIFIL faces a new task, perhaps even more difficult and dangerous than its previous one. It must be robust and effective, and ensure that no vacuum is left between the Israeli withdrawal and the deployment of Lebanese forces. Obviously, if it is to carry out this new mandate, it needs to be augmented with the utmost urgency and provided with sophisticated military capabilities. The Council cannot afford to relax for one minute. I urge its members to consult closely, and at once, with both existing and potential troop contributors, with a view to generating the additional forces needed as quickly as possible, before the situation on the ground once again spins out of control. And I urge you to make sure they have the equipment they will need.

I also appeal to all potential donors to respond swiftly to requests from the Lebanese government for financial help as it struggles to reconstruct its devastated country.

Some may well be reluctant to do so, without solid assurances that this time peace is here to stay. Such assurances are indeed essential. And they must rest, not only on the cessation of hostilities or the deployment of an expanded peace force, but on the resolution of fundamental underlying political problems, including the release of prisoners, starting with those who have been taken hostage, and a resolution of the Shebaa Farms issue in accordance with Resolution 1680.[2]

I will therefore lose no time in taking up the role assigned to me in today's resolution.[3] We have just had a terrible lesson in the dangers of allowing problems to fester. We must by now all know that unless we address unfinished business, it can and will take us unawares.

---

2. The Shebaa Farms are an area at the meeting point of Israel, Lebanon, and Syria, occupied by Israel during hostilities against Syria in 1967 but subsequently claimed by Lebanon, thereby causing a dispute about whether Israel (which continued to occupy the Farms) had fully withdrawn from Lebanon in 2000. In Resolution 1680, passed in May 2006, the Security Council had encouraged Lebanon and Syria to delineate their common border.
3. Paragraph 10 of the resolution requested the Secretary-General to develop proposals for disarmament and for delineation of Lebanon's international borders within thirty days.

The Lebanese Cabinet will meet tomorrow, and the Israeli Cabinet on Sunday, to review the resolution. Over the weekend I will undertake to establish with both parties the exact date and time at which the cessation of hostilities will come into effect.

Lebanon has been a victim for too long. Mired in an incomplete political transformation since the end of the civil war, it has remained an arena in which both domestic and regional actors could play out their self-interested schemes. Such exploitation of a vulnerable country is shameful. It has undermined the laudable effort of many Lebanese citizens to consolidate their country as a sovereign, independent and democratic State.

The country and its people deserve better. They deserve the full support of the United Nations in their effort to cast off the chains of external interference and domestic strife. Doing so will require both the establishment of national consensus among Lebanese and constructive cooperation ... by all relevant parties and actors on the regional level, including the governments of Syria and Iran.

Indeed, over the last five weeks we have been reminded yet again what a fragile, tense and crisis-ridden region the Middle East has become—probably now more complex and difficult than ever before. It is now undergoing changes, shifts and realignments on a scale, and of a strategic significance, not seen since the colonial powers withdrew at the end of the Second World War. Perhaps even more ominous than the physical destruction are the changes in perception that have been occurring, both inside the region and beyond it. The Middle East, which has long figured at the very top of this Council's agenda, is likely to remain there for years to come.

The resolution you are about to adopt is only one step towards the comprehensive approach that is needed. Other steps will need to be taken—many others. In order to prevent yet another eruption of violence and bloodshed, the international community must now be prepared to offer sustained support and assistance for the political and economic reconstruction of Lebanon, and also to address the broader context of crisis in the region.

In particular, we must not turn our backs on the bloodshed, suffering, and hardship that have continued to afflict Palestinian civilians in Gaza and the West Bank or the danger from Qassam rockets that continues to threaten the Israeli communities bordering the Gaza Strip.

Progress in the Middle East peace process would undoubtedly facilitate the resolution of conflicts elsewhere in the region, and vice versa. Therefore, the various crises in the region must henceforth be addressed not in isolation or bilaterally, but as part of a holistic and comprehensive effort, sanctioned and championed by this Council, to bring peace and stability to the region as a whole.

The parallel crises in Lebanon and Gaza over the past few weeks have demonstrated, once again, that there are no military solutions to this conflict. War is not—I repeat, war is *not*—"the continuation of politics by other means." On the contrary, it represents a catastrophic failure of political skill and imagination—a dethronement of peaceful politics from the primacy which it should enjoy. By taking the first step today towards ending the fighting in Lebanon, the Council is belatedly reasserting that primacy—as the founders of this Organization expected it to do.

Only political solutions will be sustainable in the long term. The peace treaties between Israel and Egypt, and between Israel and Jordan, are expressions of stable political arrangements and agreements. Through these treaties, the leaders of the countries concerned have courageously brought stability and peace to borders that were previously beset with violence, and thus to their peoples. Ultimately, similar arrangements, based on foundations that are well known to all of us, will have to be put in place along all the borders where there is conflict. Only comprehensive solutions can bring lasting peace.

The United Nations stands for a just solution to all these issues. We stand for security for Lebanon, for Israel, for the region. We stand for a comprehensive solution, and must therefore do our utmost to address all the separate but intertwined issues and conflicts in the region, whether manifest or latent. Delays will mean only more lost lives, more shattered hopes and a further decline in the standing and authority of this Council and the Organization.

We must spare the people of Lebanon, of Israel, and of the wider region any further bloodshed—both now and in the months and years ahead.

❉

Not Just a Regional Conflict

Address to the Security Council
New York, New York
12 December 2006

In his last month in office, Annan felt obliged to make one last statement
to the Security Council, stressing the profound importance of the Middle
East conflict and suggesting better ways to approach a solution.

As I told the General Assembly in September, the Israeli-Palestinian conflict is not just one regional conflict amongst many. No other conflict carries such a powerful symbolic and emotional charge even for people far away.

Yet, while the quest for peace has registered some important achievements over the years, a final settlement has defied the best efforts of several generations of world leaders. I, too, will leave office without an end to the prolonged agony.

The Middle East today faces grim prospects. The region is in profound crisis. The situation is more complex, more fragile and more dangerous than it has been for a very long time....

Mistrust between Israelis and Palestinians has reached new heights.

The Gaza Strip has become a cauldron of deepening poverty and frustration, despite the withdrawal of Israeli troops and settlements last year. In the West Bank, too, the situation is dire. Settlement activity and construction of the Barrier continue.[1] Israeli obstacles impede Palestinian movement throughout the area. The Palestinian Authority, paralyzed by a debilitating political and financial crisis, is no longer able to provide security or basic services.

---

1. Since 2002 Israel had been constructing a physical barrier in the occupied West Bank, ostensibly intended to protect Israeli civilians from attacks by Arab terrorists.

Israelis, for their part, continue to live in fear of terrorism. They are dismayed by the inadequacy of Palestinian efforts to halt rocket attacks into southern Israel. And they are alarmed by a Hamas-led government[2] which is, at best, ambivalent about a two-State solution and, at worst, refuses to renounce violence and rejects the basic tenets of the approach to the conflict consistently favored by a majority of Palestinians and enshrined in the Oslo Accords.

In Lebanon, the country's political transformation is incomplete, and its leaders face a campaign of intimidation and destabilization. As last summer's fighting between Israel and Hezbollah showed, Lebanon remains hostage to its own difficult history and captive to forces, from within and from beyond its borders, that wish to exploit its vulnerability.

Casting our glance to other parts of the region, we see the Syrian Golan Heights still under Israeli control and concerns about Syria's relations with militant groups beyond its borders. Iraq is mired in unrelenting violence. Iran's nuclear activities and possible ambitions have emerged as a source of deep concern.... And all of this feeds, and is fed by, an alarming rise in extremism.

Each of these conflicts has its own dynamics and causes. Each will require its own specific solution and its own process to produce a solution that will endure. And in each case, it is the parties involved who bear the primary responsibility for peace. No one can make peace for them. No peace can be imposed on them; no one should want peace more than they do.

I would therefore like to offer a few thoughts on what the parties themselves, and outsiders from the Quartet[3] to this Council and other UN bodies, might do differently in the search for peace—in particular peace between Israelis and Palestinians, which, while no panacea, would go a long way towards defusing tensions throughout the region.

One of the most frustrating aspects of the Israeli-Palestinian conflict is the apparent inability of many people on both sides to understand the position of the other and the unwillingness of some to even try. As a true friend and supporter of both sides, I would like to address frank messages to each.

---

2. The Islamist movement Hamas had won the Palestinian parliamentary elections in January 2006, after which (in March) a Hamas-led cabinet was formed.
3. Since 2002 the United Nations, United States, European Union, and Russian Federation had been meeting regularly as the Quartet in an attempt to encourage and guide the Israeli-Palestinian peace process.

It is completely right and understandable that Israel and its supporters should seek to ensure its security by persuading Palestinians, and Arabs and Muslims more broadly, to alter their attitude and behavior towards Israel. But they are not likely to succeed unless they themselves grasp and acknowledge the fundamental Palestinian grievance—namely, that the establishment of the State of Israel involved the dispossession of hundreds of thousands of Palestinian families, turning them into refugees, and was followed 19 years later by a military occupation that brought hundreds of thousands more Palestinians under Israeli rule.

Israel is justifiably proud of its democracy and its efforts to build a society based on respect for the rule of law. But Israel's democracy can thrive only if the occupation over another people ends. Former Prime Minister Ariel Sharon acknowledged as much. Israel has undergone a major cultural shift since the days of Oslo: all of Israel's major political parties now acknowledge that Israel needs to end the occupation, for its own sake and for the sake of its own security.

Yet thousands of Israelis still live in territories occupied in 1967—and more than 1,000 more are added every month. As Palestinians watch this activity, they also see a Barrier being built through their land in contravention of the Advisory Opinion of the International Court of Justice, as well as more than 500 checkpoints to control their movement, and the heavy presence of the Israeli Defense Forces. Their despair at the occupation only grows, as does their determination to resist it. As a result, some tend to invest much of their trust in those who pursue the armed struggle rather than a peace process that does not seem to yield the coveted goal of an independent State.

I agree with Israel and its supporters that there is a difference—moral as well as legal—between terrorists, who deliberately target civilians, and regular soldiers who, in the course of military operations, unintentionally kill or wound civilians despite efforts to avoid such casualties. But the larger the number of civilian casualties and wounded during these operations, and the more perfunctory the precautions taken to avoid such losses, the more this difference is diminished. The use of military force in densely populated civilian areas is a blunt instrument that only produces more death, destruction, recrimination and vengeance. And as we have seen, it does little to achieve the desired goal of stopping terrorist attacks.

Israelis may reply that they are merely protecting themselves from terrorism, which they have every right to do. But that argument will carry less weight as long as the occupation in the West Bank becomes more burdensome and the settlement expansion continues. Israel would receive more understanding if its actions were clearly designed to help end an occupation rather than to entrench it.

We should all work with Israel to move beyond the unhappy status quo and reach a negotiated end to the occupation based on the principle of "land for peace."

It is completely right and understandable to support the Palestinian people, who have suffered so much. But Palestinians and their supporters will never be truly effective if they focus solely on Israel's transgressions, without conceding any justice or legitimacy to Israel's own concerns and without being willing to admit that Israel's opponents have themselves committed appalling and inexcusable crimes. No resistance to occupation can justify terrorism. We should all be united in our unequivocal rejection of terror as a political instrument.

I also believe the actions of some UN bodies may themselves be counterproductive. The Human Rights Council, for example, has already held three special sessions focused on the Arab-Israeli conflict. I hope the Council will take care to handle the issue in an impartial way and not allow it to monopolize attention at the expense of other situations where there are no less grave violations, or even worse.

In the same vein, those who complain that the Security Council is guilty of a "double standard"—applying sanctions to Arab and Muslim governments but not to Israel—should take care that they themselves do not apply double standards in the other direction, by holding Israel to a standard of behavior they are unwilling to apply to other States, to Israel's adversaries, or indeed to themselves.

Some may feel satisfaction at repeatedly passing General Assembly resolutions or holding conferences that condemn Israel's behavior. But one should also ask whether such steps bring any tangible relief or benefit to the Palestinians. There have been decades of resolutions. There has been a proliferation of special committees, sessions and Secretariat divisions and units. Has any of this had an effect on Israel's policies, other than to strengthen the belief in Israel, and among many of its supporters, that this great Organization is too one-sided to be allowed a significant role in the Middle East peace process?

Even worse, some of the rhetoric used in connection with the issue implies a refusal to concede the very legitimacy of Israel's existence, let alone the validity of its security concerns. We must never forget that Jews have very good historical reasons for taking seriously any threat to Israel's existence. What was done to Jews and others by the Nazis remains an undeniable tragedy, unique in human history. Today, Israelis are often confronted with words and actions that seem to confirm their fear that the goal of their adversaries is to extinguish their existence as a state and as a people.

Therefore, those who want to be heard on Palestine should not deny or minimize that history, or the connection many Jews feel for their historic homeland. Rather, they should acknowledge Israel's security concerns and make clear that their criticism is rooted not in hatred or intolerance, but in a desire for justice, self-determination, and peaceful coexistence.

Perhaps the greatest irony in this sad story is that there is no serious question about the broad outline of a final settlement. The parties themselves, at various times and through various diplomatic channels, have come close to bridging almost all of the gaps between them. There is every reason for the parties to try again, with principled, concerted help from the international community. We need a new and urgent push for peace.

The road will be long, and much trust will have to be rebuilt along the way. But let us remember where this effort needs to take us. Two States, Israel and Palestine, within secure, recognized and negotiated boundaries based on those of 4 June 1967. A broader peace encompassing Israel's other neighbors, namely Lebanon and Syria. Normal diplomatic and economic relations. Arrangements that will allow both Israel and Palestine to establish their internationally recognized capitals in Jerusalem and ensure access for people of all faiths to their holy places. A solution that respects the rights of Palestinian refugees and is consistent with the two-State solution and with the character of the States in the region.

Reaching this destination is not as impossible as some might imagine. Most Israelis genuinely believe in peace with the Palestinians—perhaps not quite as the Palestinians envision it, but genuine nevertheless. Most

Palestinians do not seek the destruction of Israel, only the end of occupation, and their own State—perhaps in a slightly larger territory than Israelis would wish to concede, but a limited territory nevertheless.

Our challenge is to convince the people on each side that these majorities exist on the other side, while showing that the spoilers and rejectionists are a distinct minority.

I believe that the fundamental aspirations of both peoples can be reconciled. I believe in the right of Israel to exist, and to exist in full and permanent security—free from terrorism, free from attack, free even from the threat of attack. I believe in the right of the Palestinians to exercise their self-determination. They have been miserably abused and exploited, by Israel, by the Arab world, sometimes by their own leaders and perhaps even, at times, by the international community. They deserve to see fulfilled their simple ambition to live in freedom and dignity.

The Roadmap, endorsed by this Council in its Resolution 1515,[4] is still the reference point around which any effort to reenergize a political effort should be concentrated. Its sponsor, the Quartet, retains its validity because of its singular combination of legitimacy, political strength and financial and economic clout. But the Quartet needs to do more to restore faith not only in its own seriousness and effectiveness, but also in the Roadmap's practicability and to create the conditions for resuming a viable peace process....

Tensions in the region are near breaking point. Extremism and populism are leaving less political space for moderates, including those States that have reached peace agreements with Israel. Welcome moves towards democracy such as elections have simultaneously posed a quandary in bringing to power parties, individuals and movements that oppose the basis of current peacemaking approaches. The opportunity for negotiating a two-State solution will last for only so long. Should we fail to seize it, the people who most directly bear the brunt of this calamity will be consigned to new depths of suffering and grief. Other conflicts and problems will become that much harder to resolve. And extremists the world over will enjoy a boost to their recruiting efforts.

---

4. The "Performance-Based Roadmap to a Permanent Two-State Solution to the Israeli-Palestinian Conflict" had been issued by the Quartet in April 2003 and endorsed by the UN Security Council in November of that year.

The period ahead could well prove crucial. Every day brings defeats in the struggle for peace and reasons to give up. But we must not succumb to frustration. The principles on which peace must be based are known to all of us. Even the contours of what a solution would look like on the ground are well mapped out. I believe we can break the current stalemate and make new strides towards peace.

The United Nations and the Middle East are closely intertwined. The region has shaped this Organization like no other. The situation, the people, the thirst for peace, are all very close to my heart. I know they are close to yours as well. As a matter of urgency, let us match that concern with concerted action.

PREVENTION OF GENOCIDE AND THE RESPONSIBILITY TO PROTECT

❈

The International Criminal Court

Statement Opening the Rome Conference to
Establish the International Criminal Court
Rome, Italy
15 June 1998

The atrocities of the mid-1990s in the former Yugoslavia and in Rwanda
had led the UN Security Council to create ad hoc tribunals to try those
responsible but had also galvanized the worldwide movement for a per-
manent international court that could deal with such crimes. Although this
court would not be an organ of the United Nations, the United Nations
was charged with organizing the process for establishing it, including the
conference in Rome at which the founding statute was agreed. As Secretary-
General, Annan was invited to open the conference.

I t is said that all roads lead to Rome. But not all lead there directly. The road that has led us to this Conference in the Eternal City has been a long one. It has led through some of the darkest moments in human history. But it has also been marked by the determined belief of human beings that their true nature is to be noble and generous. When human beings maltreat each other, they call it "inhuman."

Most human societies, alas, have practiced warfare. But most have also had some kind of warrior code of honor. They have proclaimed, at least in principle, the need to protect the innocent and defenseless, and to punish those who carry violence to excess.

Unhappily, that did not prevent acts of genocide in previous centuries, such as the extermination of indigenous peoples; nor did it prevent the barbaric trade in African slaves.

Our own century has seen the invention and use of weapons of mass destruction and the use of industrial technology to dispose of millions upon millions of human beings. Gradually, the world has come to realize that relying on each State or army to punish its own transgressors is not enough. When crimes are committed on such a scale, we know that the State lacks either the power or the will to stop them. Too often, indeed, they are part of the systematic State policy, and the worst criminals may be found at the pinnacle of State power.

After the defeat of Nazism and fascism in 1945, the United Nations was set up in an effort to ensure that world war could never happen again. The victorious Powers also set up international tribunals, at Nuremberg and Tokyo, to judge the leaders who had ordered and carried out the worst atrocities. And they decided to prosecute Nazi leaders not only for "war crimes"—waging war and massacring people in occupied territories—but also for "crimes against humanity" which included the slaughter of their own fellow citizens and others in the tragedy we now know as the Holocaust.

Was it enough to make an example of a few arch-criminals in two States that had waged aggressive war and leave it at that? The General Assembly of the United Nations did not think so. In 1948, it adopted the Convention on the Prevention and Punishment of the Crime of Genocide. And it requested the International Law Commission to study the possibility of establishing a permanent international criminal court. In this area, as in so many, the cold war prevented further progress at that time. If only it had prevented further crimes against humanity as well!

Alas, this was not the case. I need only mention, as the most notorious single example in that period, the killing of more than two million people in Cambodia between 1975 and 1978. As you know, the man who organized that horror died just two months ago, without ever being brought to answer for his crimes before a court.[1]

Humanity had to wait until the 1990s for a political climate in which the United Nations could once again consider establishing an international criminal court. And, unhappily, this decade has also brought new crimes to force the issue on the world's attention. Events in the former Yugoslavia have added the dreadful euphemism of "ethnic cleansing" to our vocabulary. Perhaps a quarter of a million people died there between 1991 and 1995—the great majority of them civilians, guilty only of living on the "wrong" side of a line someone had drawn on a map.

---

1. Pol Pot, leader of the Khmer Rouge, had died on 15 April 1998.

And then, in 1994, came the genocide of Rwanda. On my visit there last month, I was able to register at first hand the terrible, irreparable damage that event has done, not only to one small country but to the very idea of an international community. In future, the United Nations and its Member States must summon the will to prevent such a catastrophe from being repeated anywhere in the world. And as part of that effort, we must show clearly that such crimes will not be left unpunished.

Events in the former Yugoslavia and in Rwanda overtook the slow processes by which the world was considering the creation of a permanent international court. Ad hoc tribunals had to be set up for those two countries, and they are now at work. They have issued indictments and international arrest warrants.... A historic milestone was passed six weeks ago when a former prime minister of Rwanda actually pleaded guilty to the charge of genocide.

These tribunals are showing, however imperfectly, that there is such a thing as international criminal justice and that it can have teeth. But ad hoc tribunals are not enough. People all over the world want to know that humanity can strike back—that whatever and whenever genocide, war crimes or other such violations are committed, there is a court before which the criminal can be held to account; a court that puts an end to a global culture of impunity; a court where "acting under orders" is no defense; a court where all individuals in a government hierarchy or military chain of command, without exception, from rulers to private soldiers, must answer for their actions....

I do not underestimate the difficulties you have to overcome in the five weeks ahead. The work of the preparatory committees has shown what a complex issue this is and how many conflicting principles and interests have to be reconciled.

Some small States fear giving pretexts for more powerful ones to set aside their sovereignty. Others worry that the pursuit of justice may sometimes interfere with the vital work of making peace. You have to take those worries into account. Obviously, you must aim for a statute accepted and implemented by as many States as possible.

But the overriding interest must be that of the victims and of the international community as a whole. I trust you will not flinch from creating a court strong and independent enough to carry out its task.

It must be an instrument of justice, not expediency. It must be able to protect the weak against the strong.

I know you are ready for long weeks of hard and detailed negotiations. But I hope you will feel, at every moment, that the eyes of the victims of the past crimes, and of the potential victims of future ones, are fixed firmly upon us.

We have before us an opportunity to take a monumental step in the name of human rights and the rule of law. We have an opportunity to create an institution that can save lives and serve as a bulwark against evil ... to bequeath to the next century a powerful instrument of justice. Let us rise to the challenge. Let us give succeeding generations this gift of hope. They will not forgive us if we fail.[2]

❉

On Intervention

35th Annual Ditchley Foundation Lecture
Ditchley Park, England
26 June 1998

Ditchley Park, a stately home near Oxford, is the home of the Ditchley Foundation, which holds conferences on issues of international concern. Its annual lecture is an opportunity to address Britain's foreign-policy establishment. Annan used it to make the first full statement of his views on a theme that was to recur many times in his subsequent career.

I expect some of you are surprised by the title I have chosen for my talk. Or if not, you may think I have come to preach a sermon *against* intervention. I suppose that would be the traditional line for a citizen of a former British colony to take in an address to senior policy makers and diplomats of the former imperial Power. And some people would also expect a sermon on those lines from the United

---

2. On 17 July 1998, the Rome Statute of the International Criminal Court was adopted by a vote of 120 to 7, with twenty-one countries abstaining. It entered into force on 1 July 2002.

Nations Secretary-General, whatever his country of origin. The United Nations is, after all, an association of sovereign States, and sovereign States do tend to be extremely jealous of their sovereignty. Small States, especially, are fearful of intervention in their affairs by great Powers. And indeed, our century has seen many examples of the strong "intervening"—or interfering—in the affairs of the weak, from the Allied intervention in the Russian civil war in 1918 to the Soviet "interventions" in Hungary, Czechoslovakia and Afghanistan. Others might refer to the American intervention in Viet Nam or even the Turkish intervention in Cyprus in 1974. The motives and the legal justification, may be better in some cases than others, but the word "intervention" has come to be used almost as a synonym for "invasion."

The Charter of the United Nations gives great responsibilities to great Powers in their capacity as permanent members of the Security Council. But as a safeguard against abuse of those powers, Article 2.7 of the Charter protects national sovereignty even from intervention by the United Nations itself—it forbids the United Nations to intervene "in matters which are essentially within the domestic jurisdiction of any State."

That prohibition is just as relevant today as it was in 1945: violations of sovereignty remain violations of the global order.

Yet, in other contexts, the word "intervention" has a more benign meaning. We all applaud the policeman who intervenes to stop a fight or the teacher who prevents big boys from bullying a smaller one. And medicine uses the word "intervention" to describe the act of the surgeon, who saves life by "intervening" to remove malignant growth or to repair damaged organs. Of course, the most intrusive methods of treatment are not always to be recommended. A wise doctor knows when to let nature take its course. But a doctor who never intervened would have few admirers and probably even fewer patients.

So it is in international affairs. Why was the United Nations established, if not to act as a benign policeman or doctor? Our job *is* to intervene: to prevent conflict where we can, to put a stop to it when it has broken out, or—when neither of those things is possible—at least to contain it and prevent it from spreading. That is what the world expects of us, even though—alas—the United Nations by no means always lives up to such expectations. It is also what the Charter requires of us, particularly in Chapter VI, which deals with the peaceful settlement of disputes, and Chapter VII, which describes the action the United Nations must take when peace comes under threat or is actually broken.

The purpose of Article 2.7, which I quoted just now, was to confine such interventions to cases where the international peace is threatened or broken and to keep the United Nations from interfering in purely domestic disputes. Yet even that article carries the important rider that "this principle shall not prejudice the application of enforcement measures under Chapter VII." In other words, even national sovereignty can be set aside if it stands in the way of the Security Council's overriding duty to preserve international peace and security. On the face of it, there is a simple distinction between international conflict, which is clearly the United Nations' business, and domestic disputes, which are not. The very phrase "domestic dispute" sounds reassuring. It suggests a little local difficulty, which the State in question can easily settle, if only it is left alone to do so.

We all know that in recent years it has not been like that. Most wars nowadays are civil wars. Or at least that is how they start. And these civil wars are anything but benign. In fact they are "civil" only in the sense that civilians—that is, non-combatants—have become the main victims.

In the First World War, roughly 90 percent of those killed were soldiers and only 10 percent civilians. In the Second World War, even if we count all the victims of Nazi death camps as war casualties, civilians made up only half, or just over half, of all those killed. But in many of today's conflicts, civilians have become the main targets of violence. It is now conventional to put the proportion of civilian casualties somewhere in the region of 75 percent.

I say "conventional" because the truth is that no one really knows. Relief agencies such as the Office of the United Nations High Commissioner for Refugees (UNHCR) and the Red Cross rightly devote their resources to helping the living rather than counting the dead. Armies count their own losses and sometimes make boasts about the number of enemies they have killed. But there is no agency whose job is to keep a tally of civilians killed. The victims of today's brutal conflicts are not merely anonymous, but literally countless. Yet, so long as the conflict rages within the borders of a single State, the old orthodoxy would require us to let it rage. We should leave it to "burn itself out" or perhaps to "fester." (You can choose your own euphemism.) We should leave it even to escalate, regardless of human consequences, at least until the point when its effects begin to spill over into neighboring States so that it becomes, in the words of so many Security Council resolutions, "a threat to international peace and security."

In reality, this "old orthodoxy" was never absolute. The Charter, after all, was issued in the name of "the peoples," not the governments, of the United Nations. Its aim is not only to preserve international peace—vitally important though that is—but also "to reaffirm faith in fundamental human rights, in the dignity and worth of the human person." The Charter protects the sovereignty of peoples. It was never meant as a license for governments to trample on human rights and human dignity. Sovereignty implies responsibility, not just power.

This year we celebrate the fiftieth anniversary of the Universal Declaration of Human Rights. That declaration was not meant as a purely rhetorical statement. The General Assembly which adopted it also decided, in the same month, that it had the right to express its concern about the apartheid system in South Africa. The principle of international concern for human rights took precedence over the claim of non-interference in internal affairs.

And the day before it adopted the Universal Declaration, the General Assembly had adopted the Convention on the Prevention and Punishment of the Crime of Genocide, which puts all States under an obligation to "prevent and punish" this most heinous of crimes. It also allows them to "call upon the competent organs of the United Nations" to take action for this purpose.

Since genocide is almost always committed with the connivance, if not the direct participation, of the State authorities, it is hard to see how the United Nations could prevent it without intervening in a State's internal affairs.

As for punishment, a very important attempt is now being made to fulfill this obligation through the Ad Hoc International Criminal Tribunals for the former Yugoslavia and Rwanda. And 10 days ago in Rome, I had the honor to open the conference which is to establish a permanent international criminal court. Within a year or two, I sincerely hope, this court will be up and running, with competence to try cases of war crimes and crimes against humanity wherever, and by whomsoever, they are committed.

State frontiers, ladies and gentlemen, should no longer be seen as a watertight protection for war criminals or mass murderers. The fact that a conflict is "internal" does not give the parties any right to disregard the most basic rules of human conduct. Besides, most "internal" conflicts do not stay internal for very long. They soon "spill over" into neighboring countries.

The most obvious and tragic way this happens is through the flow of refugees. But there are others, one of which is the spread of knowledge. News today travels around the world more rapidly than we could imagine even a few years ago. Human suffering on a large scale has become impossible to keep quiet. People in far-off countries not only hear about it, but often see it on their TV screens. That in turn leads to public outrage and pressure on governments to "do something," in other words, to intervene. Moreover, today's conflicts do not only spread across existing frontiers. Sometimes they actually give birth to new States, which of course means new frontiers. In such cases, what started as an internal conflict becomes an international one. That happens when peoples who formerly lived together in one State find each other's behavior so threatening, or so offensive, that they can no longer do so. Such separations are seldom as smooth and trouble-free as the famous "velvet divorce" between Czechs and Slovaks. All too often they happen in the midst of, or at the end of, a long and bitter conflict—as was the case with Pakistan and Bangladesh, with the former Yugoslav republics, and with Ethiopia and Eritrea. In other cases, such as the former Soviet Union, the initial separation may be largely non-violent, and yet it soon gives rise to new conflicts, which pose new problems to the international community. In many cases, the conflict eventually becomes so dangerous that the international community finds itself *obliged* to intervene. By then it can only do so in the most intrusive and expensive way, which is *military* intervention.

And yet the most effective interventions are not military. It is much better, from every point of view, if action can be taken to resolve or manage a conflict before it reaches the military stage.

Sometimes this action may take the form of economic advice and assistance. In so many cases, ethnic tensions are exacerbated by poverty and famine or by uneven economic development which brings wealth to one section of a community while destroying the homes and livelihood of another. If outsiders can help avert this by suitably targeted aid and investment, by giving information and training to local entrepreneurs, or by suggesting more appropriate State policies, their "intervention" should surely be welcomed by all concerned. That is why I see the work of the United Nations Development Program and of our sister "Bretton Woods" institutions in Washington as organically linked to the United Nations' work on peace and security.

In other cases, what is most needed is skillful and timely diplomacy. Here in Europe I would cite the example of the Organization for Security and Cooperation in Europe's High Commissioner on National Minorities, Max van der Stoel.[1] You hardly ever see him on television or read about him in the newspapers, but that surely is a measure of his success. His job is to help European States deal with their minority problems quietly and peacefully, so that they never get to the stage of featuring in banner headlines or TV news bulletins around the world.

The United Nations also does its best to "intervene" in such effective but non-military ways. When I went to Baghdad in February of this year, I did so in search of a peaceful solution to a crisis that had brought us to the brink of a new war in the Gulf. I came back with an agreement which averted that crisis, at least for the time being.[2] ...

Iraq is but one example of how, when the moment is ripe, diplomacy through the United Nations can achieve the will of the international community. We much prefer to see disputes settled under Chapter VI, rather than move to the drastic and expensive means available under Chapter VII.

For many years, the United Nations has been conducting successful peacekeeping operations—both of the traditional variety, monitoring

---

1. Max van der Stoel (1924–2011), a former foreign minister of the Netherlands, was the OSCE's first High Commissioner on National Minorities, holding that office from 1993 to 2000.
2. Annan went to Baghdad in February 1998 to defuse a crisis over Saddam Hussein's refusal to allow UN disarmament inspectors access to certain "presidential sites." He was able to negotiate an agreement, but it broke down later in the year, leading to the withdrawal of the inspectors and US air strikes against Iraq.

cease-fires and buffer zones, and the more complex multidimensional operations that helped bring peace to Namibia, Mozambique and El Salvador.

And in recent years, there has been an increasing emphasis on the United Nations' political work, as the size—though not the number—of peacekeeping operations has shrunk since its peak in the early 1990s. Early diplomatic intervention, at its best, can avert bloodshed altogether. But as you know, our resources are limited. And ... we are more than happy if disputes can be dealt with peacefully at the regional level, without the United Nations needing to be involved.

We must assume, however, that there will always be some tragic cases where peaceful means have failed: where extreme violence is being used and only forceful intervention can stop it. Even during the cold war, when the United Nations' own enforcement capacity was largely paralyzed by divisions in the Security Council, there were cases where extreme violations of human rights in one country led to military intervention by one of its neighbors. In 1971 Indian intervention ended the civil war in East Pakistan, allowing Bangladesh to achieve independence. In 1978 Viet Nam intervened in Cambodia, putting an end to the genocidal rule of the Khmer Rouge. In 1979 Tanzania intervened to overthrow Idi Amin's erratic dictatorship in Uganda.

In all three of those cases, the intervening States gave refugee flows across the border as the reason why they had to act. But what justified their action in the eyes of the world was the internal character of the regimes they acted against. And history has by and large ratified that verdict. Few would now deny that in those cases intervention was a lesser evil than allowing massacre and extreme oppression to continue. Yet, at the time, in all three cases, the international community was divided and disturbed. Why? Because these interventions were unilateral. The States in question had no mandate from anyone else to act as they did. And that sets an uncomfortable precedent.

Can we really afford to let each State be the judge of its own right, or duty, to intervene in another State's internal conflict? If we do, will we not be forced to legitimize Hitler's championship of the Sudeten Germans or Soviet intervention in Afghanistan?

Most of us would prefer, I think—especially now that the cold war is over—to see such decisions taken collectively by an international institution whose authority is generally respected. And surely the only institution competent to assume that role is the Security Council of the United Nations. The Charter clearly assigns responsibility to the Council for maintaining international peace and security. I would argue, therefore, that only the Council has the authority to decide that the internal situation in any State is so grave as to justify forceful intervention.

As you know, many Member States feel that the Council's authority now needs to be strengthened by an increase in its membership, bringing in new permanent members or possibly adding a new category of member. Unfortunately a consensus on the details of such a reform has yet to be reached.

This is a matter for the Member States. As Secretary-General I would make only three points. First, the Security Council must become more representative in order to reflect current realities, rather than the realities of 1945. Secondly, the Council's authority depends not only on the representative character of its membership but also on the quality and speed of its decisions. Humanity is ill served when the Council is unable to react quickly and decisively in a crisis. Thirdly, the delay in reaching agreement on reform, however regrettable, must not be allowed to detract from the Council's authority and responsibility in the meanwhile.

The Council in its present form derives its authority from the Charter. That gives it a unique legitimacy as the linchpin of world order, which all Member States should value and respect. It also places a unique responsibility on Council members, both permanent and non-permanent—a responsibility of which their governments and indeed their citizens should be fully conscious.

Of course the fact that the Council has this unique responsibility does not mean that the intervention itself should always be undertaken directly by the United Nations, in the sense of forces wearing blue helmets and controlled by the United Nations Secretariat. No one knows better than I do, as a former Under-Secretary-General in charge of peacekeeping, that the United Nations lacks the capacity for directing large-scale military enforcement operations.

At least for the foreseeable future, such operations will have to be undertaken by Member States or by regional organizations. But they need to have the authority of the Security Council behind them, expressed in an authorizing resolution. That formula, developed in 1990 to deal with the Iraqi aggression against Kuwait, has proved its usefulness and will no doubt be used again in future crises.

But we should not assume that intervention always needs to be on a massive scale. There are cases where the speed of the action may be far more crucial than the size of the force. Personally, I am haunted by the experience of Rwanda in 1994: a terrible demonstration of what can happen when there is no intervention, or at least none in the crucial early weeks of a crisis. General Dallaire, the commander of the United Nations mission, has indicated that with a force of even modest size and means he could have prevented much of the killing. Indeed he has said that 5,000 peace-keepers could have saved 500,000 lives. How tragic it is that at the crucial moment the opposite course was chosen and the size of the force reduced.

Surely things would have been different if the Security Council had at its disposal a small rapid-reaction force, ready to move at a few days' notice. I believe that if we are to avert further such disasters in the future we need such a capacity; that Member States must have appropriately trained standby forces immediately available and must be willing to send them quickly when the Security Council requests it.

Some have even suggested that private security firms, like the one which recently helped restore the elected President to power in Sierra Leone,[3] might play a role in providing the United Nations with the rapid-reaction capacity it needs. When we had need of skilled soldiers to separate fighters from refugees in the Rwandan refugee camps in Goma,[4] I even considered the possibility of engaging a private firm. But the world may not be ready to privatize peace.

In any case, let me stress that I am not asking for a standing army at the beck and call of the Secretary-General. The decision to intervene, I repeat, can only be taken by the Security Council. But at present the Council's authority is diminished, because it lacks the means to intervene effectively even when it wishes to do so.

---

3. Private security forces assisted the troops sent by the Economic Community of West African States (ECOWAS) to restore President Ahmed Tejane Kabbah, who had been forced into exile by a coup.
4. After the defeat of the genocidal Hutu government in Rwanda in 1994, nearly 1 million Hutu, including many perpetrators of the genocide, took refuge in and around Goma in the east of what was then Zaire (now Democratic Republic of Congo).

Let me conclude by coming back to where I started. The United Nations is an association of sovereign States, but the rights it exists to uphold belong to peoples, not governments. By the same token, it is wrong to think the obligations of United Nations membership fall only on States. Each one of us—whether as workers in government, in intergovernmental or non-governmental organizations, in business, in the media, or simply as human beings—has an obligation to do whatever he or she can to correct injustice. Each of us has a duty to halt—or, better, to prevent—the infliction of suffering.

Much has been written about the "duty to interfere" (*le devoir d'ingérence*). We should remember that the inventor of this phrase, Bernard Kouchner, coined it not as a minister in the French government but when he was still running the charity Médecins du Monde. He argued that non-governmental organizations had a duty to cross national boundaries, with or without the consent of governments, in order to reach the victims of natural disasters and other emergencies. And their right to do this has since been recognized by two resolutions of the United Nations General Assembly—in 1988 (after the earthquake in Armenia) and again in 1991.

Both these resolutions, while paying full respect to State sovereignty, assert the overriding right of people in desperate situations to receive help and the right of international bodies to provide it.

So when we recall tragic events such as those of Bosnia or Rwanda and ask, Why did no one intervene? the question should not be addressed only to the United Nations or even to its Member States. Each of us as an individual has to take his or her share of responsibility. No one can claim ignorance of what happened. All of us should recall how we responded, and ask, What did I do? Could I have done more? Did I let my prejudice, my indifference, or my fear overwhelm my reasoning? Above all, how would I react next time?

And "next time" may already be here. The last few months' events in Kosovo present the international community with what may be its severest challenge in Europe since the Dayton Agreement was concluded in 1995.[5]

As in Bosnia, we have witnessed the shelling of towns and villages, indiscriminate attacks on civilians in the name of security, the separation

---

5. The peace agreement ending the Bosnian war was reached at Wright-Patterson Air Force Base near Dayton, Ohio, in November 1995.

of men from women and children and their summary execution, and the flight of thousands from their homes, many of them across an international border. In short, events reminiscent of the whole ghastly scenario of "ethnic cleansing" again—as yet on a smaller scale than in Bosnia, but for how long?

Of course there are differences—the crucial one being, precisely, that so far this conflict is being waged within the borders of a single State,[6] recognized as such by the entire international community. I repeat: so far. But when we witness the outflow of refugees into Albania, when we hear the insistence of Kosovar Albanian spokesmen that they will settle for nothing less than full independence, and when we remember the ethnic tensions in at least one neighboring State,[7] how can we not conclude that this crisis is indeed a threat to international peace and security?

This time, ladies and gentlemen, no one will be able to say that they were taken by surprise—neither by the means employed, nor by the ends pursued. This time, ethnically driven violence must be seen for what it is, and we know all too well what to expect if it is allowed to continue....

Of course, we all hope for a peaceful solution.... But that only makes it more important to stop the violence now. And I feel confident that this time, if peaceful means fail to achieve this, the Security Council will not be slow to assume its grave responsibility.[8]

A great deal is at stake in Kosovo today—for the people of Kosovo themselves, for the overall stability of the Balkans, and for the credibility and legitimacy of all our words and deeds in pursuit of collective security. All our professions of regret, all our expressions of determination to never again permit another Bosnia, all our hopes for a peaceful future for the Balkans will be cruelly mocked if we allow Kosovo to become another killing field.

Our theme is vast, but the hour is late. Let me recall, in conclusion, that in French law there is a crime called "failure to assist a person in danger" (*non-assistance à personne en danger*).

I am sure this is what the late François Mitterrand had in mind in April 1991, when he congratulated the Security Council on its decision

---

6. The Federal Republic of Yugoslavia, of which Kosovo was then part.
7. The former Yugoslav republic of Macedonia.
8. See "The Use of Force" in Chapter 3.

to intervene in the internal affairs of Iraq in order to save the Kurds. "For the first time," President Mitterrand declared, "non-interference has stopped at the point where it was becoming failure to assist a people in danger." That, ladies and gentlemen, is what "intervention" is all about.

When people are in danger, everyone has a duty to speak out. No one has a right to pass by on the other side. If we are tempted to do so, we should call to mind the unforgettable warning of Martin Niemöller, the German Protestant theologian who lived through the Nazi persecution:

> In Germany they came first for the Communists. And I did not speak up because I was not a Communist. Then they came for the Jews. And I did not speak up, because I was not a Jew. Then they came for the trade unionists. And I did not speak up, because I was not a trade unionist. Then they came for the Catholics. And I did not speak up, because I was a Protestant. Then they came for me. And by that time there was no one left to speak up.

❋

An Emerging Norm

Speech to the UN Commission on Human Rights
Geneva, Switzerland
7 April 1999

As noted in Chapter 3 (see "The Use of Force"), Annan had reacted cautiously to the NATO attack on Yugoslavia in March 1999 because it was not authorized by the Security Council. But two weeks later the annual session of the Commission on Human Rights in Geneva gave him the opportunity to stress the underlying issue and to further articulate the principle that sovereignty is not a license for governments to massacre their own people.

This last Commission on Human Rights of the twentieth century is meeting under the dark cloud of the crime of genocide. Of all gross violations, genocide knows no parallel in human history. The tragic irony of this age of human rights—where greater numbers are enjoying human rights than perhaps ever in history—is that it has been repeatedly darkened by outbursts of indiscriminate violence and organized mass killings. In Cambodia, in the 1970s, up to two million people were killed by Pol Pot's regime. And in this decade, from Bosnia to Rwanda, thousands upon thousands of human beings were massacred for belonging to the wrong ethnicity.

Though we have no independent observers on the ground, the signs are that it may be happening, once more, in Kosovo.

Every time, though, the world says, "Never again." And yet it happens. The vicious and systematic campaign of "ethnic cleansing" conducted by the Serbian authorities in Kosovo appears to have one aim: to expel or kill as many ethnic Albanians in Kosovo as possible, thereby denying a people their most basic rights to life, liberty and security. The result is a humanitarian disaster throughout the region.

We all deeply regret that the international community, despite months of diplomatic efforts, failed to prevent this disaster. What gives me hope—and should give every future "ethnic cleanser" and every state-backed architect of mass murder pause—is that a universal sense of outrage has been provoked.

Emerging slowly, but I believe surely, is an international norm against the violent repression of minorities that will and must take precedence over concerns of sovereignty.

It is a principle that protects minorities—and majorities—from gross violations.

And let me therefore be very clear: even though we are an organization of Member States, the rights and ideals the United Nations exists to protect are those of peoples. As long as I am Secretary-General, the United Nations as an institution will always place the human being at the center of everything we do.

No government has the right to hide behind national sovereignty in order to violate the human rights or fundamental freedoms of its peoples. Whether a person belongs to the minority or the majority, that person's human rights and fundamental freedoms are sacred.

This developing international norm will pose fundamental challenges to the United Nations.

Of this there can be no doubt.

But nor can there be any doubt that if we fail this challenge, if we allow the United Nations to become the refuge of the "ethnic cleanser" or mass murderer, we will betray the very ideals that inspired the founding of the United Nations.

❋

Two Concepts of Sovereignty

Address to the General Assembly
New York, New York
20 September 1999

The Kosovo war ended in June 1999 with Yugoslavia's acceptance of a peace plan that involved ceding de facto control of Kosovo to a UN administration. Annan decided to use his annual address to the General Assembly, in September, to spell out the implications of what had happened for international order. The issue was made even more topical by events in East Timor, the former Portuguese territory that had been annexed by Indonesia in 1975. In a UN-supervised referendum on August 30, 1999, the population voted overwhelmingly for independence. But the Indonesian military and its local auxiliaries reacted with a punitive campaign of violence. International pressure on the Indonesian president, B. J. Habibie, in which Annan played an important part, led to the withdrawal of Indonesian forces and the entry of an Australian-led international force, authorized by the Security Council, which began deploying on the day of Annan's speech. This slightly abridged version of the speech appeared in The Economist *on September 16 and appears here with permission.*

T he tragedy of East Timor, coming so soon after that of Kosovo, has focused attention once again on the need for timely intervention by the international community when death and suffering are being inflicted on large numbers of people and when the State nominally in charge is unable or unwilling to stop it.

In Kosovo a group of States intervened without seeking authority from the United Nations Security Council. In Timor the Council has now authorized intervention, but only after obtaining an invitation from Indonesia. We all hope that this will rapidly stabilize the situation, but many hundreds—probably thousands—of innocent people have already perished. As in Rwanda five years ago, the international community stands accused of doing too little, too late.

Neither of these precedents is satisfactory as a model for the new millennium. Just as we have learnt that the world cannot stand aside when gross and systematic violations of human rights are taking place, we have also learnt that, if it is to enjoy the sustained support of the world's peoples, intervention must be based on legitimate and universal principles. We need to adapt our international system better to a world with new actors, new responsibilities, and new possibilities for peace and progress.

State sovereignty, in its most basic sense, is being redefined—not least by the forces of globalization and international cooperation. States are now widely understood to be instruments at the service of their peoples, and not vice versa. At the same time individual sovereignty—by which I mean the fundamental freedom of each individual, enshrined in the Charter of the UN and subsequent international treaties—has been enhanced by a renewed and spreading consciousness of individual rights. When we read the Charter today, we are more than ever conscious that its aim is to protect individual human beings, not to protect those who abuse them.

These changes in the world do not make hard political choices any easier. But they do oblige us to think anew about such questions as how the UN responds to humanitarian crises and why States are willing to act in some areas of conflict but not in others where the daily toll of death and suffering is as bad or worse. From Sierra Leone to Sudan, from Angola to Afghanistan, there are people who need more than words of sympathy. They need a real and sustained commitment to help end their cycles of violence and give them a new chance to achieve peace and prosperity.

The genocide in Rwanda showed us how terrible the consequences of inaction can be in the face of mass murder. But this year's conflict in Kosovo raised equally important questions about the consequences of action without international consensus and clear legal authority.

It has cast in stark relief the dilemma of so-called humanitarian intervention. On the one hand, is it legitimate for a regional organization to use force without a UN mandate? On the other, is it permissible to let gross and systematic violations of human rights, with grave humanitarian consequences, continue unchecked? The inability of the international community to reconcile these two compelling interests in the case of Kosovo can be viewed only as a tragedy.

To avoid repeating such tragedies in the next century, I believe it is essential that the international community reach consensus—not only on the principle that massive and systematic violations of human rights must be checked, wherever they take place, but also on ways of deciding what action is necessary, and when, and by whom. The Kosovo conflict and its outcome have prompted a debate of worldwide importance. And to each side in this debate difficult questions can be posed.

To those for whom the greatest threat to the future of international order is the use of force in the absence of a Security Council mandate, one might say, Leave Kosovo aside for a moment, and think about Rwanda. Imagine for one moment that, in those dark days and hours leading up to the genocide, there had been a coalition of States ready and willing to act in defense of the Tutsi population, but the Council had refused or delayed giving the green light. Should such a coalition then have stood idly by while the horror unfolded?

To those for whom the Kosovo action heralded a new era when States and groups of States can take military action outside the established mechanisms for enforcing international law, one might equally ask, Is there not a danger of such interventions undermining the imperfect, yet resilient, security system created after the Second World War and of setting dangerous precedents for future interventions without a clear criterion to decide who might invoke these precedents and in what circumstances? Nothing in the UN Charter precludes a recognition that there are rights beyond borders. What the Charter does say[1] is that "armed force shall not be used, save in the common interest." But what is that common interest? Who shall define it? Who shall defend it? Under whose authority? And with what means of intervention? In

---

1. In the Preamble.

seeking answers to these monumental questions, I see four aspects of intervention which need to be considered with special care.

First, *"intervention" should not be understood as referring only to the use of force.* A tragic irony of many of the crises that go unnoticed or unchallenged in the world today is that they could be dealt with by far less perilous acts of intervention than the one we saw this year in Yugoslavia. And yet the commitment of the world to peacekeeping, to humanitarian assistance, to rehabilitation and reconstruction varies greatly from region to region and crisis to crisis. If the new commitment to humanitarian action is to retain the support of the world's peoples, it must be—and must be seen to be—universal, irrespective of region or nation. Humanity, after all, is indivisible.

Second, it is clear that traditional *notions of sovereignty alone are not the only obstacle to effective action* in humanitarian crises. No less significant are the ways in which States define their national interests. The world has changed in profound ways since the end of the cold war, but I fear our conceptions of national interest have failed to follow suit. A new, broader definition of national interest is needed in the new century, which would induce States to find greater unity in the pursuit of common goals and values. In the context of many of the challenges facing humanity today, the collective interest *is* the national interest.

Third, in cases where forceful intervention does become necessary, *the Security Council*—the body charged with authorizing the use of force under international law—*must be able to rise to the challenge.* The choice must not be between Council unity and inaction in the face of genocide—as in the case of Rwanda—and Council division but regional action, as in the case of Kosovo. In both cases, the UN should have been able to find common ground in upholding the principles of the Charter and acting in defense of our common humanity.

As important as the Council's enforcement power is its deterrent power, and unless it is able to assert itself collectively where the cause is just and the means available, its credibility in the eyes of the world may well suffer. If States bent on criminal behavior know that frontiers are not an absolute defense—that the Council will take action to halt the gravest crimes against humanity—then they will not embark on such a course assuming they can get away with it. The Charter requires the

Council to be the defender of the "common interest." Unless it is seen to be so—in an era of human rights, interdependence and globalization—there is a danger that others will seek to take its place.

Fourth, when fighting stops, *the international commitment to peace must be just as strong as was the commitment to war.* In this situation, too, consistency is essential. Just as our commitment to humanitarian action must be universal if it is to be legitimate, so our commitment to peace cannot end as soon as there is a cease-fire. The aftermath of war requires no less skill, no less sacrifice, no fewer resources than the war itself, if lasting peace is to be secured.

This developing international norm in favor of intervention to protect civilians from wholesale slaughter will no doubt continue to pose profound challenges to the international community. In some quarters it will arouse distrust, skepticism, even hostility. But I believe on balance we should welcome it. Why? Because, despite all the difficulties of putting it into practice, it does show that humankind today is less willing than in the past to tolerate suffering in its midst and more willing to do something about it.

❋

An Action Plan to Prevent Genocide

Address to the UN Commission on Human Rights
Geneva, Switzerland
7 April 2004

The annual session of the Commission on Human Rights coincided, in 2004, with the tenth anniversary of the genocide in Rwanda and also with mounting evidence of large-scale atrocities in Darfur (Sudan). The General Assembly had designated April 7—the day on which the genocide started in 1994—as an annual Day of Remembrance. Annan decided that this would be the appropriate day for him to address the Commission on Human Rights, and he began by asking the delegates to observe two minutes' silence.

I t is good that we have observed those minutes of silence together. We must never forget our collective failure to protect at least eight hundred thousand defenseless men, women and children who perished in Rwanda ten years ago.

Such crimes cannot be reversed.

Such failures cannot be repaired.

The dead cannot be brought back to life.

So what can we do?

First, we must all acknowledge our responsibility for not having done more to prevent or stop the genocide.

Neither the United Nations Secretariat, nor the Security Council, nor Member States in general, nor the international media paid enough attention to the gathering signs of disaster. Still less did we take timely action.

When we recall such events and ask, Why did no one intervene? we should address the question not only to the United Nations or even to its Member States. No one can claim ignorance. All who were playing any part in world affairs at that time should ask, What more could I have done? How would I react next time—and what am I doing now to make it less likely there will be a next time?

Perhaps more than any others, those questions have dominated my thoughts since I became Secretary-General. If there is one legacy I would most wish to leave to my successors, it is an Organization both better equipped to prevent genocide and able to act decisively to stop it when prevention fails.

Many of my actions as Secretary-General have been undertaken with this in mind. But I know that my efforts are insufficient. The risk of genocide remains frighteningly real.

Therefore, as the only fitting memorial the United Nations can offer to those whom its inaction in 1994 condemned to die, and as recommended in 1999 by the Independent Inquiry into the actions of the United Nations during the genocide in Rwanda, I wish today to launch an Action Plan to Prevent Genocide, involving the whole United Nations system.

Let me summarize the plan under five headings:

First, *preventing armed conflict.*

Genocide almost always occurs during war. Even apparently tolerant individuals, once they engage in war, have categorized some of their fellow human beings as enemies, suspending the taboo which forbids the deliberate taking of human life. And in almost all cases, they accept that civilians may also be killed or hurt, whatever efforts are made to limit so-called collateral damage.

Unless we are very careful, this can be the beginning of a swift descent into a different moral universe, where whole communities are designated as the enemy and their lives held to be of no account. And from there, it is only one more step to the actual and deliberate elimination of these communities: one more step, in other words, to genocide.

So one of the best ways to reduce the chances of genocide is to address the causes of conflict.

The plan will therefore embrace and expand the recommendations already made in my report on Prevention of Armed Conflict,[1] which have been endorsed by both the Security Council and the General Assembly.

We must help countries strengthen their capacity to prevent conflict at local and national levels.

We must do more at the regional level to prevent conflict spilling over from one country to another.

We must give greater attention to environmental problems and tensions related to competition over natural resources.

We must work together with the international financial institutions, with civil society, and with the private sector to ensure that young people get the chance to better themselves through education and peaceful employment, so that they are less easily recruited into predatory gangs and militias.

We must protect the rights of minorities, since they are genocide's most frequent targets.

By all these means and more, we must attack the roots of violence and genocide: hatred, intolerance, racism, tyranny, and the dehumanizing public discourse that denies whole groups of people their dignity and their rights....

Second, *protection of civilians* in armed conflict.

Wherever we fail to prevent conflict, one of our highest priorities must be to protect civilians. The parties to conflict—not only States but also

---

1. Published in 2001 (A/55/985-S/2001/574).

non-State actors—need to be constantly reminded of their responsibility, under international humanitarian law, to protect civilians from violence.

This has now been accepted by the Security Council, and the UN system is working on a platform of action for the protection of civilians. But translating it into concrete results will not be easy. In more and more conflicts we see that civilians, including women and children, are no longer just "caught in the cross fire." They become the direct targets of violence and rape, as war is waged against a whole society.

Wherever civilians are deliberately targeted because they belong to a particular community, we are in the presence of potential, if not actual, genocide.

We can no longer afford to be blind to this grim dynamic. Nor should we imagine that appeals to morality or compassion will have much effect on people who have adopted a deliberate strategy of killing and forcible expulsion.

That is why many of our United Nations peacekeepers today are no longer restricted to using force only in self-defense. They are also empowered to do so in defense of their mandate, and that mandate often explicitly includes the protection of local civilians threatened with imminent violence....

Third, *ending impunity.*

We have little hope of preventing genocide or reassuring those who live in fear of its recurrence if people who have committed this most heinous of crimes are left at large and not held to account. It is therefore vital that we build and maintain robust judicial systems, both national and international—so that, over time, people will see there is no impunity for such crimes.

Working in parallel with a Rwandan justice system that has prosecuted many people who committed acts of genocide, the International Criminal Tribunal for Rwanda has handed down landmark verdicts, which send a message to those who may be contemplating genocide in other countries.

It was the first international court to convict anyone for this crime, the first court of any kind to hold a former head of government responsible for genocide, the first to determine that rape was used as an act of genocide, and the first to find that journalists who incite the population to genocide are themselves guilty of that crime.

The plan calls for a review of the work of this tribunal and others, both national and international, in punishing and suppressing genocide, so that we can learn lessons for the future. It calls for special attention to countries that have experienced conflict or are at risk from it. And it calls for greater efforts to achieve wide ratification of the Rome Statute, so that the new International Criminal Court can deal effectively with crimes against humanity, whenever national courts are unable or unwilling to do so.

Fourth, *early and clear warning.*

One of the reasons for our failure in Rwanda was that beforehand we did not face the fact that genocide was a real possibility. And once it started, for too long we could not bring ourselves to recognize it or call it by its name.

If we are serious about preventing or stopping genocide in future, we must not be held back by legalistic arguments about whether a particular atrocity meets the definition of genocide or not. By the time we are certain, it may often be too late to act. We must recognize the signs of approaching or possible genocide, so that we can act in time to avert it.

Here, civil society groups can play a vital role. Often it is their reports that first draw attention to an impending catastrophe—and far too often, they are ignored.

The United Nations human rights system, too, has a special responsibility. This Commission, through the work of its Special Rapporteurs, independent experts and working groups, as well as the treaty bodies and the Office of the High Commissioner, should be well placed to sound the alarm. Indeed, your Special Rapporteur on Extrajudicial Killings described many warning signs in Rwanda the year before the genocide happened.[2] Alas, no one paid attention.

The challenge is to bring all this information together in a focused way, so as to better understand complex situations and thus be in a position to suggest appropriate action. At present there are still conspicuous gaps in our capacity to analyze and manage the information we have. The plan seeks to correct this.

One decision I have already taken is to create a new post of Special Adviser on the Prevention of Genocide, who will report through me

---

2. Report by Mr. B. W. Ndiaye, Special Rapporteur, on his mission to Rwanda from April 8 to 17, 1993 (E/CN.4/1994/7/Add.1, 11 August 1993).

to the Security Council and the General Assembly, as well as to this Commission.

This adviser's mandate will refer not only to genocide but also to mass murder and other large-scale human rights violations, such as ethnic cleansing. His or her functions will be:

* First, to work closely with the High Commissioner[3] to collect information on potential or existing situations or threats of genocide and their links to international peace and security;
* Second, to act as an early-warning mechanism to the Security Council and other parts of the UN system;
* And third, to make recommendations to the Security Council on actions to be taken to prevent or halt genocide.

That brings me to the fifth and final heading of the action plan, which is the need for *swift and decisive action* when, despite all our efforts, we learn that genocide is happening or about to happen.

Too often, even when there is abundant warning, we lack the political will to act.

Anyone who embarks on genocide commits a crime against humanity. Humanity must respond by taking action in its own defense. Humanity's instrument for that purpose must be the United Nations, and specifically the Security Council.

In this connection, let me say here and now that I share the grave concern expressed last week by eight independent experts appointed by this Commission at the scale of reported human rights abuses and at the humanitarian crisis unfolding in Darfur, Sudan.

Last Friday, the United Nations Emergency Relief Coordinator reported to the Security Council that "a sequence of deliberate actions has been observed that seem aimed at achieving a specific objective: the forcible and long-term displacement of the targeted communities, which may also be termed 'ethnic cleansing.'" His assessment was based on reports from our international staff on the ground in Darfur ... and from my own Special Envoy for Humanitarian Affairs in Sudan.

---

3. For human rights.

Such reports leave me with a deep sense of foreboding. Whatever terms it uses to describe the situation, the international community cannot stand idle.

At the invitation of the Sudanese government, I propose to send a high-level team to Darfur to gain a fuller understanding of the extent and nature of this crisis and to seek improved access to those in need of assistance and protection. It is vital that international humanitarian workers and human rights experts be given full access to the region, and to the victims, without further delay. If that is denied, the international community must be prepared to take swift and appropriate action.

By "action" in such situations I mean a continuum of steps, which may include military action. But the latter should always be seen as an extreme measure, to be used only in extreme cases.

We badly need clear guidelines on how to identify such extreme cases and how to react to them. Such guidelines would ensure that we have no excuse to ignore a real danger of genocide when it does arise. They would also provide greater clarity and thus help to reduce the suspicion that allegations of genocide might be used as a pretext for aggression.

A serious attempt to provide such guidelines was made by the International Commission on Intervention and State Sovereignty[4] in its report on the responsibility to protect. That Commission did very useful groundwork for the High-Level Panel on Threats, Challenges and Change,[5] which surely cannot avoid this issue as it considers how to improve our collective security system. I earnestly hope that the Panel's recommendations will bring consensus within reach, and I urge all Member States to make a real effort to achieve it.[6]

But let us not wait until the worst has happened or is already happening.

Let us not wait until the only alternatives to military action are futile hand-wringing or callous indifference.

---

4. An independent commission appointed by the Canadian government and cochaired by Gareth Evans (former foreign minister of Australia) and Mohamed Sahnoun (a senior Algerian diplomat who had headed several important UN missions). The report, which first developed the concept of responsibility to protect (and coined the phrase), was published in December 2001.
5. See "A Fork in the Road" in Chapter 3.
6. Indeed, the High-Level Panel's report embraced the concept of responsibility to protect. Annan took it up in his *In Larger Freedom* report, and it was endorsed by the World Summit in September 2005.

Let us, Mr. Chairman, be serious about preventing genocide.

Only so can we honor the victims whom we remember today. Only so can we save those who might be victims tomorrow.

※

Remembering the Holocaust

*Statement to the Special Session of the General Assembly Commemorating the Sixtieth Anniversary of the Liberation of the Nazi Death Camps
New York, New York
24 January 2005*

With Annan's encouragement, the General Assembly marked the 60th anniversary of the liberation of Auschwitz on January 27, 1945, by holding a special session; later that year it designated January 27 as an annual International Holocaust Remembrance Day.

T he date for this session was chosen to mark the sixtieth anniversary of the liberation of Auschwitz. But, as you know, there were many other camps, which fell one by one to the Allied forces in the winter and spring of 1945.

Only gradually did the world come to know the full dimensions of the evil that those camps contained. The discovery was fresh in the minds of the delegates at San Francisco, when this Organization was founded. The United Nations must never forget that it was created as a response to the evil of Nazism or that the horror of the Holocaust helped to shape its mission. That response is enshrined in our Charter and in the Universal Declaration of Human Rights.

The camps were not mere "concentration camps." Let us not use the euphemism of those who built them. Their purpose was not to "concentrate" a group in one place, so as to keep an eye on them. It was to exterminate an entire people.

There were other victims, too. The Roma, or Gypsies, were treated with the same utter disregard for their humanity as the Jews. Nearly a quarter of the one million Roma living in Europe were killed.

Poles and other Slavs, Soviet prisoners of war, and mentally or physically handicapped people were likewise massacred in cold blood. Groups as disparate as Jehovah's Witnesses and homosexuals, as well as political opponents and many writers and artists, were treated with appalling brutality.

To all these we owe respect, which we can show by making special efforts to protect all communities that are similarly threatened and vulnerable, now and in the future.

But the tragedy of the Jewish people was unique. Two-thirds of all Europe's Jews, including one and a half million children, were murdered. An entire civilization, which had contributed far beyond its numbers to the cultural and intellectual riches of Europe and the world, was uprooted, destroyed, laid waste.

In a moment, you will have the honor of hearing from one of the survivors, my dear friend Elie Wiesel. As Elie has written, "Not all victims were Jews, but all Jews were victims." It is fitting, therefore, that the first State to speak today will be the State of Israel—which rose, like the United Nations itself, from the ashes of the Holocaust.

The Holocaust came as the climax of a long, disgraceful history of anti-Semitic persecution, pogroms, institutionalized discrimination and other degradation. The purveyors of hatred were not always, and may not be in the future, only marginalized extremists.

How could such evil happen in a cultured and highly sophisticated nation-state, in the heart of a Europe whose artists and thinkers had given the world so much? Truly it has been said, "All that is needed for evil to triumph is that good men do nothing."

There were good men—and women—who did do something: Germans like Gertrude Luckner[1] and Oskar Schindler;[2] foreigners like Miep

---

1. Catholic anti-Nazi who saved many Jews and herself spent nineteen months as a prisoner in Ravensbrück.
2. Businessman who rescued more than a thousand Jews; hero of the film *Schindler's List*.

Gies,[3] Chiune Sugihara,[4] Selahattin Ülkümen,[5] and Raoul Wallenberg.[6] But not enough. Not nearly enough.

Such an evil must never be allowed to happen again. We must be on the watch out for any revival of anti-Semitism and ready to act against the new forms of it that are happening today.

That obligation binds us not only to the Jewish people, but to all others that have been, or may be, threatened with a similar fate. We must be vigilant against all ideologies based on hatred and exclusion, whenever and wherever they may appear.

On occasions such as this, rhetoric comes easily. We rightly say, "Never again." But action is much harder. Since the Holocaust the world has, to its shame, failed more than once to prevent or halt genocide—for instance, in Cambodia, in Rwanda, and in the former Yugoslavia.

Even today we see many horrific examples of inhumanity around the world. To decide which deserves priority, or precisely what action will be effective in protecting victims and giving them a secure future, is not simple. It is easy to say that "something must be done." To say exactly what, and when, and how, and to do it, is much more difficult.

But what we must not do is deny what is happening or remain indifferent, as so many did when the Nazi factories of death were doing their ghastly work.

Terrible things are happening today in Darfur, Sudan. Tomorrow I expect to receive the report of the international commission of inquiry, which I established at the request of the Security Council.

That report will determine whether or not acts of genocide have occurred in Darfur. But also, and no less important, it will identify the gross violations of international humanitarian law and human rights which undoubtedly *have* occurred.

---

3. Dutch citizen who helped to hide Anne Frank and her family.
4. Japanese vice-consul in Lithuania during World War II, who helped several thousand Jews escape by giving them transit visas to Japan.
5. Turkish consul in Rhodes (Greece), who also helped many Jews to escape.
6. Swedish diplomat who saved tens of thousands of Jews from the Nazis in Hungary, then disappeared after being arrested by Soviet forces; uncle of Annan's wife, Nane Lagergren.

The Security Council, once it has that report in its hands, will have to decide what action to take, with a view to ensuring that the perpetrators are held accountable. It is a very solemn responsibility.[7]

Dear friends,

Today is a day to honor the victims of the Holocaust—to whom, alas, no reparation can ever be made, at least in this world.

It is a day to honor our founders—the allied nations whose troops fought and died to defeat Nazism. Those troops are represented here today by veteran liberators of the camps, including my dear friend and colleague Sir Brian Urquhart.[8]

It is a day to honor the brave people who risked, and sometimes sacrificed, their own lives to save fellow human beings. Their examples redeem our humanity and must inspire our conduct.

It is a day to honor the survivors, who heroically thwarted the designs of their oppressors, bringing to the world and to the Jewish people a message of hope. As time passes, their numbers dwindle. It falls to us, the successor generations, to lift high the torch of remembrance and to live our own lives by its light.

It is, above all, a day to remember not only the victims of past horrors, whom the world abandoned, but also the potential victims of present and future ones. A day to look them in the eye, and say: "You, at least, we must not fail."

---

7. On 31 March 2005 the Security Council referred the situation in Darfur to the International Criminal Court, which in 2009 issued an arrest warrant for the president of Sudan, Omar Al Bashir.
8. Brian Urquhart served the United Nations from 1945, retiring in 1985 as Under-Secretary-General for Special Political Affairs. In April 1945, as a British officer, he had taken part in the liberation of Bergen-Belsen. He was one of the speakers at this special session of the General Assembly.

❀ CHAPTER NINE ❀

THE VALUE OF DIVERSITY

✼

A Dialogue among and within Societies

Lecture to the Oxford Centre for Islamic Studies
Oxford, England
28 June 1999

In 1998 President Mohammad Khatami of Iran had proposed a "dialogue among civilizations" as a way of averting the "clash of civilizations" predicted by the American political scientist Samuel P. Huntington. The idea proved popular with other states, and the UN General Assembly decided to proclaim 2001 as the Year of Dialogue among Civilizations. An invitation to lecture on "The Dialogue of Civilizations and the Need for a World Ethic" at the Oxford Centre for Islamic Studies, in the United Kingdom, gave Annan the opportunity to examine this idea in some depth.

I slam is not only one of the world's great religions. In the course of history it has also been the guiding spirit of more than one great civilization....

No one doubts that in the past there were distinct human "civilizations," in the plural. They rose and fell; they blossomed, and they declined. One of the first writers to perceive this was the great Islamic historian and philosopher Ibn Khaldun.

Some civilizations existed at the same time, in different parts of the world, and had little or no contact with each other. Others did come into contact, and often into conflict, seeking to dominate or conquer one another.

This second pattern, of interaction and competition between civilizations, became more common over the last two millennia. Perhaps the clearest example was the competition between Islamic and Christian civilizations. They, after all, were closely related to each other, being both derived from the ancient monotheistic tradition of the Middle East, which Muslims call *deen al-Ibraheem*—the religion of Abraham.

In the medieval Crusades, Christians and Muslims fought each other for control of Jerusalem, for the city and the Land which were Holy to both of them, as well as to the Jews. But at different times their competition affected many other parts of the world, from Spain to Indonesia and from Russia to sub-Saharan Africa, where I come from.

Yet their interaction did not only take the form of conflict. There was also "dialogue," as different civilizations learned from each other.

In the Middle Ages, the Christians had much to learn from the Muslims: medicine, science, mathematics—even the works of ancient Greek philosophers, lost in the European Dark Ages but preserved and translated into Arabic by Muslim scholars.

Later, the Christian world developed superior organization and technology, and used these assets to conquer or dominate all the other civilizations in the world. The dialogue of civilizations became, to all intents and purposes, a monologue.

As a result of that Western expansion and the spectacular improvements in transport and communications which have followed it, the peoples of the world today are much more closely interconnected than they used to be. In some respects at least, whether we like it or not, all of us are now living in a single, global civilization.

And, yet, in the last few years we seem to have heard more and more about "civilizations" in the plural—and not in the past but in the present. Samuel Huntington's prediction of a "clash of civilizations" has stimulated an enormous amount of discussion since it first appeared in 1993.

All sensible people must wish to avoid such a clash. Certainly most Muslim leaders do.

Last September one farsighted leader of a Muslim country, President Mohammed Khatami of Iran, made a memorable speech on the subject to the United Nations General Assembly. He said that "the Islamic Revolution of the Iranian people ... calls for a dialogue among civilizations and cultures instead of a clash between them."

At his suggestion, the Assembly has since decided to proclaim the year 2001 as the United Nations Year of Dialogue among Civilizations.

So what are these separate civilizations in the world today, and what form can their dialogue take?

Professor Huntington was right to point out that, with the end of the cold war, we are passing into a phase where there is no longer a clear-cut global conflict between ideologies, such as socialism and liberalism. Instead there are conflicts between identities, where the issue is not so much what you believe as what you are.

But is it right to see these conflicts as happening between different "civilizations"? I am not so sure. Sometimes the groups in conflict have very similar cultures. Some even share the same language.

Such was the case, for instance, with Serbs, Croats and Bosnian Muslims in the former Yugoslavia and with Hutus and Tutsis in Rwanda.

On the other hand, it is true that outsiders often identify with one or the other side in these conflicts on the basis of religion or culture. There is a degree of fellow feeling among Muslims across the world, as there is among Jews or, indeed, white Anglo-Saxons, when they see members of their own group in conflict with people from other groups.

In this way historical traditions, values and stereotypes continue to bring some peoples together while driving others apart.

"Civilizations" no longer exist as separate entities in the way they once did. But modern societies still bear the strong stamp of history and still identify with each other along cultural fault lines.

Among these fault lines, the one that generates most discussion today runs between Islamic and Western societies.

Objectively, it may seem somewhat artificial—especially to an audience like this, in which it would be hard to say who is Muslim and who is Western, and I'm sure many are both. But subjectively it can be very real, especially perhaps to Islamic peoples whose view of themselves has been strongly affected by the history of the last millennium.

Most Muslims are acutely aware that their religion and civilization were once dominant in large parts of Europe, Africa and Asia.

They know that this empire was gradually lost and that almost all Muslim countries fell under direct or indirect Western domination. Today colonialism has ended, but many Muslims still resent their manifest inequality with the West in power politics. Many of them have a sense of defeat and disadvantage.

Their resentment has been fed by the unjust treatment of the Palestinians and, more recently, by atrocities committed against Muslims in the former Yugoslavia.

Muslims today would like to see their culture and civilization duly respected, by themselves and by others, as was the case in the past. That surely, is a hope we should all share, provided we understand that respect today is no longer to be earned by military conquest.

Modern societies are too closely linked with each other, and modern weapons are too terrifyingly destructive, for interaction between modern "civilizations" to take the form of armed conflict, as that between past civilizations often did.

Today's dialogue must be a peaceful one. That is one reason why I believe it has to proceed on the basis of a set of shared values.

Even the most extreme moral relativist is condemned to be a universalist in this sense. The doctrine of "live and let live" will only work if all cultures and all societies accept it as the norm.

Personally, however, I do not believe that "live and let live" is a sufficient norm for today's global society. And that, perhaps, is where I part company from Professor Huntington.

I do think it is vital that we preserve and cherish diversity wherever we can. But not, as he suggests, by identifying "civilizations" with geographically distinct cultural blocs.

That might perhaps preserve an appearance of cultural diversity at the global level. But each bloc would have a depressingly closed and monolithic culture on the local level.

Professor Huntington himself seems to advocate a world like that, at the end of his book, when he warns against the danger of America becoming a multi-civilizational country, or in his terms a "torn" society.

I think most of us would disagree with that. Most of us feel that America's openness and diversity are its best qualities and that if it tried to impose cultural conformity it would be embarking, like other great powers before it, on the road of decline.

The conventional view is that civilizations are destroyed by internal conflict, which weakens their defenses, causing them to fall prey to the barbarians at the gates. But in so far as that is true, I suspect it is because rulers and leaders have too often tried to deal with internal conflict in ways which end up making it worse.

They have suppressed dissent and ignored genuine grievances, and so driven more and more people to rebel, even in alliance with those dreaded "barbarians."

In fact the very notion that foreigners are barbarians, without any civilization or ideas of their own worth studying, may be one of the things that saps the strength of a supposedly superior civilization and eventually brings about its downfall.

The history of Islamic civilization illustrates this point. For hundreds of years the Muslim world was in the forefront of scientific and technical progress, as well as artistic achievement....

A great Jewish scholar like Maimonides could flourish in the service of Muslim rulers. And later the Ottoman Empire gave asylum to both Jews and Christians fleeing from persecution in Christian States.

Indeed, the Ottomans for several centuries brought good administration to regions which have too often lacked it since—the southern and eastern Mediterranean and the Balkans. Their empire was for long a splendid example of cultural and ethnic pluralism, from which we still have much to learn.

Yet, sadly, the same Ottoman Empire allowed Islamic thought to become dominated by conservative theologians who opposed all innovations—from coffee to the printing press—equating them with heresy. The result was that—even while the West was surging ahead through the embrace of rationalism and science—in the leading Islamic State of the time religion came to be seen as an obstacle to reform and modernization as something inherently anti-religious.

Some of the current attempts to restore Islamic greatness are, I fear, doomed to fail because—instead of loosening these shackles of obscurantism—they are trying to fasten them even more tightly.

This is especially true of those movements that resort to violence as a means of enforcement, ignoring the clear message of the Quran that "there is no compulsion in religion." I fear this can only lead to even greater alienation.

Yet I am sure there is no necessary conflict between belief and modernity in Islam any more than in other religions. The challenge for

Muslim thinkers must be to live up to the finest traditions of Islamic thought—including the tradition of *ijtihad,* or free interpretation, not just in theology and law but in all the arts and sciences. They should encourage their fellow Muslims to enquire freely what is good and bad in other cultures, as in their own.

All of us who come from developing countries need to understand that the greatest gap between the developed and the developing world is the "knowledge gap." It can only be bridged by open-minded research and free, courageous thought.

The way forward, while preserving the bedrock of our traditions in belief and custom, is to free our minds to absorb and understand a world that is constantly changing.

If Ibn Khaldun were alive today, I am sure this would be his message to the Muslim peoples: live up to the best traditions of your past and play your full part in a future of coexistence and constant interaction between different traditions.

In short, our world ethic cannot be simply a matter of "live and let live," in the sense of letting each State enforce its own orthodoxy on all its citizens. Still less can it consist of letting one or two powerful "core States" enforce their will on others which are deemed to share their culture.

On the contrary, we must accept—and even cultivate—the presence of different traditions within each region of the world, and indeed within each society.

That is why I am glad to be speaking today, not just at a center of Islamic studies, but at a center of Islamic studies in Britain—a major Western country....

Muslim communities are an essential part of Western society today. They represent one of many traditions that are coming together in the modern West.

Their presence makes possible a dialogue of civilizations—or at least of traditions—within the West. They bring their own traditions to this dialogue, and they are well placed to study other traditions, some of which have a longer history in Western societies.

They can absorb what they find valuable in those traditions, incorporate it into their own outlook and way of life, and also transmit it to fellow Muslims in other countries, particularly those where they have close family ties.

These Western Muslim communities will, I suspect, be seen by future generations as an important source of renewal and inspiration in Islamic thought.

So the dialogue among civilizations must be a dialogue within societies as well as between them....

And it must be a dialogue of mutual respect. The aim is not to eliminate differences between human beings, but to preserve and even celebrate them as a source of joy and strength.

That is the world ethic that we need: a framework of shared values—a sense of our common humanity—within which different traditions can coexist.

People must be able to follow their own traditions without making war on each other. They must have sufficient freedom to exchange ideas. They must be able to learn from each other.

As the Quran says, "O mankind! We created you from a single pair of a male and female, and made you into nations and tribes, that you may know each other"[1]—"not," a leading commentator[2] adds, "that you may despise each other."

And that means that each nation must not only respect the culture and traditions of others, but must also allow its own citizens—women and men alike—the freedom to think for themselves. As President Khatami told the General Assembly,

> We should recognize that both men and women are valuable components of humanity that equally possess the potential for intellectual, social, cultural and political development, and that comprehensive and sustainable development is only possible through the active participation of both men and women in social life.

All the great religions and traditions overlap when it comes to the fundamental principles of human conduct: charity, justice, compassion, mutual respect, the equality of human beings in the sight of God.

That is what has made it possible for States in all parts of the world, representing many different religious and cultural traditions, to espouse the Universal Declaration of Human Rights and other more detailed international agreements which flow from it.

1. Quran, 49:13.
2. The Indian Islamic scholar Abdullah Yusuf Ali (1872–1953).

It may be presumptuous to single out any of these rights and obligations for special emphasis, but in this context none can be more important than freedom of thought and of expression.

Those freedoms enable human beings to listen to each other, respect each other's traditions, and learn from each other. Whatever else we define as specific to a particular culture or civilization, those freedoms are vital to us all, and we must never part with them.

❋

Unity in Diversity

Speech to the Indonesian Council on World Affairs
Jakarta, Indonesia
16 February 2000

In 1999 Annan had helped persuade Indonesia's President B. J. Habibie to relinquish control of East Timor, the former Portuguese colony annexed by Indonesia in 1975, respecting the wish for independence expressed by the Timorese people. (See "Two Concepts of Sovereignty" in Chapter 8.) Early the following year he visited Indonesia, which was going through a period of rapid political change after the fall of Suharto in 1998. Many Indonesians feared that the loss of East Timor would lead to the secession of other territories and even the breakup of their vast and diverse country. Annan offered them some advice on how to avoid this, using their national motto "Unity in Diversity."

L et me begin by saying how impressed I am by what I have seen so far during my first visit to Indonesia. And how conscious I am of the tremendous work the government and people of your country have accomplished against some formidable odds....

Under difficult circumstances and in a short space of time, you have made significant progress in restoring macroeconomic stability, advancing structural reforms, and assuring food security. Of course, economic development has been a priority since the birth of your nation. But, in the past two years, because you have understood that people are the most precious resource of any nation, this work has taken on new dimensions.

You have understood that economic and social recovery cannot take hold without a system based on transparency, accountability and the rule of law. And so you are carrying out economic reform in tandem with political, legal and institutional reform. You have opted for a foreign policy built not on competition with your neighbors, not on confrontation with the rest of the world, but on cooperation and friendship. You have championed non-alignment and South-South cooperation. You have set an example to other developing countries....

Thanks to last year's free and peaceful general election—which, I am pleased to recall, the United Nations Development Program helped you organize—you now have a government with a broad popular mandate....

Already, political reform has opened the door to a free and vibrant press. Civil society is becoming increasingly active and effective. Parliament has grown more assertive. The challenge now for Indonesia, its people and its friends—including the United Nations—is to build on the democratic institutions that have so gloriously emerged, so that they grow stronger tomorrow.

No one is born a good citizen; no nation is born a democracy. Rather, both are processes that continue to evolve over a lifetime. As your Foreign Minister[1] has rightly noted, democracy is a habit that we need to cultivate consciously in ourselves. That is how we build enduring political, economic and social institutions. That is how we develop government that is answerable to citizens and citizenry that is fully engaged in decisions that affect their country's future.

Strong institutions, underpinned by the will of the people and the rule of law, are crucial at all times and in all countries, but perhaps never more so than here and now, at this decisive time in Indonesia's history: a time when freedom and openness are bringing to the forefront a wide range of challenges....

Among these challenges, probably none seems more threatening than the issue of separatism. It may well feel to some of you as if Indonesia's

---

1. Alwi Shihab, a leading authority on Muslim-Christian relations.

very existence is under attack from covert forces which believe the country is too large and want to break it up.

But, in fact, your case is not unique at all. Separatism is a challenge facing many countries. Each case involves different realities and conditions; each requires a different approach. But most of them do have one thing in common: although they may have security implications, they are, in essence, not security problems. They are political problems, and, as such, they require political solutions.

Separatism is a much more complex issue than terrorism—though it is often identified with terrorism, because some separatists use terrorism to promote their cause. We cannot say that separatism is always wrong. After all, many Member States of the United Nations today owe their existence to separatist movements in the past. But please do not think that that means the United Nations is predisposed in favor of separatism or that its purpose is to break up large States into smaller ones.

On the contrary, the purpose of the United Nations is to enable peoples to live together without conflict. If there is one thing we hate in the modern world, it is so-called ethnic cleansing—the idea that people can live safely only among their own kind and that the price of survival is to expel or exterminate anyone whose language or religion or culture is different from their own. The United Nations will oppose that idea wherever we are given political responsibilities—from the Balkans to East Timor.[2]

The truth is that many separatist movements are wrong. Breaking up large States into smaller ones is often a wasteful and unimaginative way of resolving political differences.

But those who oppose separatism have got to show that their solution is less wasteful and more imaginative. Minorities have to be convinced that the State really belongs to them, as well as to the majority, and that both will be the losers if it breaks up. Conflict is almost certain to result if the State's response to separatism causes widespread suffering in the region or among the ethnic group concerned. The effect then is to make more people feel that the State is not their State, and so to provide separatism with new recruits.

---

2. At this time both Kosovo and East Timor were under temporary UN administration.

Like other political problems, separatism can be resolved successfully only through patient and painstaking confidence building and dialogue. By showing that staying together is the best solution for all concerned. There are no quick fixes, no short cuts. Wounds that have festered for a long time cannot heal overnight. Nor can confidence be built or dialogue develop while fresh wounds are being inflicted. It is a process that requires all parties to renounce violence. And it requires special efforts to uphold human rights. If innocent civilians are not protected, if their rights are not safeguarded, their suffering can only breed further hatred.

Therefore, let me pay tribute to President Wahid[3] and his government for the emphasis they are putting on good governance, on the rule of law, on improved civil-military relations and on accountability for corruption and violations of human rights. Let me congratulate them on their courage in seeking to come to terms with the past, as an essential part of the search for a new way forward.

Let me also thank the government for its clearly expressed desire to open a new chapter in Indonesia's relations with East Timor. However difficult these relations may have been in the past 25 years when they were imposed by one side without regard for the wishes of the other, it remains true that East Timor and Indonesia are bound together by geography and history.

Now that the right of the Timorese people to their own State has been clearly recognized, their own leaders—showing great magnanimity and statesmanship—have been the first to recognize how important it will be for that State to have good relations with Indonesia.

An independent East Timor is therefore not a threat to Indonesia's security. Rather, it can enhance the stability and prospects of your region. By the very fact of its history and location, East Timor is connected with Portugal, Europe and the Iberian world, with Australia and the South Pacific. These countries and regions are crucial in assisting East Timor's transition to independence. And all of them, I believe, understand that East Timor has a far better chance to prosper as an independent State if Indonesia, too, is prosperous and successful.

---

3. Abdurrahman Wahid, popularly known as Gus Dur, had been elected president of Indonesia by the People's Consultative Assembly in October 1999.

But the world's stake in your success is far from being confined to the success of East Timor. As the world's fourth most populous country, as its largest Muslim-majority State, and as its largest nation of islands, straddling major shipping lanes, you carry great political weight and strategic importance. And you have used that position wisely.

You have staked the success of your economic recovery on a successful transition to democracy, and vice versa. This brave choice is not only the best hope for the people of Indonesia. It is also a shining example for the whole region and indeed the world. Your success will have implications reaching far beyond your borders. Your country's well-being is critical to long-term political stability in South-East Asia and beyond....

I wanted to entitle this speech "Unity in Diversity" not only because the words are enshrined on Indonesia's coat of arms, but also because the reality behind the words is the foundation of Indonesia's past, present and future. Ever since this old Javanese motto was introduced by a saint of the Majapahit Kingdom in the fifteenth century, it has signified the unity of the Indonesian people despite their diverse culture and ethnicity. It has summed up the meaning of our common humanity.

In this globalized world, it is more relevant than ever. Because in our interdependent world ... what affects one nation affects us all. What defines us as human beings is not race, creed or geography. What gives most people's lives purpose and content is the chance of a decent life in freedom from fear and freedom from want; a successful part in the global economy, for their children and their grandchildren.

Surely, that is what makes up our common humanity and the foundations of our unity. Surely, that is why we should honor and celebrate our diversity. And so, if there are any words I will always remember from this visit to Indonesia, it is "Bhinneka Tunggal Ika."[4] Indeed, I cannot think of a better motto for the world as a whole—and particularly for our United Nations. I wish you every success on the road ahead, and I pledge that the United Nations will walk beside you on your journey.

---

4. The Old Javanese phrase inscribed in Indonesia's national symbol and translated as "Unity in Diversity."

✿

The Faith We Must Have in Each Other

Address at the Interfaith Service of
Commitment to the United Nations
New York, New York
13 September 2001

The Interfaith Service at St. Bartholomew's Church, on Park Avenue, is
an annual event timed to coincide with the opening of the UN General
Assembly. It is traditional for the Secretary-General to attend and make
short remarks. In 2001 it took on special significance, being Annan's first
public appearance after the 9/11 attacks, which had happened only two
days before.

T hank you for welcoming us today to this interfaith service of
commitment to the United Nations. As always in difficult
times, it is comforting to be among friends.

I take heart especially at the sight of so many individuals of so many
creeds praying side by side in the cause of peace. Heaven knows how much
we at the United Nations need the hope and comfort of your prayers.
Heaven knows how deeply we wish all of our prayers today may bring some
comfort to the people whose lives have been touched by this week's tragedy.

The events of the last two days must have tested the faith of every
one of us.

At times like this, it is all too tempting to jump to conclusions about
the kind of people who must be behind such appalling acts and to
identify them with some faith or community different from our own.

Instead, we should remember that, whoever they are, they must be
human beings. We like to think of such acts as inhuman, but the truth
is that human nature can sink to the depths of horror, as well as rise to
the highest level of nobility. It is up to each of us to cultivate the best
in his or her nature and to struggle against the worst.

That is why I esteem so highly the efforts of the Interfaith Centre: to find the common ground of mutual respect and love, which goes with true spirituality.

Those efforts proceed, I know, from a shared faith—faith in a dimension of life beyond the material and in the obligation, binding on all human beings, to strive to understand each other and to live in peace. That is the faith that sustains all of us here today. That is the faith we must have in each other—now and in the days ahead.

※

Naming Evil

Lecture at the 35th National Conference of the Trinity Institute
New York, New York
2 May 2004

The Trinity Institute is a theological center based at Trinity Church, Wall Street, close to the World Trade Center. "Naming Evil" was the theme of its 2004 annual conference, at which Annan was invited to speak.

I am certainly honored to be the first speaker at your conference. But I am also somewhat intimidated by the title you have chosen for it, "Naming Evil," and by the way you have described me in your brochure:

"Kofi Annan," it says, "is a man whose global experience has exposed him, over and over again, to the pervasiveness of evil and the precariousness of civilization. He will discuss the character, scope, and implications of evil in the emergent global reality. His job is to name the evils that afflict us."

Well, I have heard my job described in many ways, but never quite like that! And I'm not sure that my life has been quite as grim as you make it sound.

In fact, to be frank with you, I don't even think that the word "evil" is a regular part of my vocabulary. There is something about the word, when we apply it to another human being—and more especially to a group of human beings—that makes me uncomfortable.

It is too absolute. It seems to cut off any possibility of redemption, of dialogue, or even coexistence. It is the moral equivalent of declaring war.

When we think of other people as evil, we are perilously close to depriving them of any rights and releasing ourselves from any obligations towards them. We are poised at the top of a slippery slope that leads to violence, murder, even genocide.

And there, of course, is the paradox. Who can avoid using the word "evil," when confronted with genocide?

Unquestionably, some very evil things happen in the world. And you are right: it has been my fate to come face to face with such things at certain points in my career. I think particularly of the genocide in Rwanda and the massacre at Srebrenica, in Bosnia—the climax of a brutal war, which brought the horrible euphemism "ethnic cleansing" into everyday speech.

Both those disasters happened when I was head of the United Nations peacekeeping department. In both cases we had peacekeeping troops on the ground at the very place and time where genocidal acts were being committed.

In both cases I had subsequently to examine my conscience, as did many others who were involved. All of us had to ask what more we might have done, and why we did not do more, to stop this horror in its tracks—or, better still, before it started.

And one of the conclusions we came to, in the UN Secretariat, was that we had—to quote my report to the General Assembly on the fall of Srebrenica—"an institutional ideology of impartiality even when confronted with attempted genocide."

In other words, we were reluctant to face up to evil when we saw it. As peacekeepers and peacemakers, we were trained to listen, to see both sides of the case, to look for common ground, to work for reconciliation. Our experience told us that in no conflict is one side entirely to blame and that all parties, in every conflict, will sometimes violate the laws of war.

We were not immune to moral indignation. But we had learnt that, in peacekeeping and peacemaking, moral indignation is seldom a good guide to action. One often has to swallow one's indignation and talk very calmly to men of violence—men who, one knows or strongly suspects, have committed horrible crimes.

That can be unpleasant, but I don't think we should be ashamed of it. Often it is the only way to save lives. The difficulty is to know where to draw the line.

With hindsight, of course, it may be easy. But at the time it is usually not at all easy to judge the precise point where violence becomes so deliberate and systematic that to carry on talking achieves nothing, except to give the perpetrators more time to carry out their ghastly work. The point, that is, where impartial peacekeepers or peacemakers are no longer the answer—where force has to be met with force. Which means—dare I say it?—that evil has to be met with evil.

Because, yes, use of force is an evil, even in the best of causes. There is no such thing as a war in which only the guilty are killed, or wounded, or see their homes destroyed and their loved ones perish. Even in the best of causes, young men are sacrificed. Even those who are clearly fighting on the side of right inflict terrible pain and injury on others.

Sometimes I wish I could share the moral certainty of the pacifist—of the person for whom the prohibition of violence is absolute, so that no matter what is being done to innocent people, even to one's own family, one must always turn the other cheek rather than fight back.

That is not an easy position to take, but it does have the merit of simplicity. Those who really stick to it undoubtedly deserve our respect.

But it is not my position, and it is not the position of the United Nations. The Charter provides very clearly, in Article 42, that when the Security Council considers other measures inadequate, "it may take such action by air, sea, or land forces as may be necessary to maintain or restore international peace and security."

So there are times when the use of force is legitimate and necessary, because it is the lesser of two evils. But the lesser of two evils is still an evil, and we should not forget that.

I think it may be helpful if we resolve, when we use the word "evil" as an adjective, to apply it to actions rather than to people. Of course it is tempting, when someone commits many evil acts, to say that that person is evil in himself or herself. But I am not sure that it is right.

I do believe, very firmly, that people must be held responsible for their actions and sometimes must be punished for them. Nothing is more dangerous than to let people think they can literally get away with murder—that because they have superior force in their hands, at a particular place or time, they can do what they like and will never be called to account. We call that "the culture of impunity," and the United Nations is strongly committed to fighting against it. That is why we are doing whatever we can to help build and maintain robust judicial systems, both national and international.

But to say that any human being is irredeemably evil in himself or herself—that is a different matter, and one probably better left to theologians....

Personally I do not feel—either as a Christian or even as a simple human being—that I have the right to make such an absolute judgment about any of my fellow human beings, however evil the acts they may have committed. Indeed, that is why, personally, I have never felt able to support the death penalty. I tend to think there is some evil even in the best of us, and some chink of light and hope and human feeling even in the worst of us.

But what I am sure of is that, whatever we think about individuals, we must not allow ourselves to generalize and attribute evil characteristics to whole groups of people. That is contrary to natural justice, because it amounts to finding people guilty without even examining their individual beliefs and actions. It is also very dangerous, because once we have classified people as evil, we may easily think ourselves entitled and obliged to suppress them. Thinking of people as evil can lead to us to become evil, or at least to do evil, ourselves....

One of the great dangers of our time is that the politics of fear and anger and intolerance may force us into an artificial "clash of civilizations," in which people of different faiths and cultures perceive each other as enemies.

Acts of violence and terror, committed by a small number of individuals, are blamed on "Islam," and all Muslims become suspects.

Acts of dispossession or disproportionate use of force undertaken by the State of Israel, in what it sees as legitimate self-defense, are used to justify a resurgence of anti-Semitism, and all Jews become potential targets.

The use of force by certain Western governments is used to revive anti-Christian sentiments in the Muslim world, and all Christians, including local Christian communities, are made to feel insecure.

We have to get away from such unjust and sweeping reactions.

We must learn to see each other as individuals, each with the right to define our own identity and to belong to the faith or culture of our choice.

Tolerance is essential, but it is not enough. We must be curious about each other's traditions, anxious to find what is positive in them and what we can learn from them....

If we are intent on naming evil, as the title of your conference tells us to, then let us name it as intolerance.

Let us name it as exclusion.

Let us name it as the false assumption that we have nothing to learn from beliefs and traditions different from our own.

That, I believe, is the true evil of our time, and I urge you all to join forces against it.

❊

A Small Confession

Remarks at the Farewell Concert
New York, New York
18 December 2006

The UN Alliance of Civilizations, aimed at galvanizing international action against extremism through international, intercultural, and inter-religious dialogue and cooperation, was launched in 2005 as a joint initiative of the Spanish and Turkish governments. To define the Alliance's agenda, Annan had appointed a High-Level Group of experts, which reported in November 2006. To mark the launch of the Alliance, and as a farewell present to the Secretary-General, the Spanish government sponsored a concert in the General Assembly hall, given by the West-East Divan Orchestra—an ensemble of Arab and Israeli musicians formed and conducted by Daniel Barenboim.

W hat can I say—except, "Thank you"? … A big thank you to the government and people of Spain for sponsoring this concert, which is the nicest going-away present Nane and I could ever have wished for. And thank you especially to the Regional Government of Andalusia, whose support for the Barenboim-Said Foundation has made it possible.

Maybe this is the moment to make a small confession. I have always had some slight misgivings about the phrase "Alliance of Civilizations," as I did about the "Dialogue of Civilizations."

Of course, I am very much in favor of dialogue, and I think it is very important that people of reason and goodwill in different communities come together to combat extremism and intolerance. But I don't believe that, in the twenty-first century, humankind is really divided into separate civilizations. I think that today, for better or worse, we are all living in one civilization.

Unfortunately, that civilization has some barbaric features. We are much too prone to magnify our differences and ready to tear each other's eyes out on almost any pretext. The Alliance of Civilizations is really about fighting those tendencies in ourselves and showing what wonderful things we can do when we come together.

I cannot think of a better example than the one set by Daniel Barenboim and Edward Said—an Israeli and a Palestinian, two intellectual and artistic giants, as well as close friends. Together, they represented all that is best in their respective nations and cultures. They were both dedicated to the cause of peace and justice for their peoples. And they created this marvelous orchestra, composed of young musicians from Israel and from other Middle Eastern countries.

Their example reminds us that our civilization today is composed of many strands and that the Arab and Jewish strands are among the most important.

So my final thank you is to Daniel, to Edward—who alas is no longer with us—and to the young performers who are very much with us tonight. Their talent, their enthusiasm and their courage give us a glimpse of a future worth living for.

I know you are all as impatient to hear them as I am. So I will leave it at that.

Index

❋

PHOTO CREDITS

Cover:
Portrait of Secretary-General Kofi Annan, appointed to a second term of office, beginning on 1 January 2002 and ending 31 December 2006.
UN Photo/Sergey Bermeniev

Chapter 1: The United Nations
Secretary-General Kofi Annan addresses the Global Compact Summit in the General Assembly hall.
UN Photo/Evan Schneider

Chapter 2: Development and the Global Community
Secretary-General Kofi Annan (left) greeting assembled children at the Mayoral Palace while on official visit in Chile.
UN Photo/Milton Grant

Chapter 3: Peace and Security
Secretary-General Kofi Annan made his first state visit to Canada to meet with senior officials and address the opening ceremony for the signing of the Convention on the Prohibition of the Use, Stockpiling, Production and Transfer of Anti-Personnel Mines and on Their Destruction.
UN Photo/Evan Schneider

Chapter 4: Human Rights
Secretary-General Kofi Annan and Mrs. Nane Annan comforting some of the children who attended the wreath-laying ceremony in memory of those who had died during the previous April's massacre at a village church in Liquica.
UN Photo/Eskinder Debebe

Chapter 5: Peacekeeping and Peace-Building
Secretary-General Kofi Annan (right) addressing the staff of the United Nations Mission in Bosnia and Herzegovina (UNMIBH).
UN Photo/Milton Grant

Chapter 6: Africa
Secretary-General Kofi Annan (top left), accompanied by his wife, Nane Annan, tour a child feeding center run by Médecins sans Frontières, where they both met with many malnourished children and their mothers.
UN Photo/Evan Schneider

Chapter 7: The Middle East
A picture of a south Beirut suburb ruined in the recent conflict between Israel and Hezbollah, which Secretary-General Kofi Annan toured with the prime minister of Lebanon, Fouard Siniora.
UN Photo/Mark Garten

Chapter 8: Prevention of Genocide and the Responsibility to Protect
Kofi Annan, Secretary-General of the United Nations, and spouse, Nane Annan, are shown the burial site of genocide victims of the École Technique.
UN Photo/Milton Grant

Chapter 9: The Value of Diversity
Secretary-General Kofi Annan (second from right) meets with Eritrean religious leaders.
UN Photo/Jorge Aramburu

❋

ABOUT THE AUTHOR

Kofi Annan was the seventh Secretary-General of the United Nations, serving two terms from January 1, 1997, to December 31, 2006, and was the first to emerge from the ranks of United Nations staff. In 2001 Kofi Annan and the United Nations were jointly awarded the Nobel Prize for Peace with the citation praising Annan's leadership for "bringing new life to the organization."

Mr. Annan joined the UN system in 1962 as an administrative and budget officer with the World Health Organization in Geneva. He later served with the Economic Commission for Africa in Addis Ababa, the UN Emergency Force (UNEF II) in Ismailia, and the United Nations High Commissioner for Refugees (UNHCR) in Geneva, as well as in various senior posts in New York dealing with human resources, budget, finance, and staff security. Immediately before becoming Secretary-General, he was Under-Secretary-General for Peacekeeping. Kofi Annan facilitated the repatriation from Iraq of more than nine hundred international staff and other non-Iraqi nationals (1990) and also served as Special Representative of the Secretary-General to the former Yugoslavia and Special Envoy to NATO (1995-1996).

Since leaving the United Nations, Kofi Annan has established the Kofi Annan Foundation and continued to press for better policies to meet the needs of the poorest and most vulnerable, particularly in Africa. He has also continued to use his experience to mediate and resolve conflict. In Kenya in early 2008, Mr. Annan led the African Union's Panel of Eminent African Personalities to help find a peaceful resolution to the postelection violence. From February to August 2012, he served as Joint Special Envoy of the UN and the Arab League for Syria.

In addition to his work with the Kofi Annan Foundation, Mr. Annan serves as the Chairman of The Elders and the Africa Progress Panel (APP). He is also the founding Chairman of the Alliance for a Green Revolution in Africa (AGRA). Mr. Annan is a board member, patron, or honorary member of a number of organizations, including the United Nations Foundation. He is currently Chancellor of the University of Ghana and has held a number of positions at universities around the world.

ABOUT THE EDITOR

Edward Mortimer is a Fellow of All Souls College, Oxford, and a writer and activist specializing in human rights, global governance, and contemporary history. He was a journalist with the London *Times* (1967–1985) and the *Financial Times* (1987–1998). From 1998 to 2006, he served as Chief Speechwriter and Director of Communications to UN Secretary-General Kofi Annan, and from 2007 to 2011 as Chief Program Officer of the Salzburg Global Seminar. He is currently chair of the Sri Lanka Campaign for Peace and Justice. His books include *Faith and Power: The Politics of Islam* (Random House Vintage 1982) and *The World That FDR Built* (Scribner's 1989). In 2010 he was named CMG (Companion of the Order of St Michael and St George) for services to international communications and journalism.

✳

Editor's Note

It has been a great privilege to work on these statements—first in the original drafting (along with my colleagues Richard Amdur, Nader Mousavizadeh, and Annika Savill) and now in selecting and preparing them for publication. They have been selected as statements that still have some significance and which may merit the attention of posterity. In most cases I have provided one or two introductory sentences to explain the context, and in some a few footnotes to elucidate references to particular people or things. But my hope is that they can be read and understood without detailed knowledge of the specific circumstances in which they were given.

Thanks are due to Dr. David Hamburg, without whose tireless support and advocacy this volume would certainly never have seen the light of day. Also to Ruth McCoy and Fabian Lange for their help and advice in preparing the text; to Paradigm Publishers, and especially Jennifer Knerr, for the enthusiasm with which she accepted the book, advised on its shape and content, and shepherded it through the publication process; and to the Kofi Annan Foundation for indispensable financial support. Should there be any proceeds from the book, Mr. Annan has asked that they be donated to UNAIDS.

Edward Mortimer
Oxford, 2013